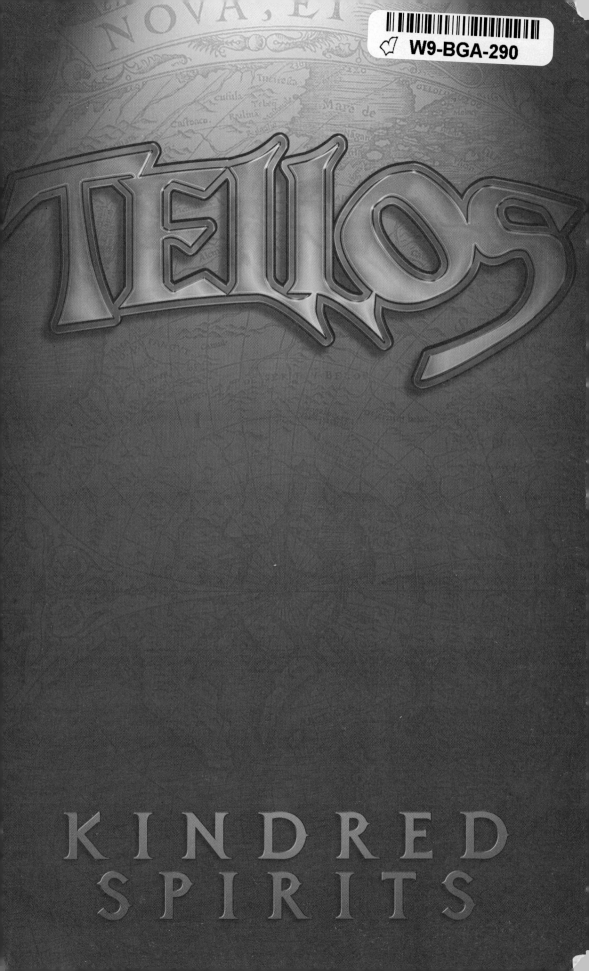

NOVA, ET

TELLOS

KINDRED
SPIRITS

For Image Comics:
Jim Valentino—Publisher
Anthony Bozzi—Director of Marketing
Brent Braun—Director of Production
Traci Hale—Controller
Kenny Felix—Graphic Designer
Doug Griffith—Art Director

Special Thanks once again t
Jim, Brent, Bozzi, and Kenny an
Everyone at Image for a
of their help and suppor

TELLOS: Vol.2. Kindred Spirits, December 2001. First Printing. Published by Image Comics, 1071 N. Batavia St. Ste. A, Orange CA 92867. Direct Market: $17.95 US/ $24.50 Can.

TELLOS
KINDRED
SPIRITS

STORY
Todd Dezago and Mike Wieri[ngo]

WRITER
Todd Dezago

ARTIST
Mike Wieringo

INKS
Rob Stull
with Rick Ketchum
Nathan Massengill
Derek Fridolfs

COLORS
Bongotone's
Paul Mounts and Ken Wolak

LETTERING & DESIGN
Paul Mounts

FILM OUTPUT
Kell-O-Graphics

INTRODUCTION AND PINUP
Tom DeFalco and Ron Lim

PINUPS
Thor Badendyck,
Tom Bancroft/Howard Shum,
and Kelly Yates

TELLOS created by
Todd Dezago and Mike Wieringo

Originally published in Tellos #'s 6-10.

Scatterjack originally published in Section Zero #1.

BY THY SIDE--!

Welcome aboard, mate!

If this is your first journey into the wonder that is Tellos, you're in for a special treat. If you've already experienced this magical patchwork world, you might as well skip this intro and cut right to the good stuff. Jarek, Koj, Serra and the rest of the gang await thee, and shall ever be by thy side.

Ever since the proliferation of fantasy role-playing games, anyone who can roll a die honestly believes that he can also create new worlds and interesting heroes. He is lulled into thinking that fantasy is easy. In some respects, he's right. It isn't all that difficult to come up with a half dozen flashy names and paste them on a like number of archetypes. The hard part comes when you try to transform these ciphers into real people with real emotions, concerns and problems.

Tellos has a wonderful cast of characters who will haunt your dreams long after you've finished their story, and who will ever be by thy side! We empathize with Jarek and his struggles, and are stunned when his true connection with the evil Malesur is finally revealed. (Whatever you do, please don't spoil your enjoyment by jumping to the end of the story!) It takes a certain amount of skill to layer enough depth and nuance into the personality of a sleazy fox so that we're actually touched when he suddenly (and uncharacteristically) joins the cause. There are dozen of talking dragons, but only one who's a deadhead, surfer-dude type. (If you don't know who I'm talking about, you'll find out in the coming pages and--trust me--he's worth the wait!)

Todd Dezago and Mike Wieringo have done an incredible job. Tellos is one part Arabian Nights, one part Lord of the Rings, a little Star Wars, some Wizard of Oz and a hearty dose of Edgar Rice Burroughs. Like all the very best adventure stories, Tellos engages both our hearts and minds, giving us some interesting insights into the human condition.

Go, read and enjoy!

Hoo-Ha!
Tom DeFalco
October, 2001

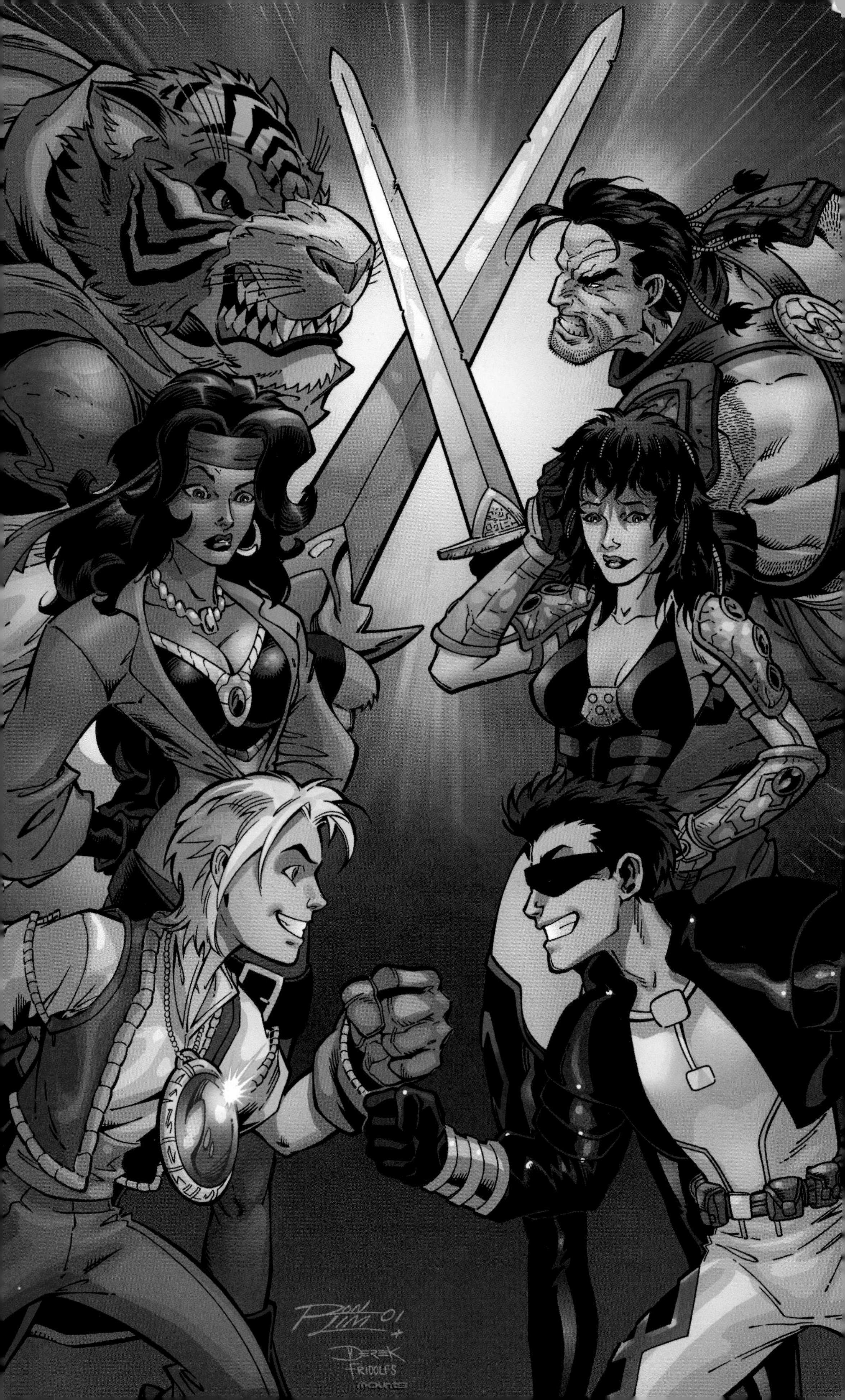

DON LIM '01 +
DEREK FRIDOLFS
mounts

THE STORY SO FAR...

TELLOS is a magikal patchwork world made up of a myriad of countless lands and realms, populated by mythical and legendary creatures, filled with adventure...and danger!!

Drawn together by a common enemy--Jarek, a young adventurer with a hazy past, his partner, the tiger warrior Koj, and Serra, Captain of the Pirate Ship, the Sheva Nova--soon find themselves on a collision course with destiny as they try to discover why they're being pursued by both Frogsoldiers and the dread ShadowJumpers, AND what strange connection Jarek has with Serra's Amulet that released a powerful D'Jinn at his bidding...!

Set on their way by Thomestharustra, the enigmatic Mage of Shades, the three soon learn that the prophecies say that Jarek, possessed of the Warrior of the Light, is to be the savior of the Lands, vanquishing the evil Malesur and halting his Campaign of Darkness. They set out on a quest to find 'The Other'--Jarek's counterpart--whose added strength will give them the power to defeat the Forces of Darkness.

But soon, the trio find themselves ambushed by a quintet of Malesur's Bounty Hunters, and the battle is joined! Outnumbered and defenseless, Jarek, Koj, and Serra are soon joined by Hawke and Rikk, Serra's thief of a boyfriend and his wiley fox partner! The sides now evenly matched, our reluctant heroes win the day...but not without taking some serious hits...

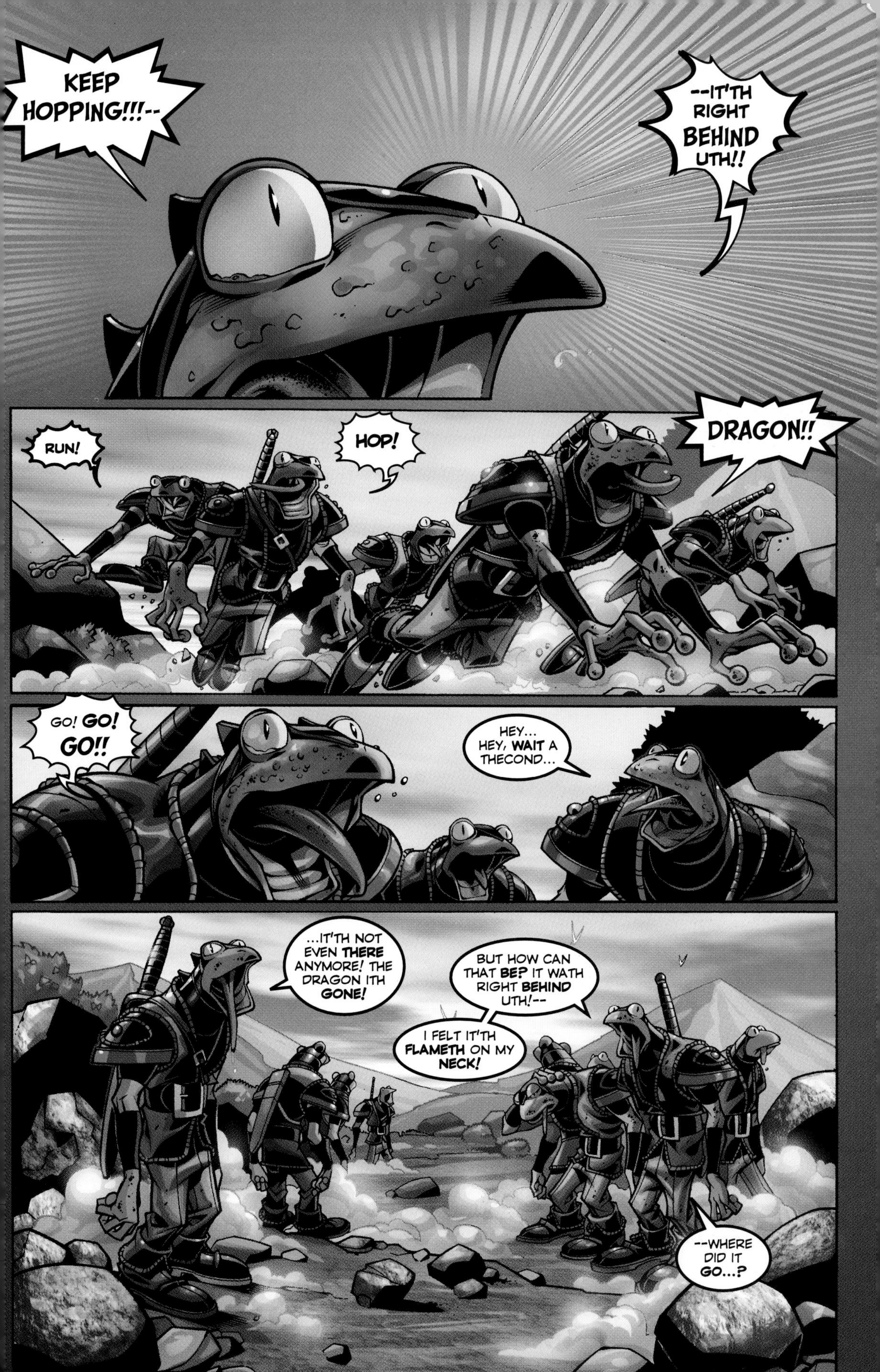
KEEP HOPPING!!!--
--IT'TH RIGHT BEHIND UTH!!
RUN!
HOP!
DRAGON!!
GO! GO! GO!!
HEY... HEY, WAIT A THECOND...
...IT'TH NOT EVEN THERE ANYMORE! THE DRAGON ITH GONE!
BUT HOW CAN THAT BE? IT WATH RIGHT BEHIND UTH!--
I FELT IT'TH FLAMETH ON MY NECK!
--WHERE DID IT GO...?

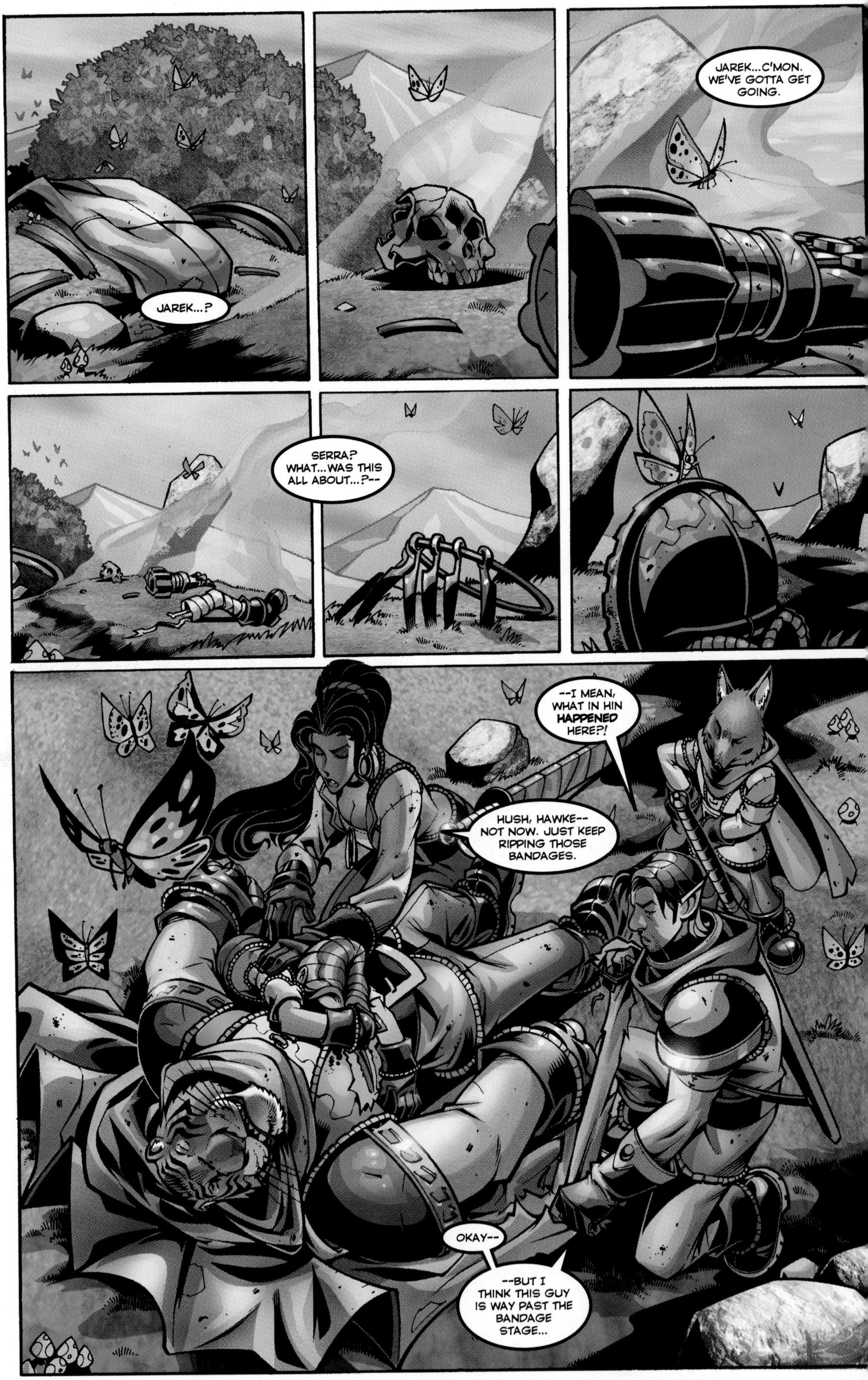
JAREK...?
JAREK...C'MON. WE'VE GOTTA GET GOING.
SERRA? WHAT...WAS THIS ALL ABOUT...?--
--I MEAN, WHAT IN HIN **HAPPENED** HERE?!
HUSH, HAWKE-- NOT NOW. JUST KEEP RIPPING THOSE BANDAGES.
OKAY--
--BUT I THINK THIS GUY IS WAY PAST THE BANDAGE STAGE...

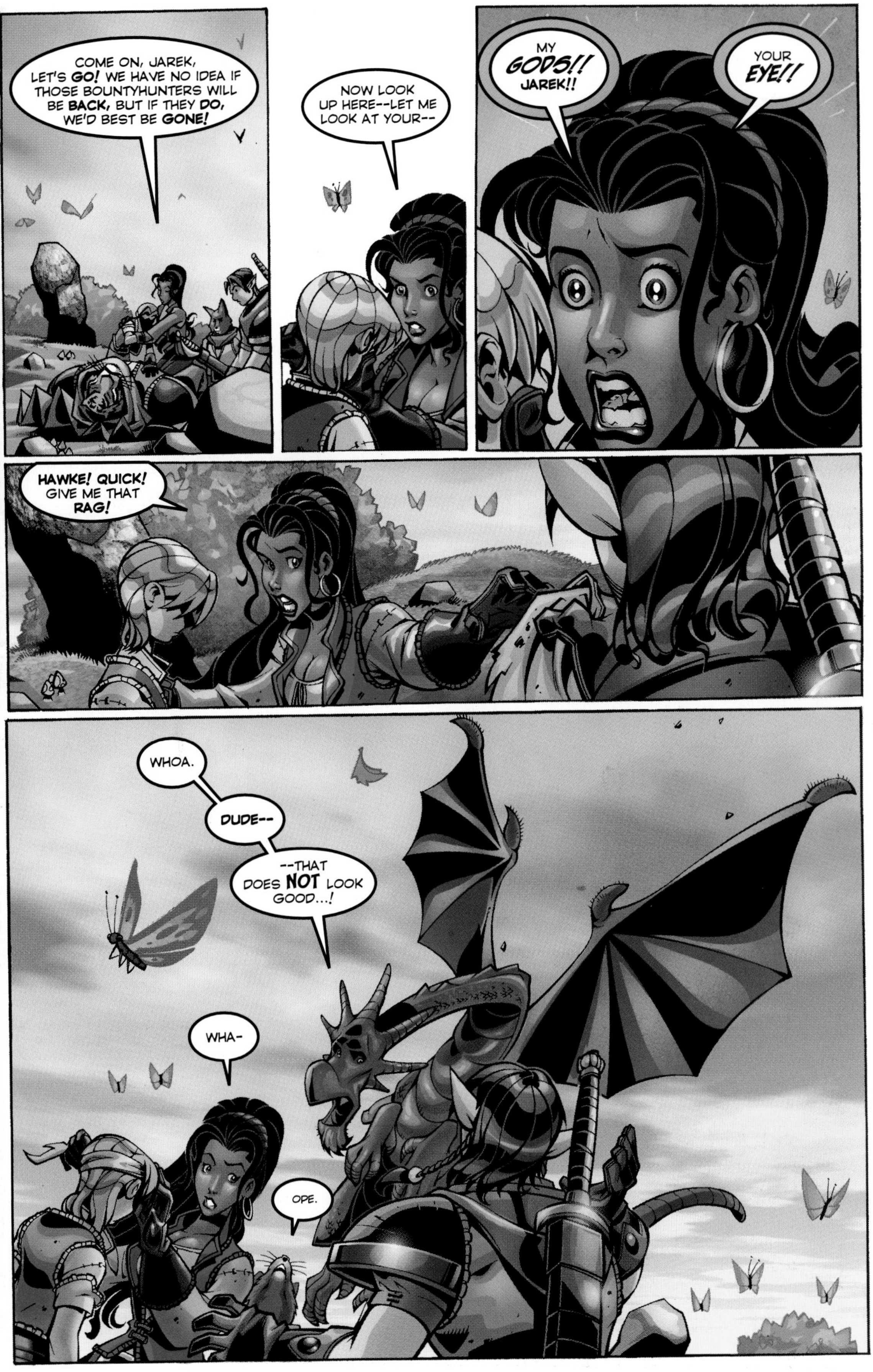
COME ON, JAREK, LET'S GO! WE HAVE NO IDEA IF THOSE BOUNTYHUNTERS WILL BE BACK, BUT IF THEY DO, WE'D BEST BE GONE!
NOW LOOK UP HERE--LET ME LOOK AT YOUR--
MY GODS!! JAREK!!
YOUR EYE!!
HAWKE! QUICK! GIVE ME THAT RAG!
WHOA.
DUDE--
--THAT DOES NOT LOOK GOOD...!
WHA-
OPE.

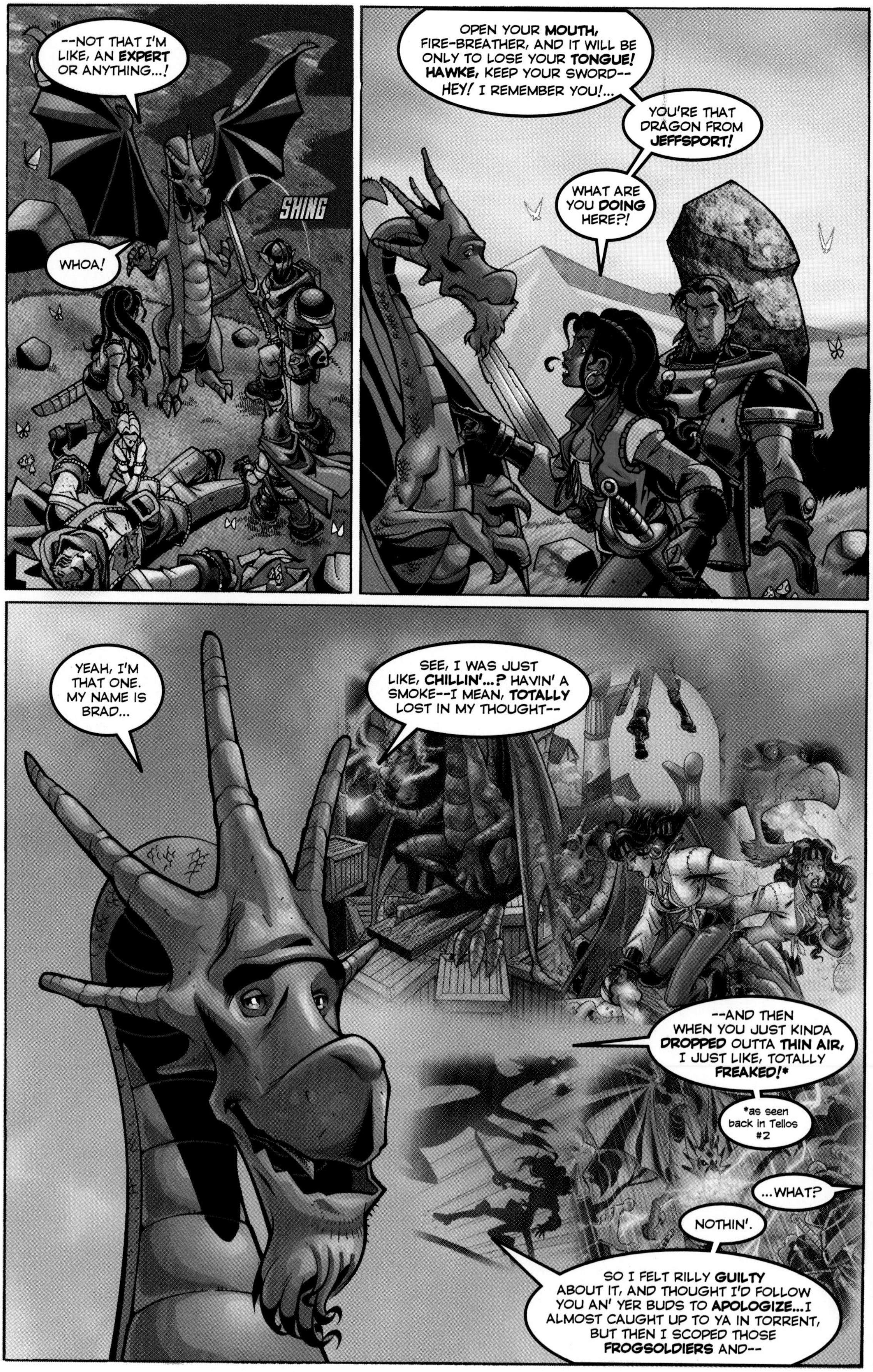
--NOT THAT I'M LIKE, AN EXPERT OR ANYTHING...!
SHING
WHOA!
OPEN YOUR MOUTH, FIRE-BREATHER, AND IT WILL BE ONLY TO LOSE YOUR TONGUE! HAWKE, KEEP YOUR SWORD-- HEY! I REMEMBER YOU!...
YOU'RE THAT DRAGON FROM JEFFSPORT!
WHAT ARE YOU DOING HERE?!
YEAH, I'M THAT ONE. MY NAME IS BRAD...
SEE, I WAS JUST LIKE, CHILLIN'...? HAVIN' A SMOKE--I MEAN, TOTALLY LOST IN MY THOUGHT--
--AND THEN WHEN YOU JUST KINDA DROPPED OUTTA THIN AIR, I JUST LIKE, TOTALLY FREAKED!*
*as seen back in Tellos #2
...WHAT?
NOTHIN'.
SO I FELT RILLY GUILTY ABOUT IT, AND THOUGHT I'D FOLLOW YOU AN' YER BUDS TO APOLOGIZE...I ALMOST CAUGHT UP TO YA IN TORRENT, BUT THEN I SCOPED THOSE FROGSOLDIERS AND--

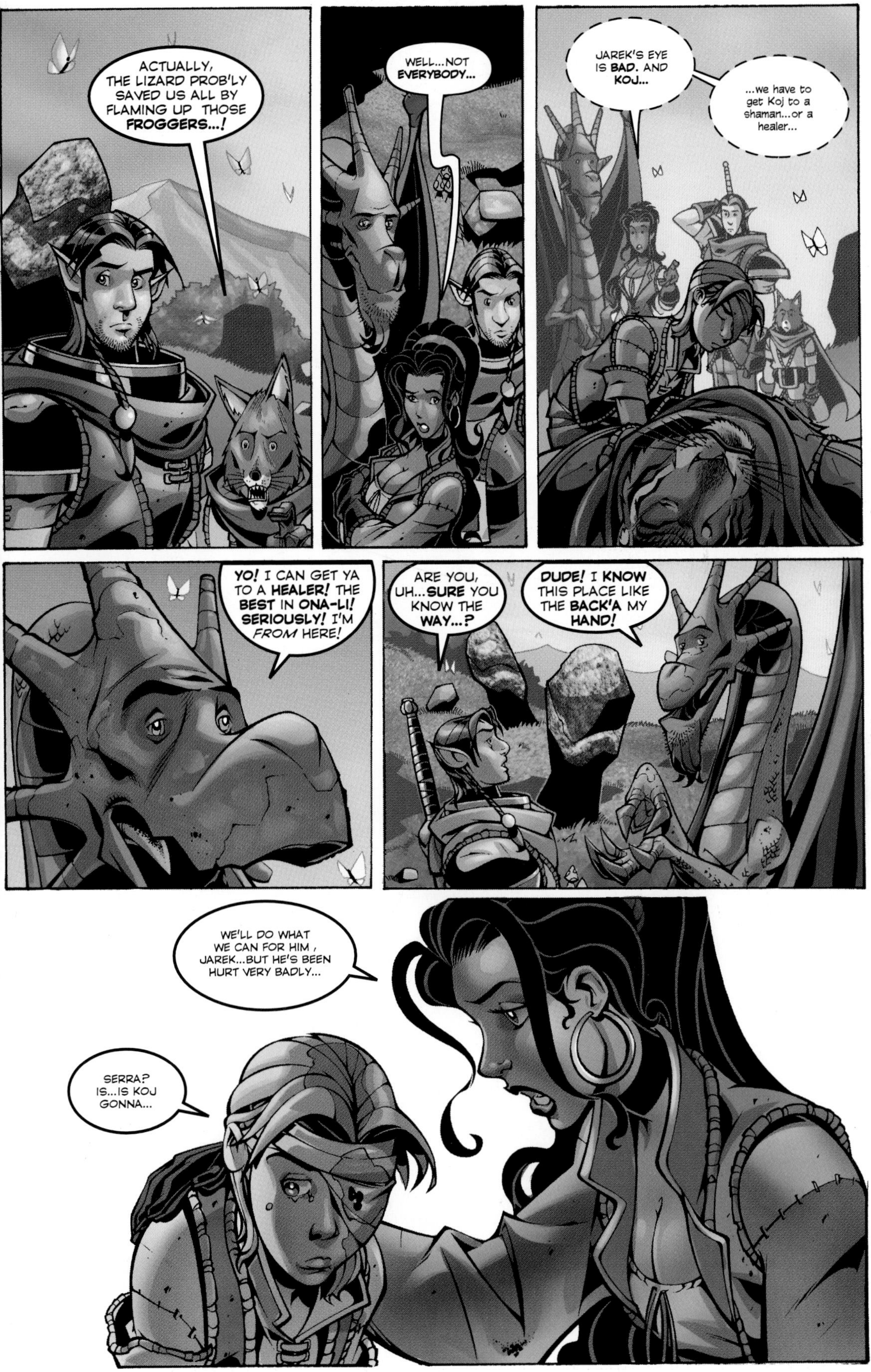

ACTUALLY, THE LIZARD PROB'LY SAVED US ALL BY FLAMING UP THOSE FROGGERS...!
WELL...NOT EVERYBODY...
JAREK'S EYE IS BAD. AND KOJ...
...we have to get Koj to a shaman...or a healer...
YO! I CAN GET YA TO A HEALER! THE BEST IN ONA-LI! SERIOUSLY! I'M FROM HERE!
ARE YOU, UH...SURE YOU KNOW THE WAY...?
DUDE! I KNOW THIS PLACE LIKE THE BACK'A MY HAND!
WE'LL DO WHAT WE CAN FOR HIM, JAREK...BUT HE'S BEEN HURT VERY BADLY...
SERRA? IS...IS KOJ GONNA...

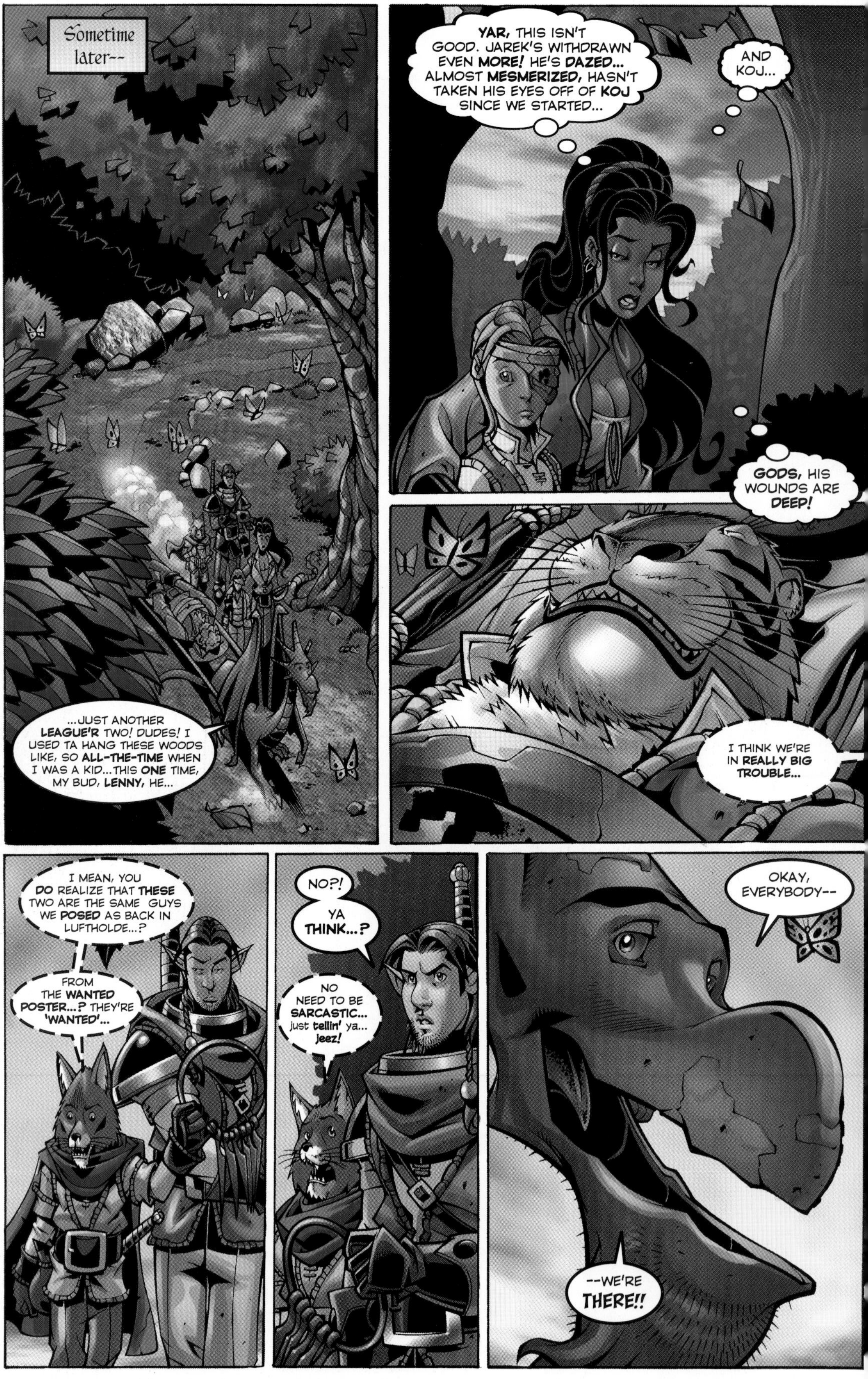
Sometime later--
...JUST ANOTHER LEAGUE'R TWO! DUDES! I USED TA HANG THESE WOODS LIKE, SO ALL-THE-TIME WHEN I WAS A KID...THIS ONE TIME, MY BUD, LENNY, HE...
YAR, THIS ISN'T GOOD. JAREK'S WITHDRAWN EVEN MORE! HE'S DAZED... ALMOST MESMERIZED, HASN'T TAKEN HIS EYES OFF OF KOJ SINCE WE STARTED...
AND KOJ...
GODS, HIS WOUNDS ARE DEEP!
I THINK WE'RE IN REALLY BIG TROUBLE...
I MEAN, YOU DO REALIZE THAT THESE TWO ARE THE SAME GUYS WE POSED AS BACK IN LUFTHOLDE...?
FROM THE WANTED POSTER...? THEY'RE 'WANTED'...
NO?!
YA THINK...?
NO NEED TO BE SARCASTIC... just tellin' ya... jeez!
OKAY, EVERYBODY--
--WE'RE THERE!!

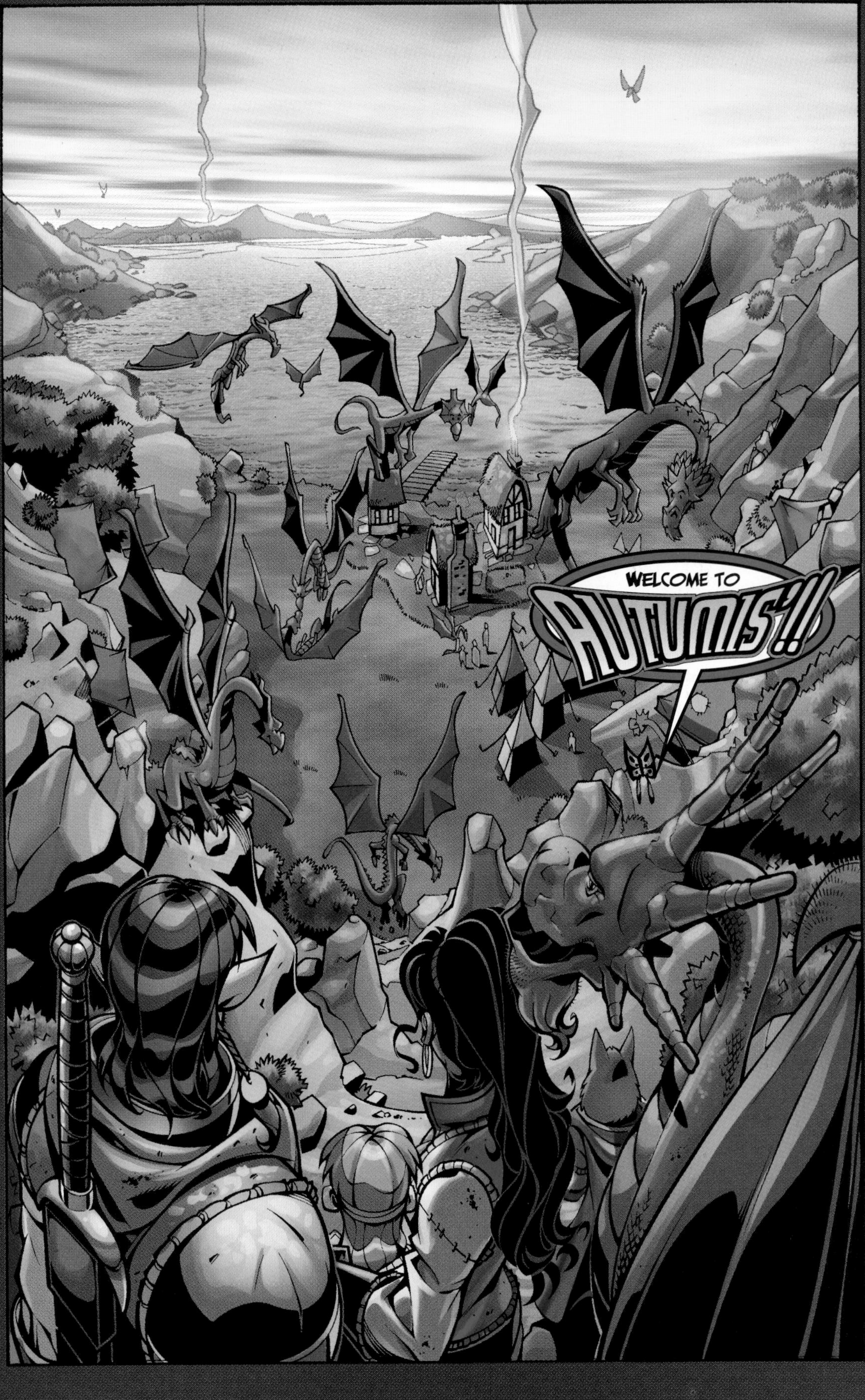
WELCOME TO AUTUMIS!!

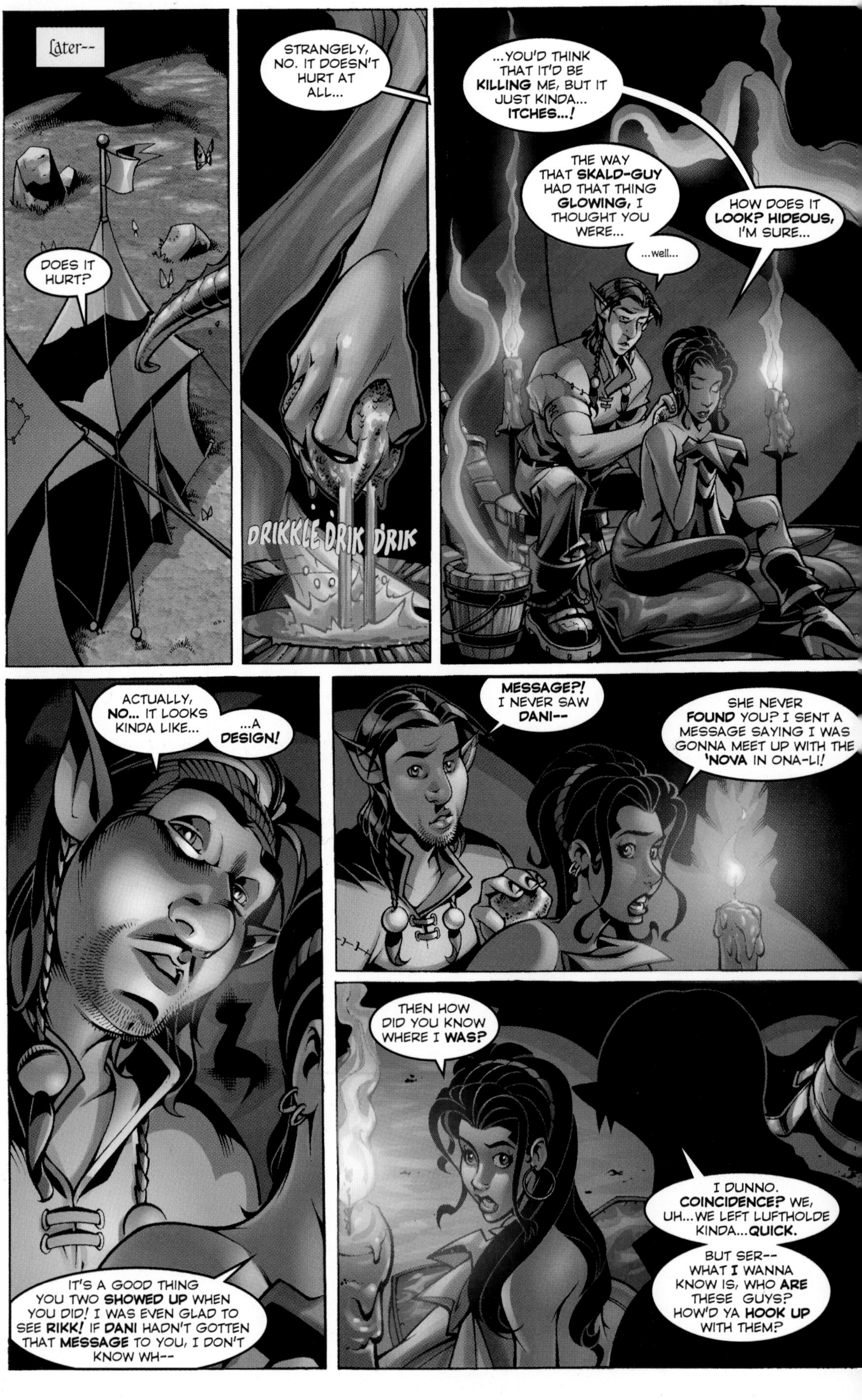

Later--
DOES IT HURT?
STRANGELY, NO. IT DOESN'T HURT AT ALL...
DRIKKLE DRIK DRIK
...YOU'D THINK THAT IT'D BE KILLING ME, BUT IT JUST KINDA... ITCHES...!
HOW DOES IT LOOK? HIDEOUS, I'M SURE...
THE WAY THAT SKALD-GUY HAD THAT THING GLOWING, I THOUGHT YOU WERE...
...well...
ACTUALLY, NO... IT LOOKS KINDA LIKE...
...A DESIGN!
IT'S A GOOD THING YOU TWO SHOWED UP WHEN YOU DID! I WAS EVEN GLAD TO SEE RIKK! IF DANI HADN'T GOTTEN THAT MESSAGE TO YOU, I DON'T KNOW WH--
MESSAGE?! I NEVER SAW DANI--
SHE NEVER FOUND YOU? I SENT A MESSAGE SAYING I WAS GONNA MEET UP WITH THE 'NOVA IN ONA-LI!
THEN HOW DID YOU KNOW WHERE I WAS?
I DUNNO. COINCIDENCE? WE, UH...WE LEFT LUFTHOLDE KINDA...QUICK.
BUT SER-- WHAT I WANNA KNOW IS, WHO ARE THESE GUYS? HOW'D YA HOOK UP WITH THEM?

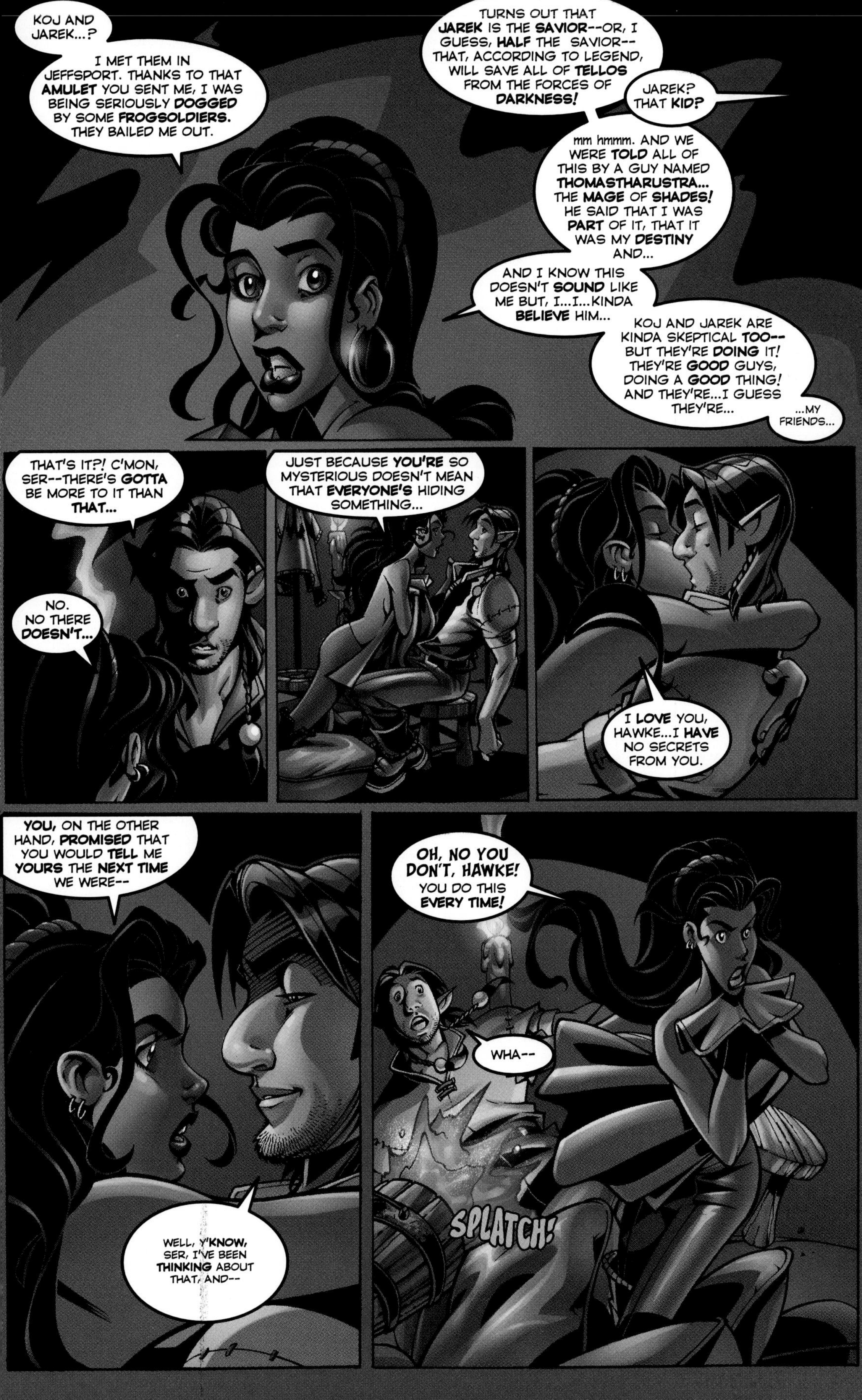
KOJ AND JAREK...?
I MET THEM IN JEFFSPORT. THANKS TO THAT AMULET YOU SENT ME, I WAS BEING SERIOUSLY DOGGED BY SOME FROGSOLDIERS. THEY BAILED ME OUT.
TURNS OUT THAT JAREK IS THE SAVIOR--OR, I GUESS, HALF THE SAVIOR--THAT, ACCORDING TO LEGEND, WILL SAVE ALL OF TELLOS FROM THE FORCES OF DARKNESS!
JAREK? THAT KID?
mm hmmm. AND WE WERE TOLD ALL OF THIS BY A GUY NAMED THOMASTHARUSTRA... THE MAGE OF SHADES! HE SAID THAT I WAS PART OF IT, THAT IT WAS MY DESTINY AND...
AND I KNOW THIS DOESN'T SOUND LIKE ME BUT, I...I...KINDA BELIEVE HIM...
KOJ AND JAREK ARE KINDA SKEPTICAL TOO--BUT THEY'RE DOING IT! THEY'RE GOOD GUYS, DOING A GOOD THING! AND THEY'RE...I GUESS THEY'RE...
...MY FRIENDS...
THAT'S IT?! C'MON, SER--THERE'S GOTTA BE MORE TO IT THAN THAT...
NO. NO THERE DOESN'T...
JUST BECAUSE YOU'RE SO MYSTERIOUS DOESN'T MEAN THAT EVERYONE'S HIDING SOMETHING...
I LOVE YOU, HAWKE...I HAVE NO SECRETS FROM YOU.
YOU, ON THE OTHER HAND, PROMISED THAT YOU WOULD TELL ME YOURS THE NEXT TIME WE WERE--
WELL, Y'KNOW, SER, I'VE BEEN THINKING ABOUT THAT, AND--
OH, NO YOU DON'T, HAWKE! YOU DO THIS EVERY TIME!
WHA--
SPLATCH!

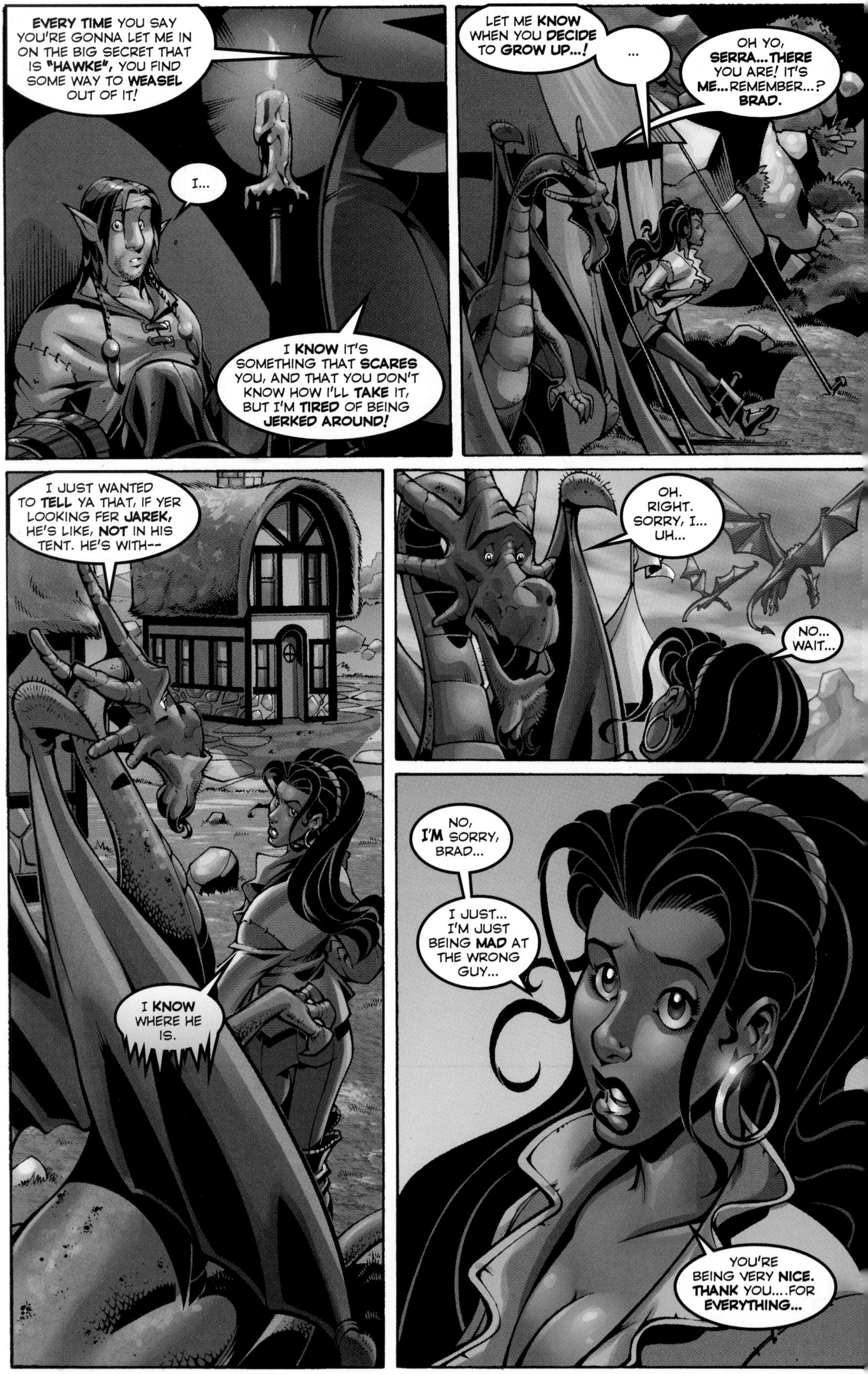
EVERY TIME YOU SAY YOU'RE GONNA LET ME IN ON THE BIG SECRET THAT IS "HAWKE", YOU FIND SOME WAY TO WEASEL OUT OF IT!
I...
I KNOW IT'S SOMETHING THAT SCARES YOU, AND THAT YOU DON'T KNOW HOW I'LL TAKE IT, BUT I'M TIRED OF BEING JERKED AROUND!
LET ME KNOW WHEN YOU DECIDE TO GROW UP...!
...
OH YO, SERRA...THERE YOU ARE! IT'S ME...REMEMBER...? BRAD.
I JUST WANTED TO TELL YA THAT, IF YER LOOKING FER JAREK, HE'S LIKE, NOT IN HIS TENT. HE'S WITH--
I KNOW WHERE HE IS.
OH. RIGHT. SORRY, I... UH...
NO... WAIT...
NO, I'M SORRY, BRAD...
I JUST... I'M JUST BEING MAD AT THE WRONG GUY...
YOU'RE BEING VERY NICE. THANK YOU....FOR EVERYTHING...

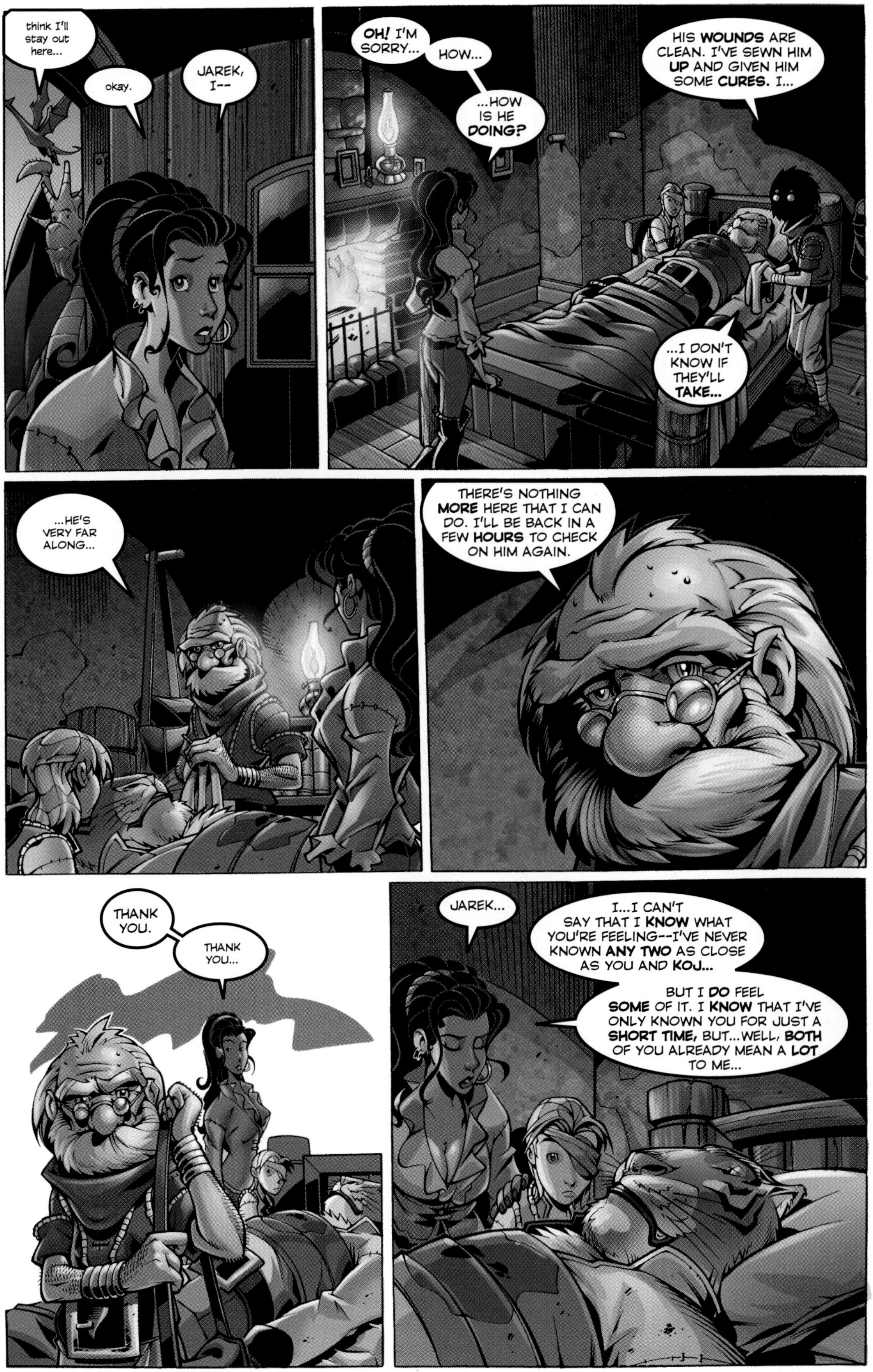
think I'll stay out here...
okay.
JAREK, I--
OH! I'M SORRY...
HOW...
...HOW IS HE DOING?
HIS WOUNDS ARE CLEAN. I'VE SEWN HIM UP AND GIVEN HIM SOME CURES. I...
...I DON'T KNOW IF THEY'LL TAKE...
...HE'S VERY FAR ALONG...
THERE'S NOTHING MORE HERE THAT I CAN DO. I'LL BE BACK IN A FEW HOURS TO CHECK ON HIM AGAIN.
THANK YOU.
THANK YOU...
JAREK...
I...I CAN'T SAY THAT I KNOW WHAT YOU'RE FEELING--I'VE NEVER KNOWN ANY TWO AS CLOSE AS YOU AND KOJ...
BUT I DO FEEL SOME OF IT. I KNOW THAT I'VE ONLY KNOWN YOU FOR JUST A SHORT TIME, BUT...WELL, BOTH OF YOU ALREADY MEAN A LOT TO ME...

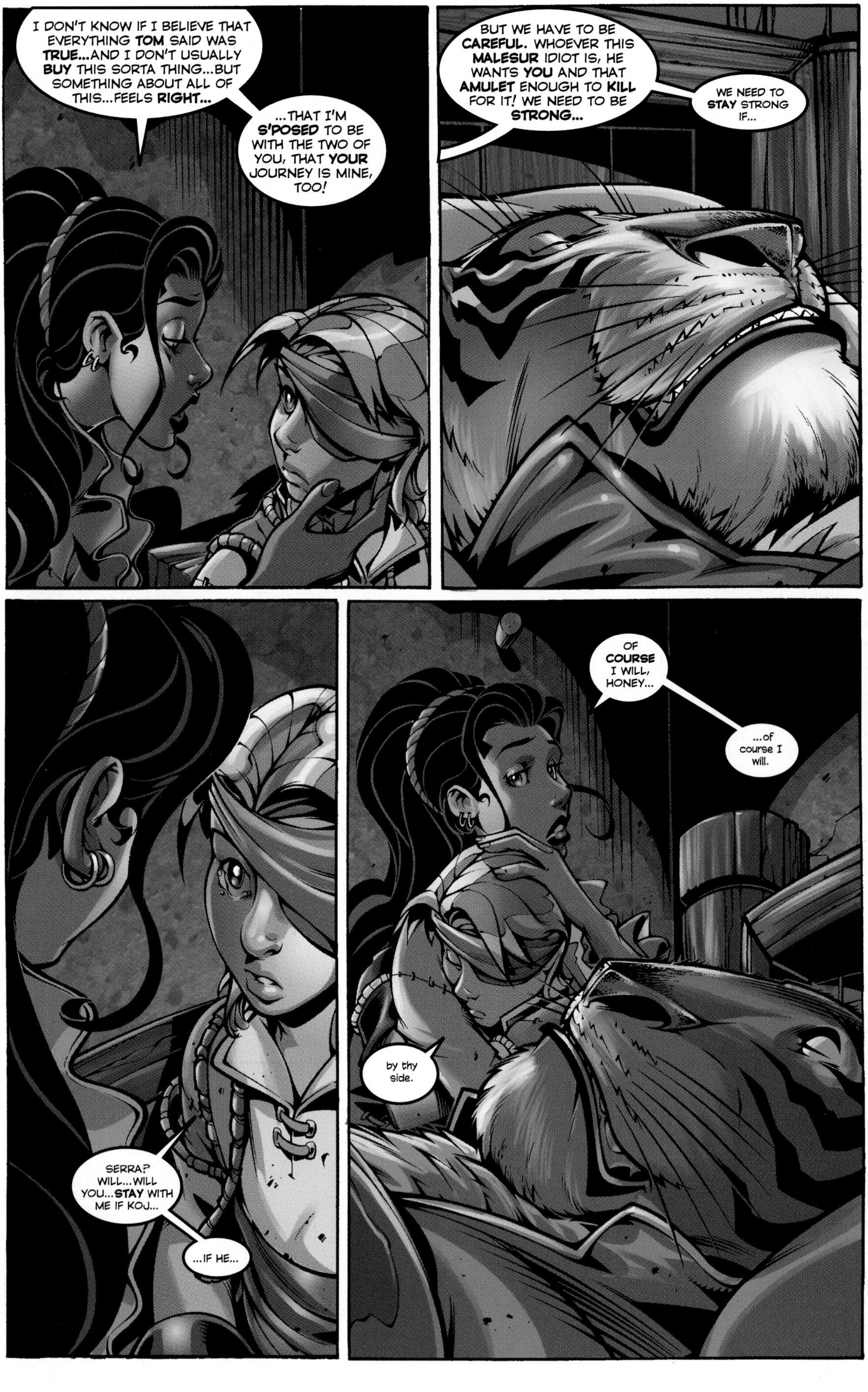
I DON'T KNOW IF I BELIEVE THAT EVERYTHING TOM SAID WAS TRUE...AND I DON'T USUALLY BUY THIS SORTA THING...BUT SOMETHING ABOUT ALL OF THIS...FEELS RIGHT...
...THAT I'M S'POSED TO BE WITH THE TWO OF YOU, THAT YOUR JOURNEY IS MINE, TOO!
BUT WE HAVE TO BE CAREFUL. WHOEVER THIS MALESUR IDIOT IS, HE WANTS YOU AND THAT AMULET ENOUGH TO KILL FOR IT! WE NEED TO BE STRONG...
WE NEED TO STAY STRONG IF...
SERRA? WILL...WILL YOU...STAY WITH ME IF KOJ...
...IF HE...
OF COURSE I WILL, HONEY...
...of course I will.
by thy side.

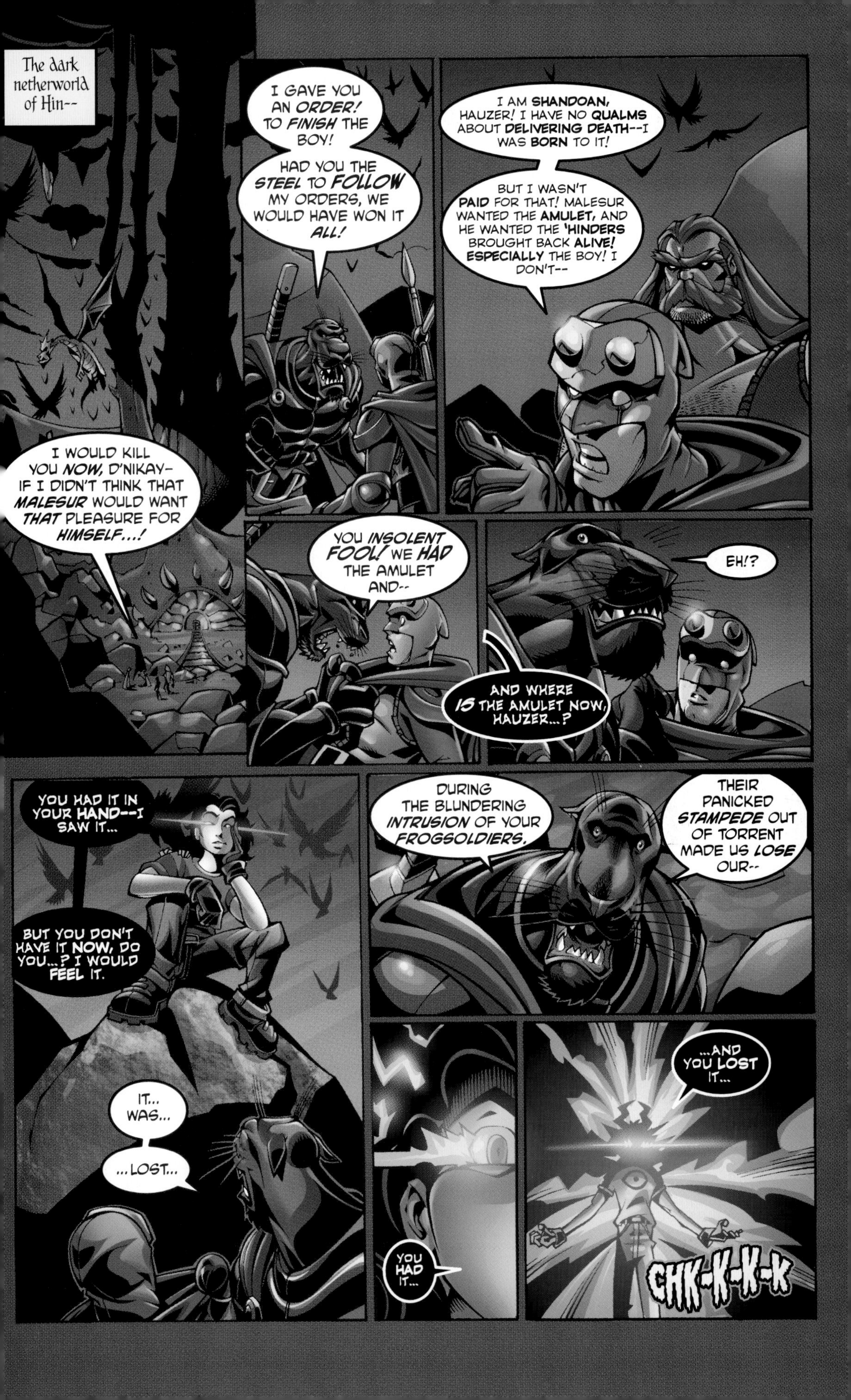
The dark netherworld of Hin--
I GAVE YOU AN ORDER! TO FINISH THE BOY!
HAD YOU THE STEEL TO FOLLOW MY ORDERS, WE WOULD HAVE WON IT ALL!
I AM SHANDOAN, HAUZER! I HAVE NO QUALMS ABOUT DELIVERING DEATH--I WAS BORN TO IT!
BUT I WASN'T PAID FOR THAT! MALESUR WANTED THE AMULET, AND HE WANTED THE 'HINDERS BROUGHT BACK ALIVE! ESPECIALLY THE BOY! I DON'T--
I WOULD KILL YOU NOW, D'NIKAY-- IF I DIDN'T THINK THAT MALESUR WOULD WANT THAT PLEASURE FOR HIMSELF...!
YOU INSOLENT FOOL! WE HAD THE AMULET AND--
EH!?
AND WHERE IS THE AMULET NOW, HAUZER...?
YOU HAD IT IN YOUR HAND--I SAW IT...
BUT YOU DON'T HAVE IT NOW, DO YOU...? I WOULD FEEL IT.
IT... WAS...
...LOST...
DURING THE BLUNDERING INTRUSION OF YOUR FROGSOLDIERS.
THEIR PANICKED STAMPEDE OUT OF TORRENT MADE US LOSE OUR--
YOU HAD IT...
...AND YOU LOST IT...
CHK-K-K-K

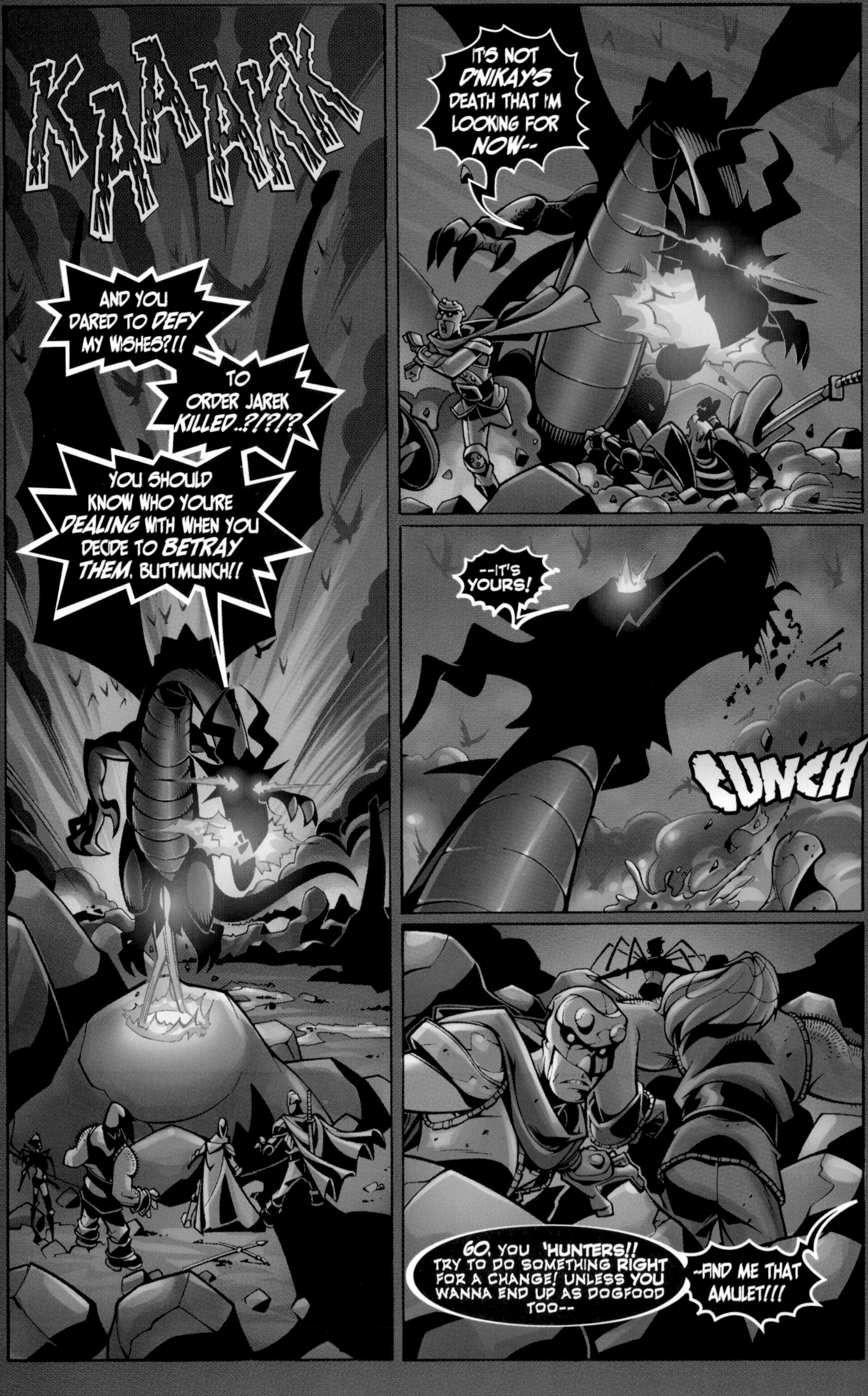
KAAAKK
AND YOU DARED TO DEFY MY WISHES?!!
TO ORDER JAREK KILLED..?!?!?
YOU SHOULD KNOW WHO YOU'RE DEALING WITH WHEN YOU DECIDE TO BETRAY THEM, BUTTMUNCH!!
IT'S NOT D'NIKAY'S DEATH THAT I'M LOOKING FOR NOW--
--IT'S YOURS!
CUNCH
GO, YOU 'HUNTERS!! TRY TO DO SOMETHING RIGHT FOR A CHANGE! UNLESS YOU WANNA END UP AS DOGFOOD TOO--
--FIND ME THAT AMULET!!!

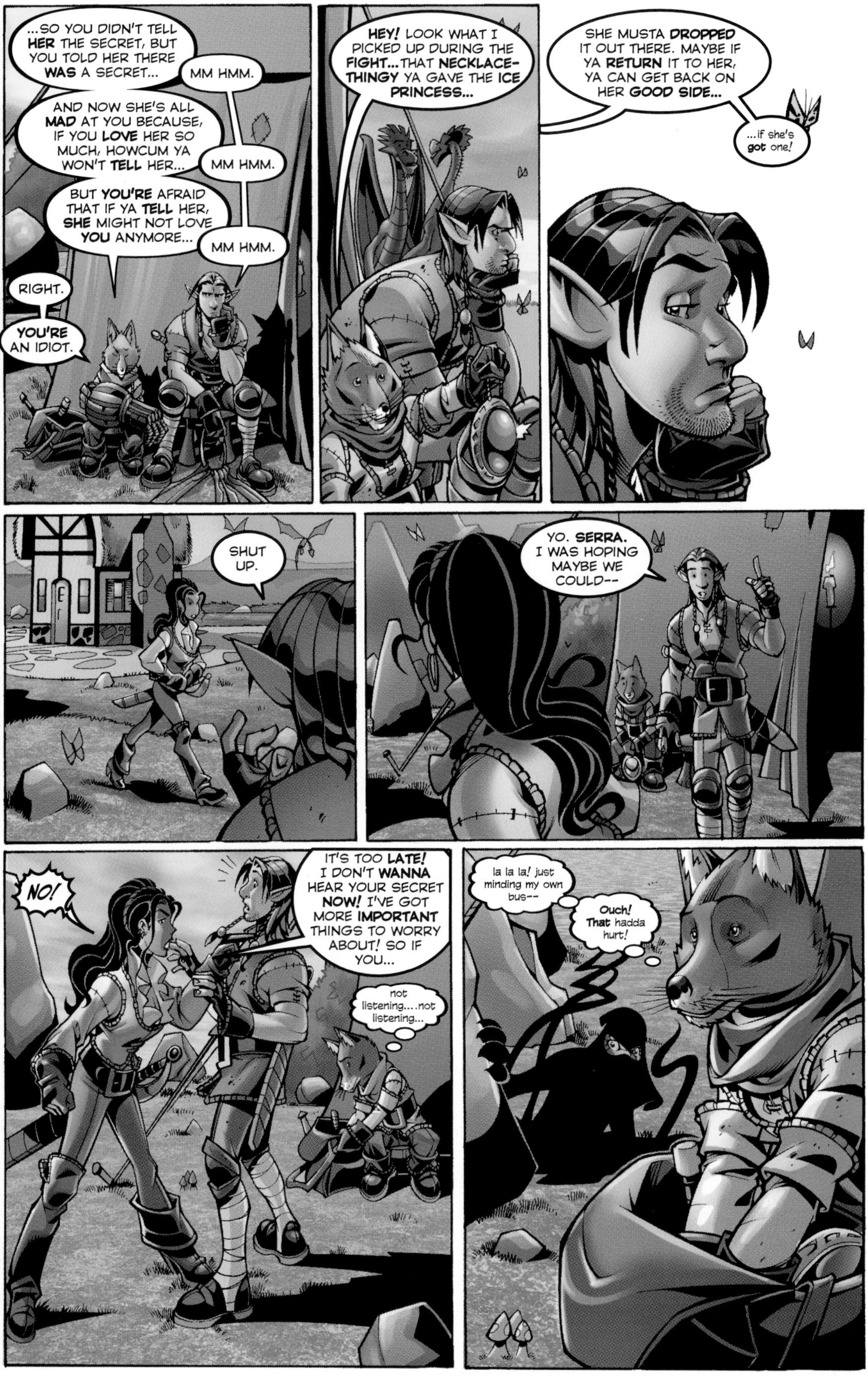
...SO YOU DIDN'T TELL HER THE SECRET, BUT YOU TOLD HER THERE WAS A SECRET...
MM HMM.
AND NOW SHE'S ALL MAD AT YOU BECAUSE, IF YOU LOVE HER SO MUCH, HOWCUM YA WON'T TELL HER...
MM HMM.
BUT YOU'RE AFRAID THAT IF YA TELL HER, SHE MIGHT NOT LOVE YOU ANYMORE...
MM HMM.
RIGHT.
YOU'RE AN IDIOT.
HEY! LOOK WHAT I PICKED UP DURING THE FIGHT...THAT NECKLACE-THINGY YA GAVE THE ICE PRINCESS...
SHE MUSTA DROPPED IT OUT THERE. MAYBE IF YA RETURN IT TO HER, YA CAN GET BACK ON HER GOOD SIDE...
...if she's got one!
SHUT UP.
YO. SERRA. I WAS HOPING MAYBE WE COULD--
NO!
IT'S TOO LATE! I DON'T WANNA HEAR YOUR SECRET NOW! I'VE GOT MORE IMPORTANT THINGS TO WORRY ABOUT! SO IF YOU...
not listening....not listening...
la la la! just minding my own bus--
Ouch! That hadda hurt!

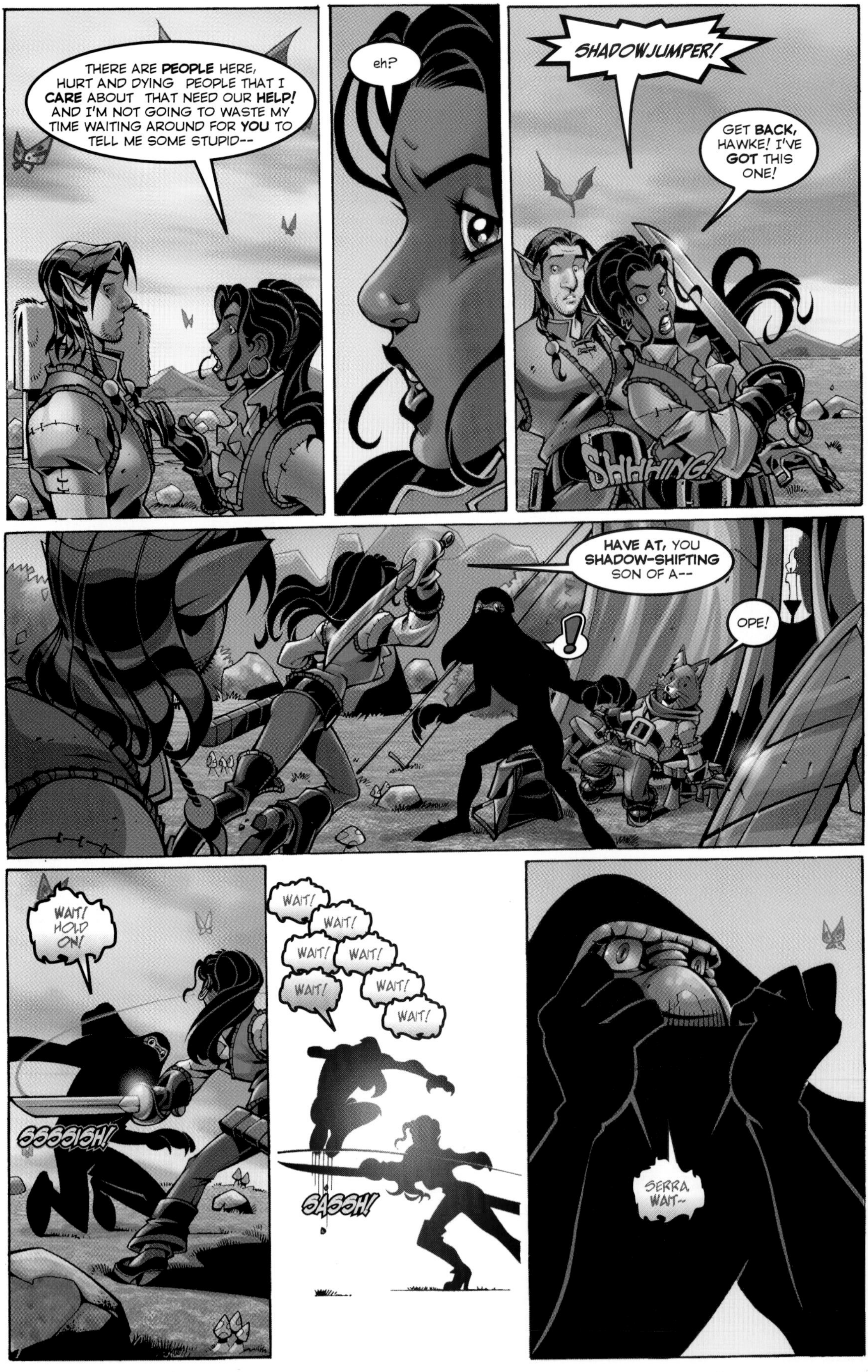
THERE ARE **PEOPLE** HERE, HURT AND DYING PEOPLE THAT I **CARE** ABOUT THAT NEED OUR **HELP!** AND I'M NOT GOING TO WASTE MY TIME WAITING AROUND FOR **YOU** TO TELL ME SOME STUPID--
eh?
SHADOWJUMPER!
GET **BACK,** HAWKE! I'VE **GOT** THIS ONE!
SHHHING!
HAVE AT, YOU **SHADOW-SHIFTING** SON OF A--
!
OPE!
WAIT! HOLD ON!
SSSSISH!
WAIT!
WAIT!
WAIT!
WAIT!
WAIT!
WAIT!
WAIT!
SASSH!
SERRA, WAIT--

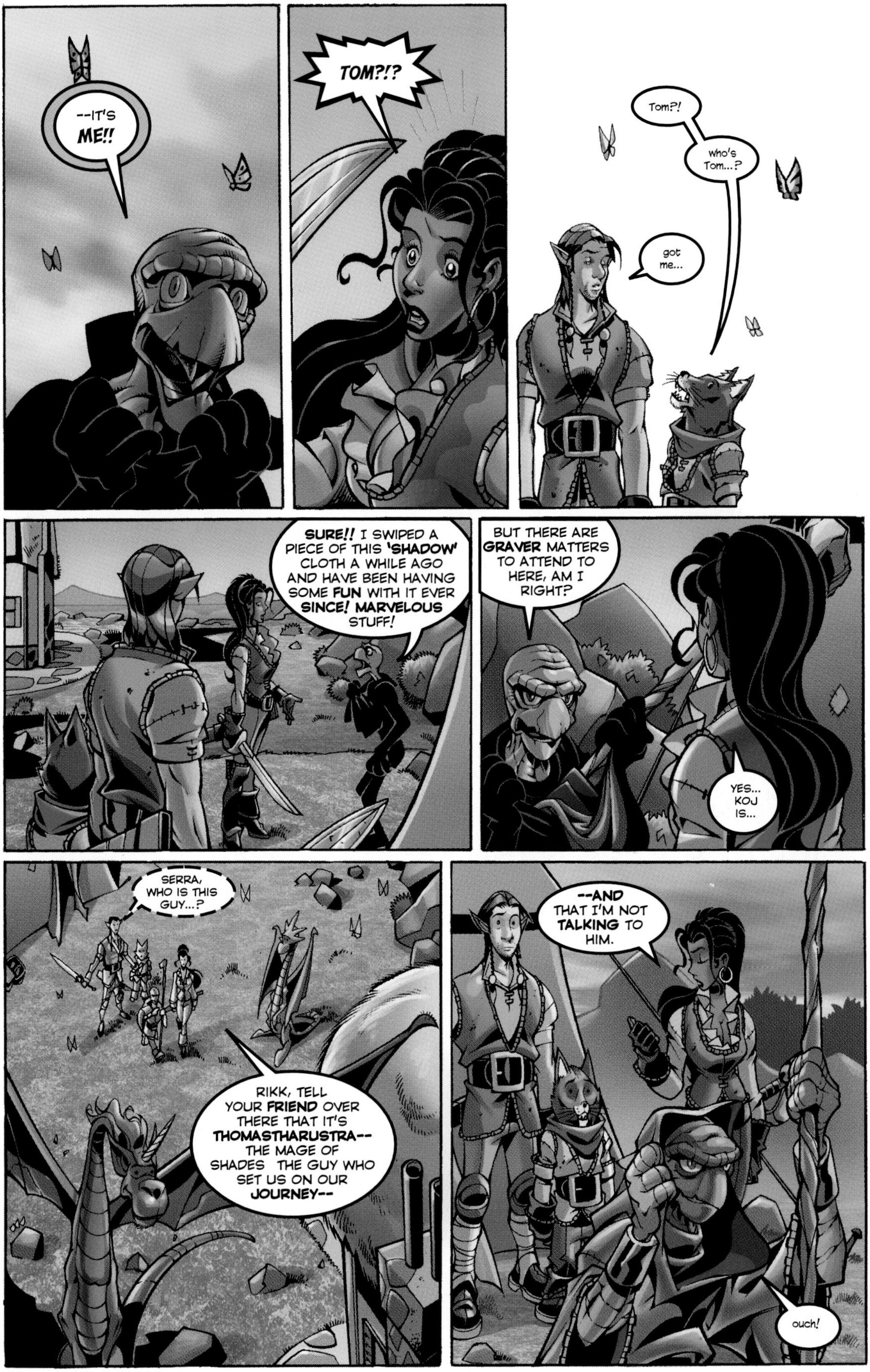
--IT'S
ME!!
TOM?!?
Tom?!
who's
Tom...?
got
me...
SURE!! I SWIPED A PIECE OF THIS 'SHADOW' CLOTH A WHILE AGO AND HAVE BEEN HAVING SOME FUN WITH IT EVER SINCE! MARVELOUS STUFF!
BUT THERE ARE GRAVER MATTERS TO ATTEND TO HERE, AM I RIGHT?
YES... KOJ IS...
SERRA, WHO IS THIS GUY...?
RIKK, TELL YOUR FRIEND OVER THERE THAT IT'S THOMASTHARUSTRA-- THE MAGE OF SHADES THE GUY WHO SET US ON OUR JOURNEY--
--AND THAT I'M NOT TALKING TO HIM.
ouch!

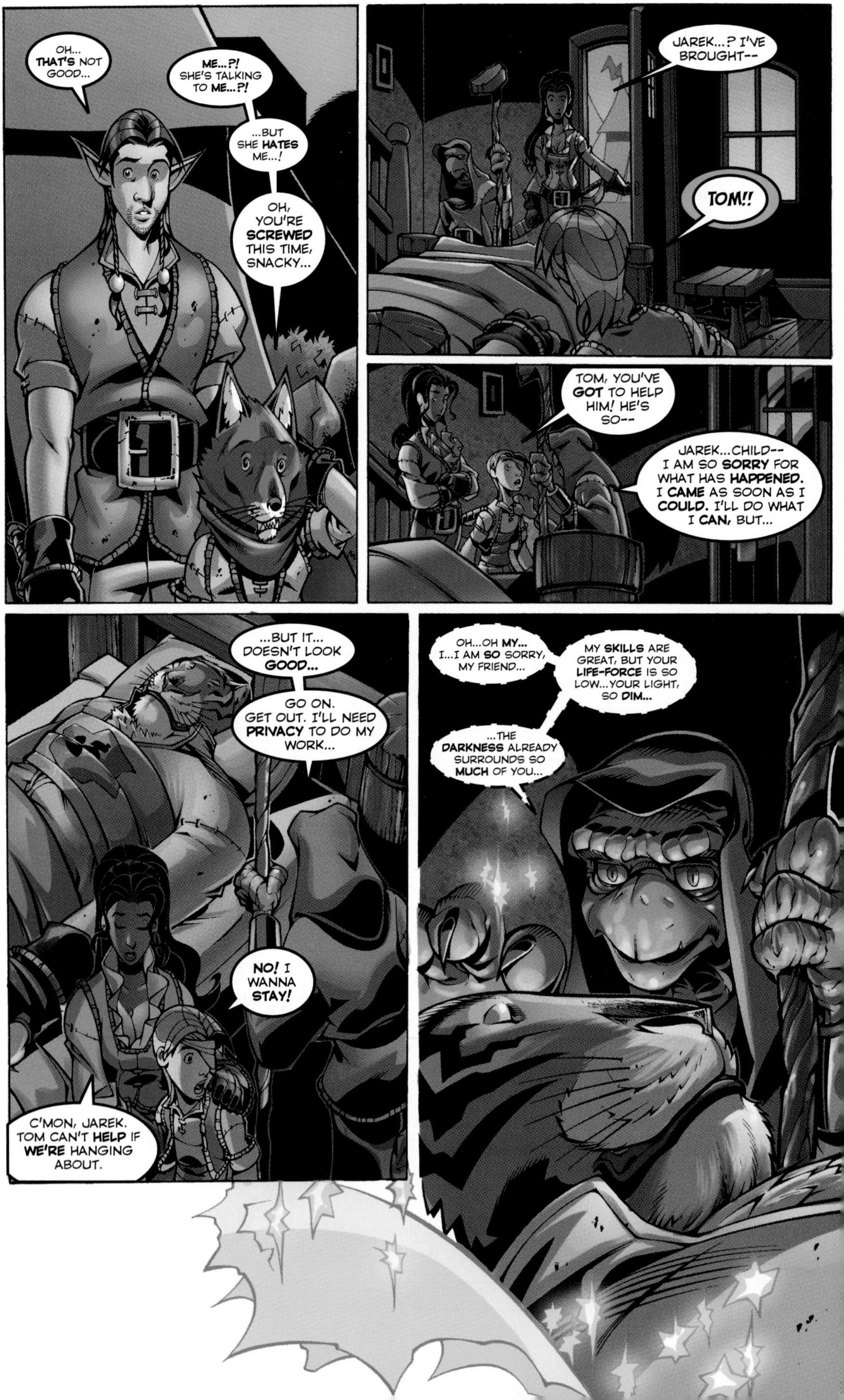
OH... THAT'S NOT GOOD...
ME...?! SHE'S TALKING TO ME...?!
...BUT SHE HATES ME...!
OH, YOU'RE SCREWED THIS TIME, SNACKY...
JAREK...? I'VE BROUGHT--
TOM!!
TOM, YOU'VE GOT TO HELP HIM! HE'S SO--
JAREK...CHILD-- I AM SO SORRY FOR WHAT HAS HAPPENED. I CAME AS SOON AS I COULD. I'LL DO WHAT I CAN, BUT...
...BUT IT... DOESN'T LOOK GOOD...
GO ON. GET OUT. I'LL NEED PRIVACY TO DO MY WORK...
NO! I WANNA STAY!
C'MON, JAREK. TOM CAN'T HELP IF WE'RE HANGING ABOUT.
OH...OH MY... I...I AM SO SORRY, MY FRIEND...
MY SKILLS ARE GREAT, BUT YOUR LIFE-FORCE IS SO LOW...YOUR LIGHT, SO DIM...
...THE DARKNESS ALREADY SURROUNDS SO MUCH OF YOU...

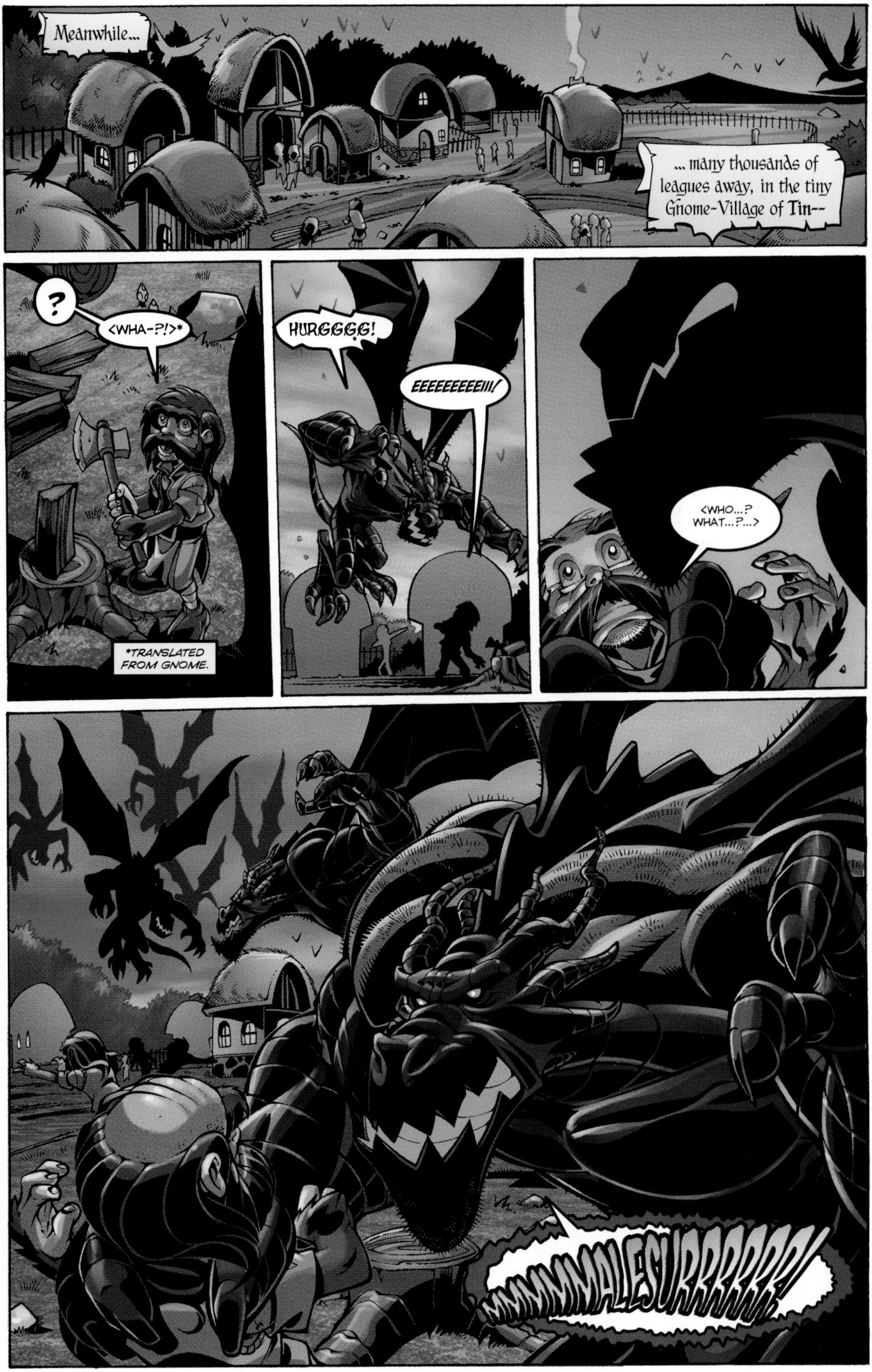
Meanwhile...
... many thousands of leagues away, in the tiny Gnome-Village of Tin--
?
<WHA-?!>*
*TRANSLATED FROM GNOME.
HURGGGG!
EEEEEEEEEIII!
<WHO...? WHAT...?...>
MMMMMMALESURRRRRRR!

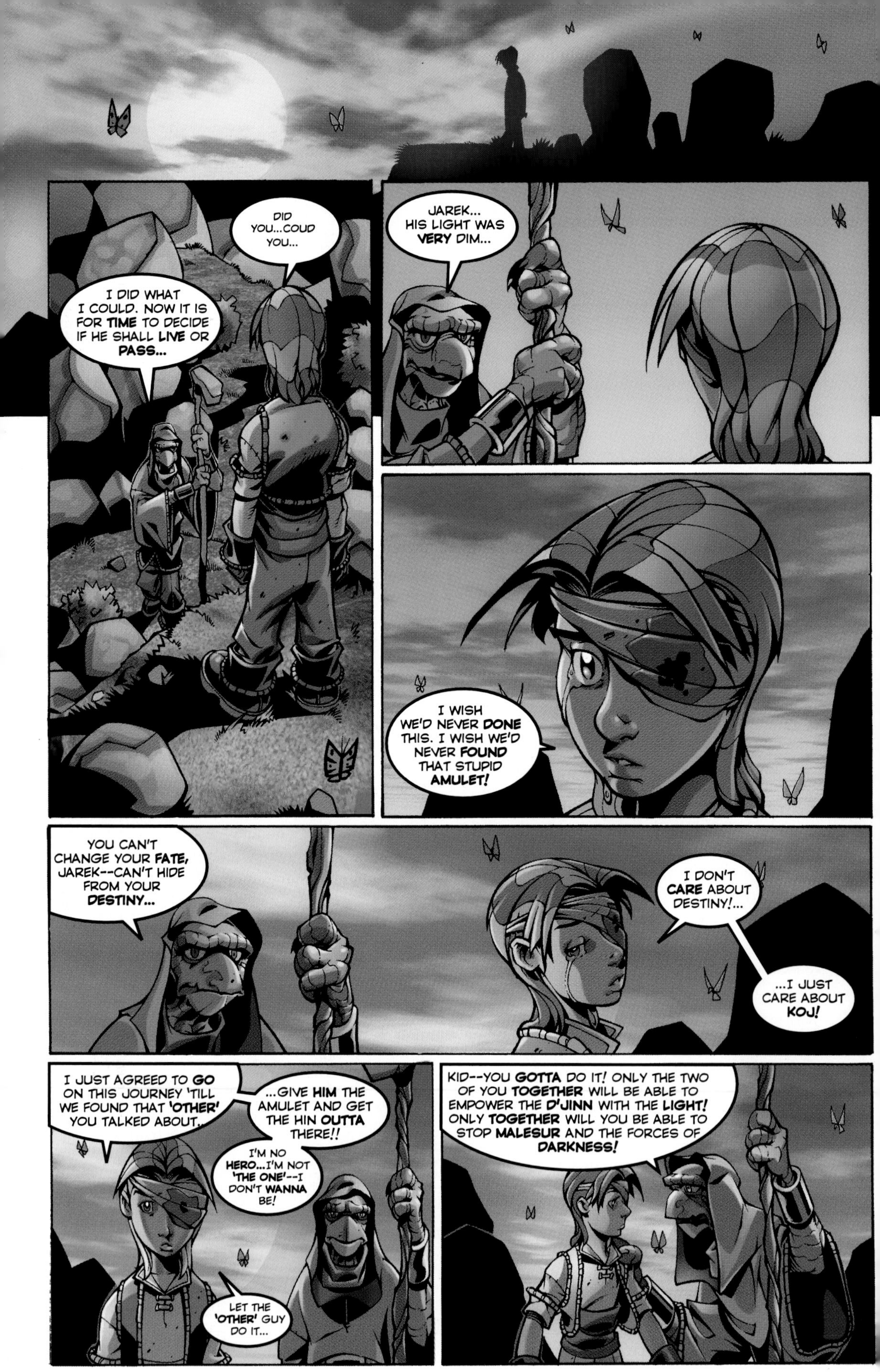
DID YOU...COUD YOU...
I DID WHAT I COULD. NOW IT IS FOR TIME TO DECIDE IF HE SHALL LIVE OR PASS...
JAREK... HIS LIGHT WAS VERY DIM...
I WISH WE'D NEVER DONE THIS. I WISH WE'D NEVER FOUND THAT STUPID AMULET!
YOU CAN'T CHANGE YOUR FATE, JAREK--CAN'T HIDE FROM YOUR DESTINY...
I DON'T CARE ABOUT DESTINY!...
...I JUST CARE ABOUT KOJ!
I JUST AGREED TO GO ON THIS JOURNEY 'TILL WE FOUND THAT 'OTHER' YOU TALKED ABOUT...
...GIVE HIM THE AMULET AND GET THE HIN OUTTA THERE!!
I'M NO HERO...I'M NOT 'THE ONE'--I DON'T WANNA BE!
LET THE 'OTHER' GUY DO IT...
KID--YOU GOTTA DO IT! ONLY THE TWO OF YOU TOGETHER WILL BE ABLE TO EMPOWER THE D'JINN WITH THE LIGHT! ONLY TOGETHER WILL YOU BE ABLE TO STOP MALESUR AND THE FORCES OF DARKNESS!

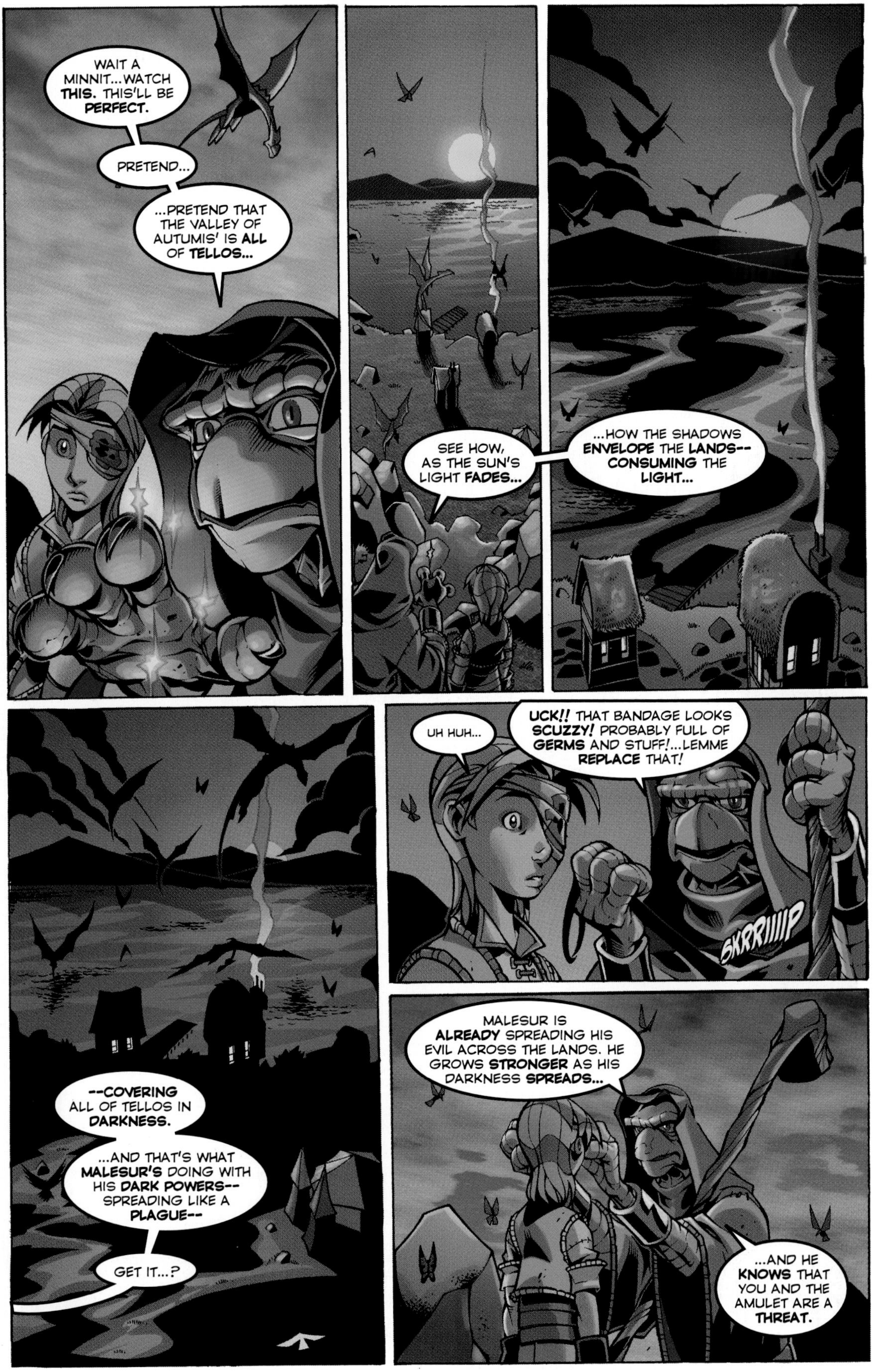
WAIT A MINNIT...WATCH **THIS.** THIS'LL BE **PERFECT.**
PRETEND...
...PRETEND THAT THE VALLEY OF AUTUMIS' IS **ALL** OF **TELLOS...**
SEE HOW, AS THE SUN'S LIGHT **FADES...**
...HOW THE SHADOWS **ENVELOPE** THE **LANDS--** **CONSUMING** THE **LIGHT...**
--COVERING ALL OF TELLOS IN **DARKNESS.**
...AND THAT'S WHAT **MALESUR'S** DOING WITH HIS **DARK POWERS--** SPREADING LIKE A **PLAGUE--**
GET IT...?
UH HUH...
UCK!! THAT BANDAGE LOOKS **SCUZZY!** PROBABLY FULL OF **GERMS** AND STUFF!...LEMME **REPLACE** THAT!
SKRRIIIIP
MALESUR IS **ALREADY** SPREADING HIS EVIL ACROSS THE LANDS. HE GROWS **STRONGER** AS HIS DARKNESS **SPREADS...**
...AND HE **KNOWS** THAT YOU AND THE AMULET ARE A **THREAT.**

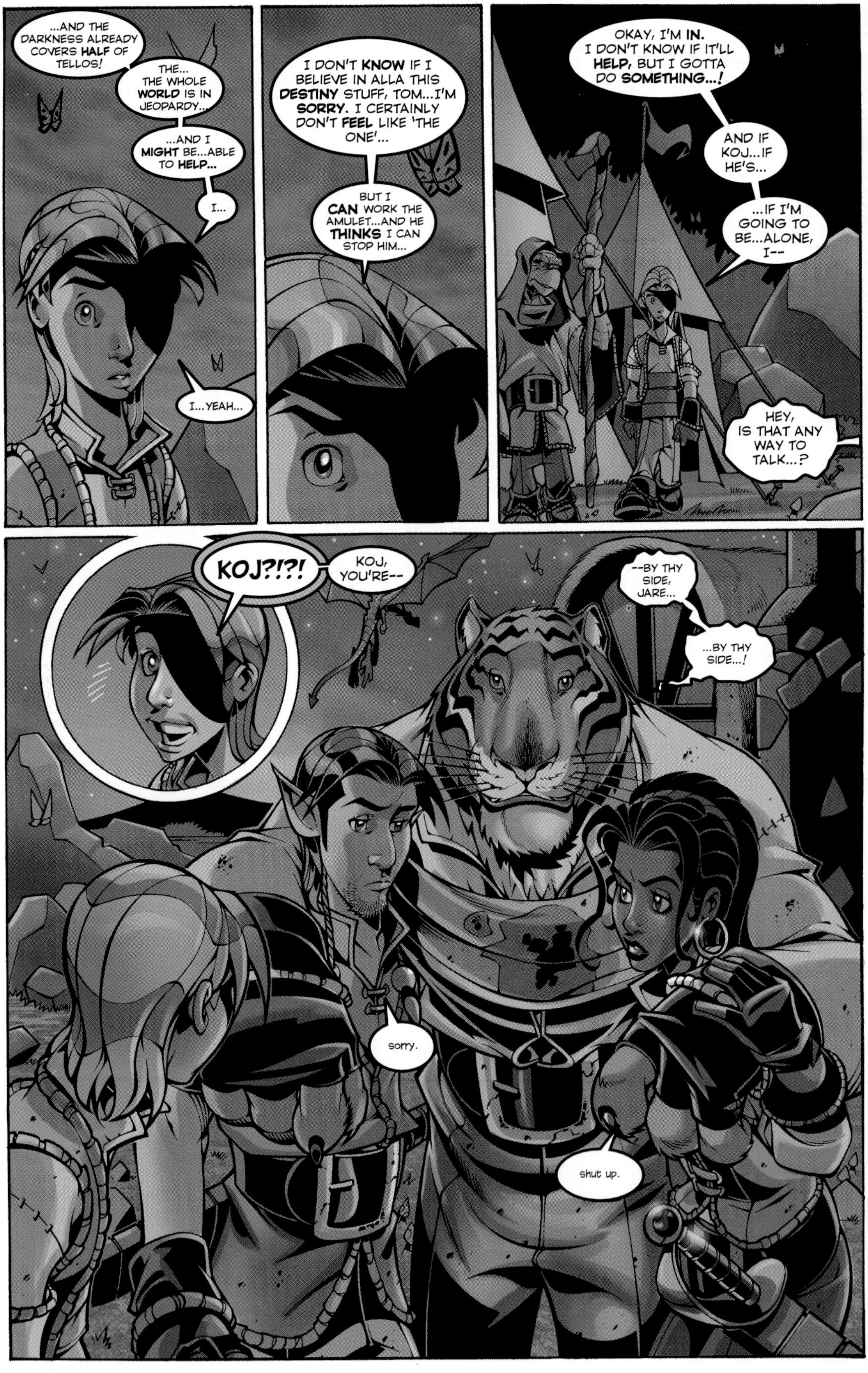
...AND THE DARKNESS ALREADY COVERS HALF OF TELLOS!
THE... THE WHOLE WORLD IS IN JEOPARDY...
...AND I MIGHT BE...ABLE TO HELP...
I...
I...YEAH...
I DON'T KNOW IF I BELIEVE IN ALLA THIS DESTINY STUFF, TOM...I'M SORRY. I CERTAINLY DON'T FEEL LIKE 'THE ONE'...
BUT I CAN WORK THE AMULET...AND HE THINKS I CAN STOP HIM...
OKAY, I'M IN. I DON'T KNOW IF IT'LL HELP, BUT I GOTTA DO SOMETHING...!
AND IF KOJ...IF HE'S...
...IF I'M GOING TO BE...ALONE, I--
HEY, IS THAT ANY WAY TO TALK...?
KOJ?!?!
KOJ, YOU'RE--
--BY THY SIDE, JARE...
...BY THY SIDE...!
sorry.
shut up.

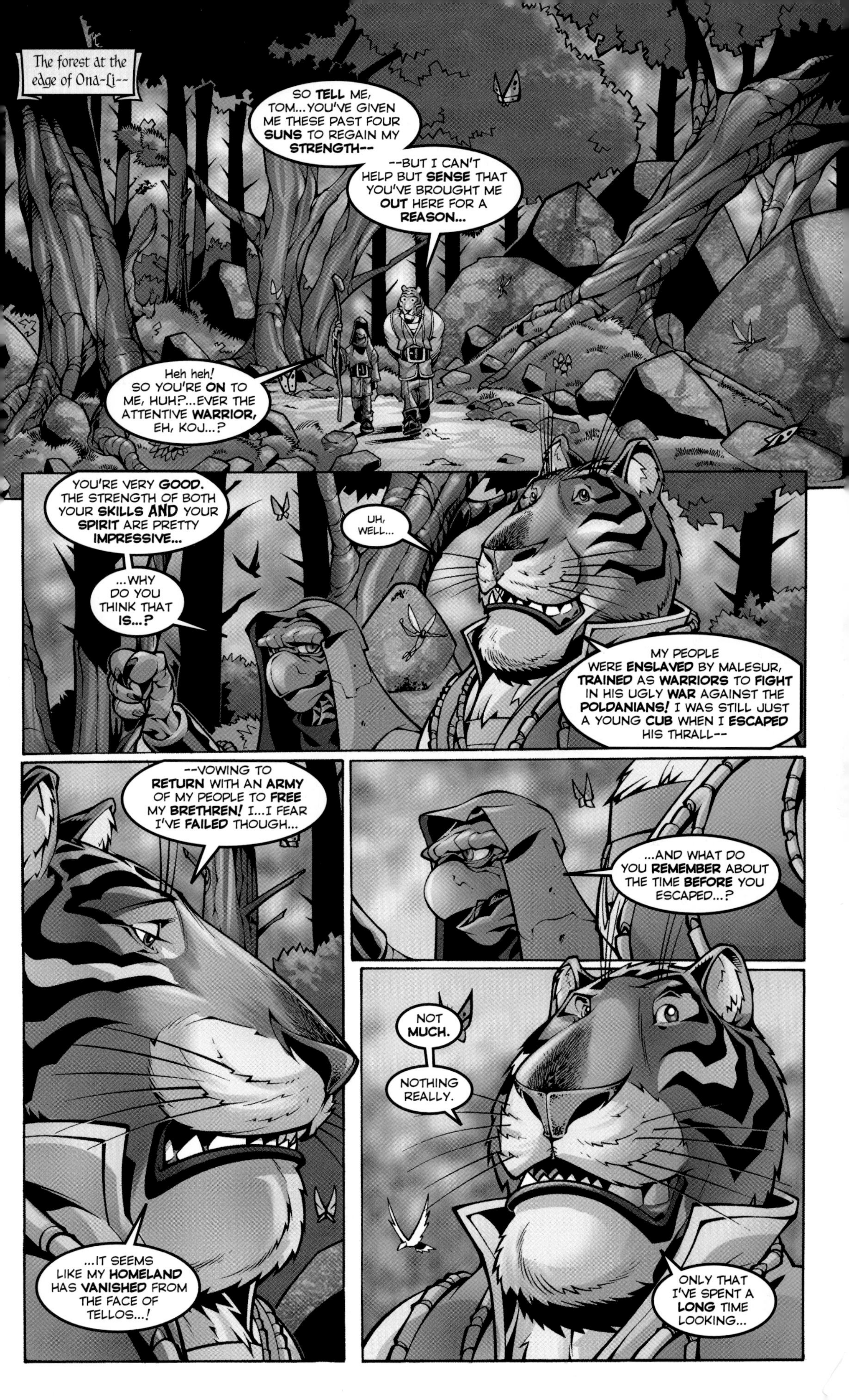
The forest at the edge of Ona-Li--
SO TELL ME, TOM...YOU'VE GIVEN ME THESE PAST FOUR SUNS TO REGAIN MY STRENGTH--
--BUT I CAN'T HELP BUT SENSE THAT YOU'VE BROUGHT ME OUT HERE FOR A REASON...
Heh heh! SO YOU'RE ON TO ME, HUH?...EVER THE ATTENTIVE WARRIOR, EH, KOJ...?
YOU'RE VERY GOOD. THE STRENGTH OF BOTH YOUR SKILLS AND YOUR SPIRIT ARE PRETTY IMPRESSIVE...
UH, WELL...
...WHY DO YOU THINK THAT IS...?
MY PEOPLE WERE ENSLAVED BY MALESUR, TRAINED AS WARRIORS TO FIGHT IN HIS UGLY WAR AGAINST THE POLDANIANS! I WAS STILL JUST A YOUNG CUB WHEN I ESCAPED HIS THRALL--
--VOWING TO RETURN WITH AN ARMY OF MY PEOPLE TO FREE MY BRETHREN! I...I FEAR I'VE FAILED THOUGH...
...IT SEEMS LIKE MY HOMELAND HAS VANISHED FROM THE FACE OF TELLOS...!
...AND WHAT DO YOU REMEMBER ABOUT THE TIME BEFORE YOU ESCAPED...?
NOT MUCH.
NOTHING REALLY.
ONLY THAT I'VE SPENT A LONG TIME LOOKING...

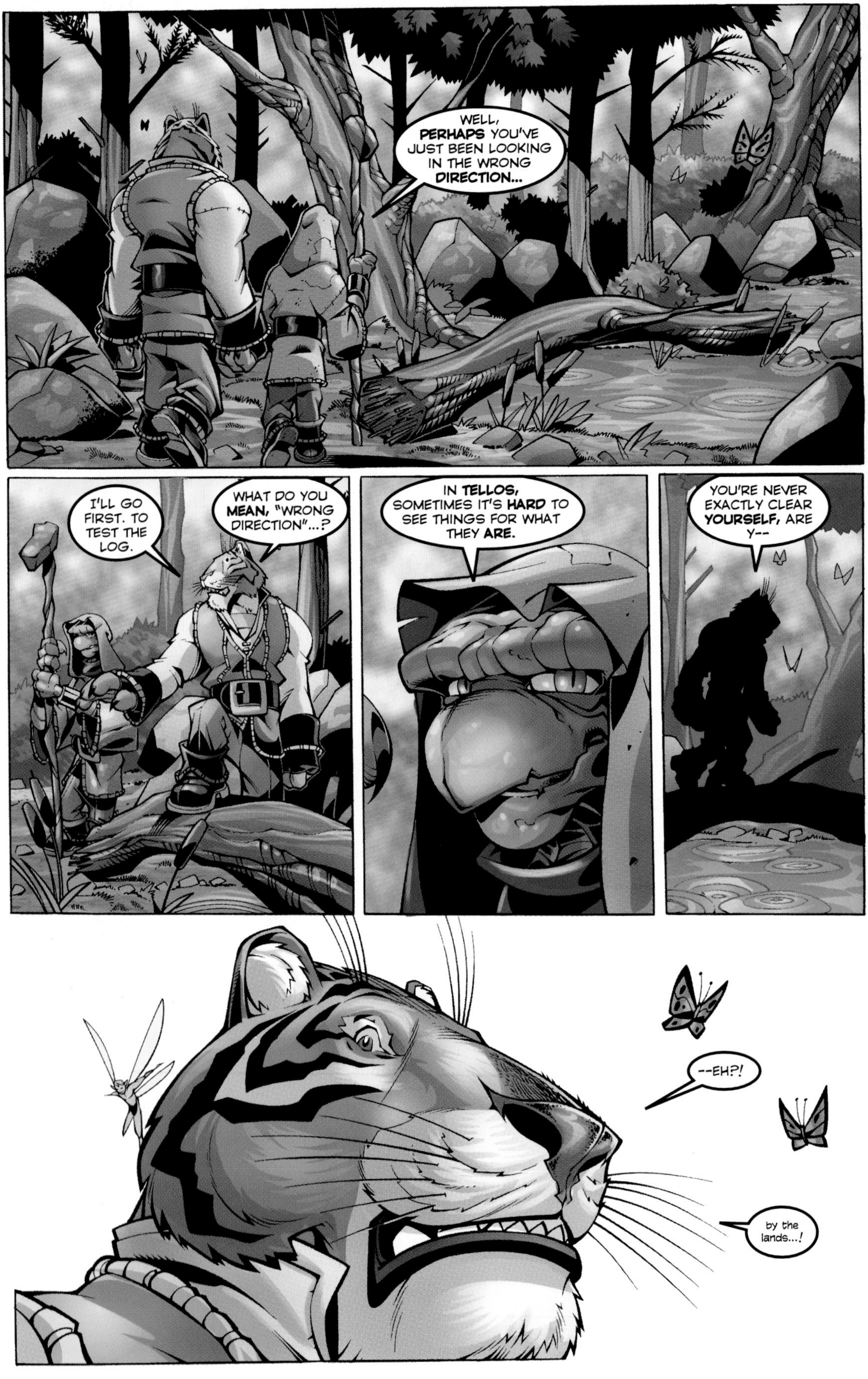
WELL, **PERHAPS** YOU'VE JUST BEEN LOOKING IN THE WRONG **DIRECTION...**
I'LL GO FIRST. TO TEST THE LOG.
WHAT DO YOU **MEAN,** "WRONG DIRECTION"...?
IN **TELLOS,** SOMETIMES IT'S **HARD** TO SEE THINGS FOR WHAT THEY **ARE.**
YOU'RE NEVER EXACTLY CLEAR **YOURSELF,** ARE Y--
--EH?!
by the lands...!

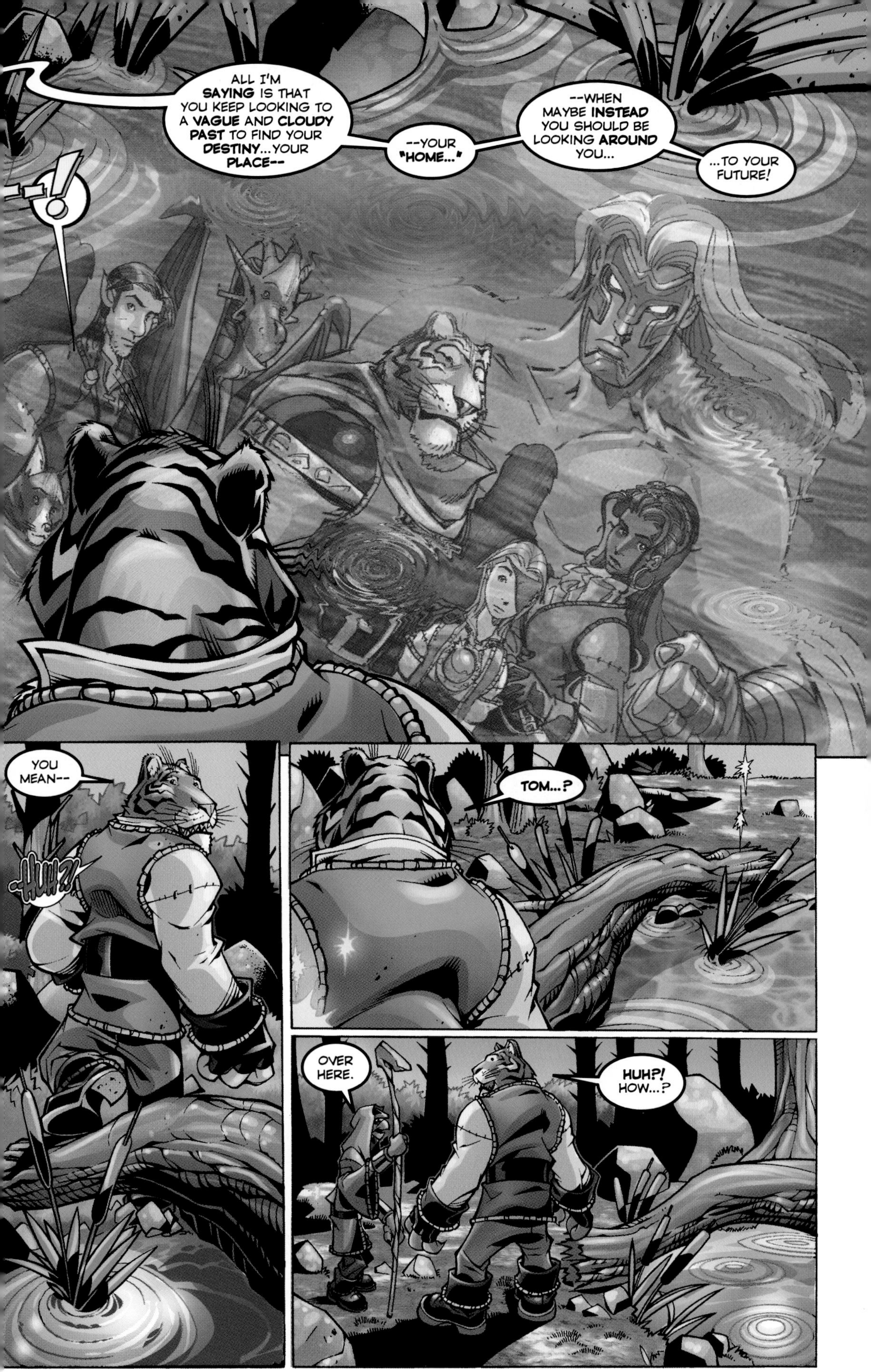
ALL I'M SAYING IS THAT YOU KEEP LOOKING TO A VAGUE AND CLOUDY PAST TO FIND YOUR DESTINY...YOUR PLACE--
--YOUR "HOME..."
--WHEN MAYBE INSTEAD YOU SHOULD BE LOOKING AROUND YOU...
...TO YOUR FUTURE!
--!
YOU MEAN--
-HUH?!
TOM...?
OVER HERE.
HUH?! HOW...?

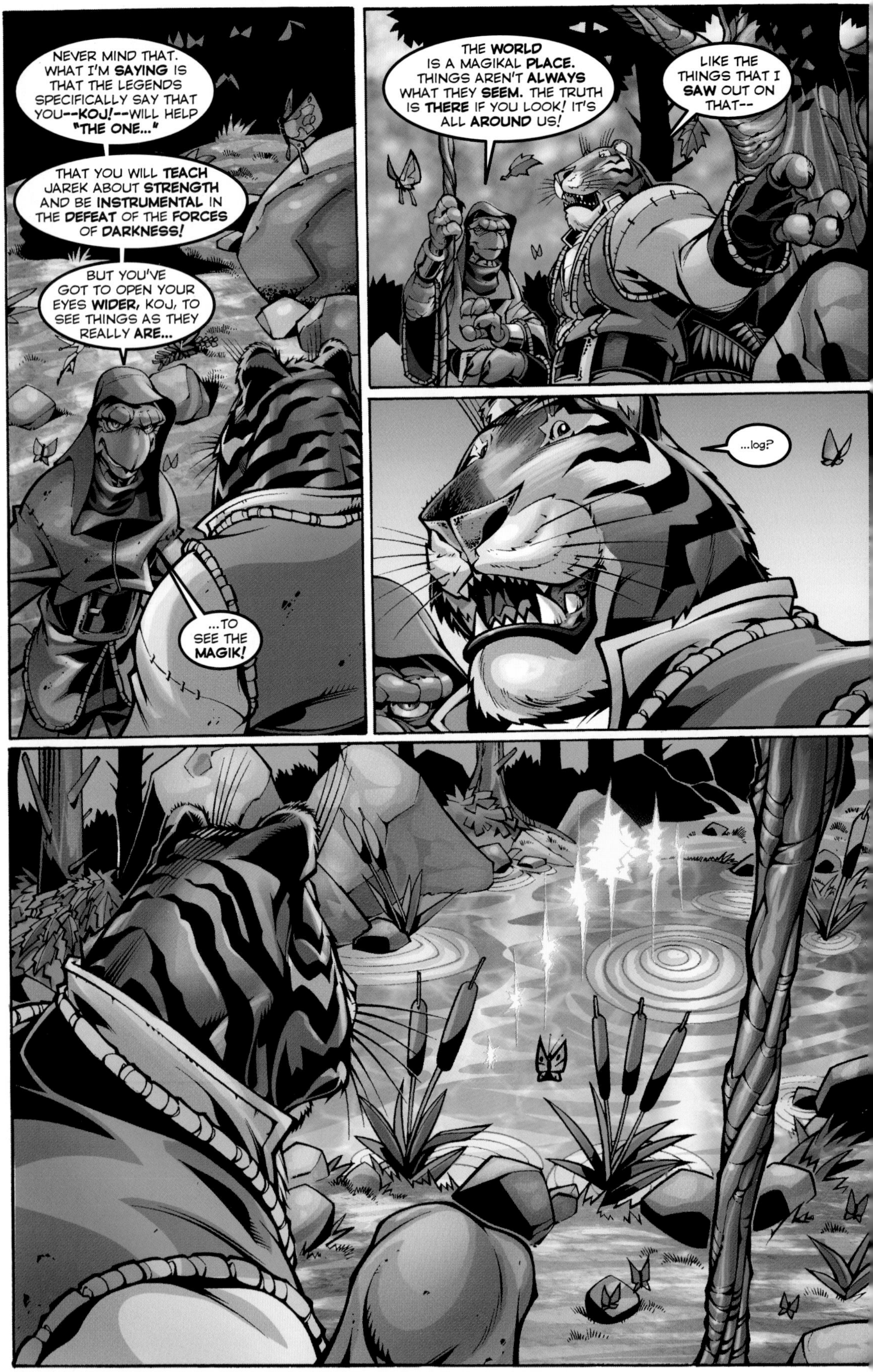

NEVER MIND THAT. WHAT I'M SAYING IS THAT THE LEGENDS SPECIFICALLY SAY THAT YOU--KOJ!--WILL HELP "THE ONE..."
THAT YOU WILL TEACH JAREK ABOUT STRENGTH AND BE INSTRUMENTAL IN THE DEFEAT OF THE FORCES OF DARKNESS!
BUT YOU'VE GOT TO OPEN YOUR EYES WIDER, KOJ, TO SEE THINGS AS THEY REALLY ARE...
...TO SEE THE MAGIK!
THE WORLD IS A MAGIKAL PLACE. THINGS AREN'T ALWAYS WHAT THEY SEEM. THE TRUTH IS THERE IF YOU LOOK! IT'S ALL AROUND US!
LIKE THE THINGS THAT I SAW OUT ON THAT--
...log?

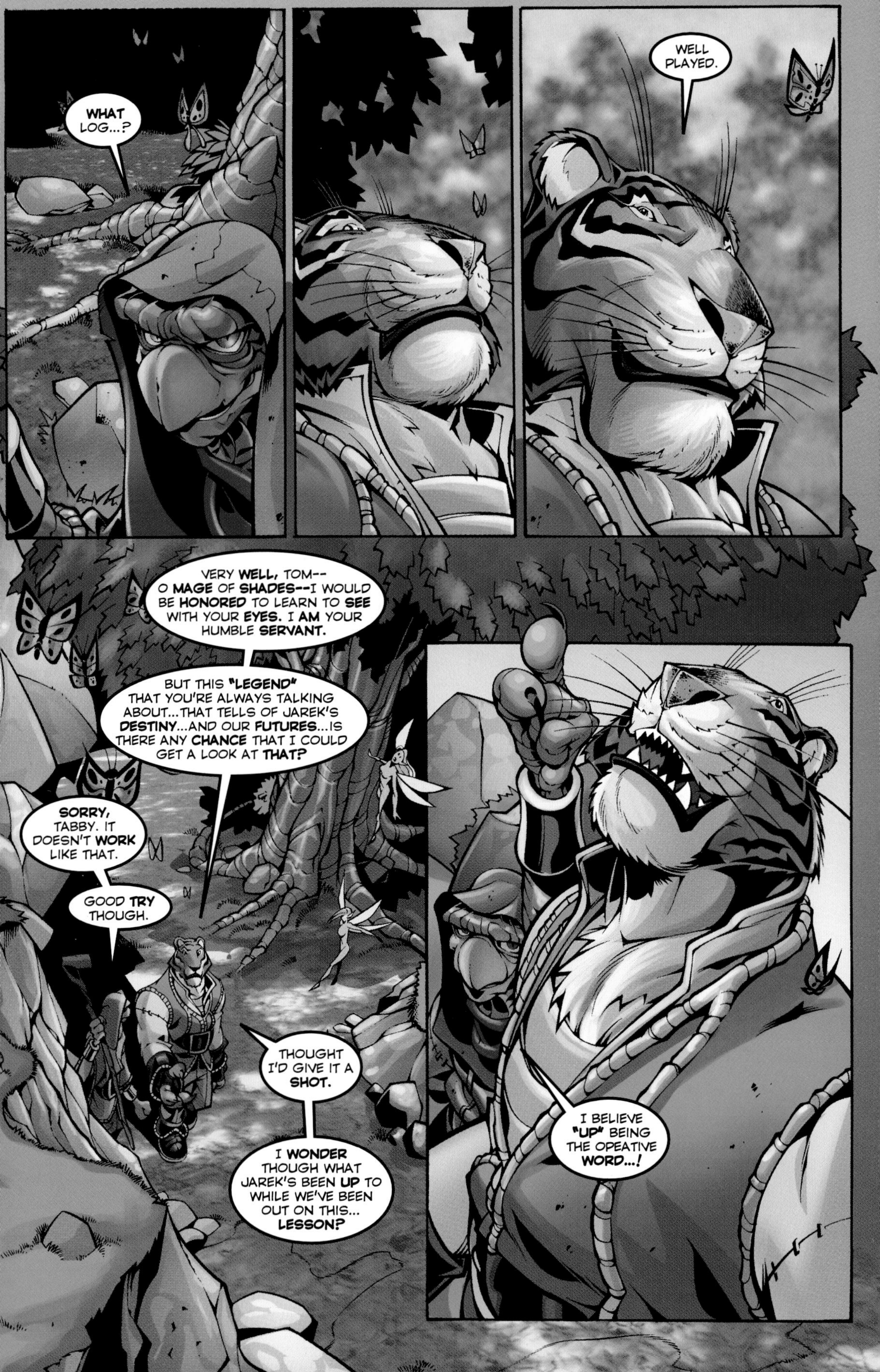
WHAT LOG...?
WELL PLAYED.
VERY WELL, TOM-- O MAGE OF SHADES--I WOULD BE HONORED TO LEARN TO SEE WITH YOUR EYES. I AM YOUR HUMBLE SERVANT.
BUT THIS "LEGEND" THAT YOU'RE ALWAYS TALKING ABOUT...THAT TELLS OF JAREK'S DESTINY...AND OUR FUTURES...IS THERE ANY CHANCE THAT I COULD GET A LOOK AT THAT?
SORRY, TABBY. IT DOESN'T WORK LIKE THAT.
GOOD TRY THOUGH.
THOUGHT I'D GIVE IT A SHOT.
I WONDER THOUGH WHAT JAREK'S BEEN UP TO WHILE WE'VE BEEN OUT ON THIS... LESSON?
I BELIEVE "UP" BEING THE OPEATIVE WORD...!

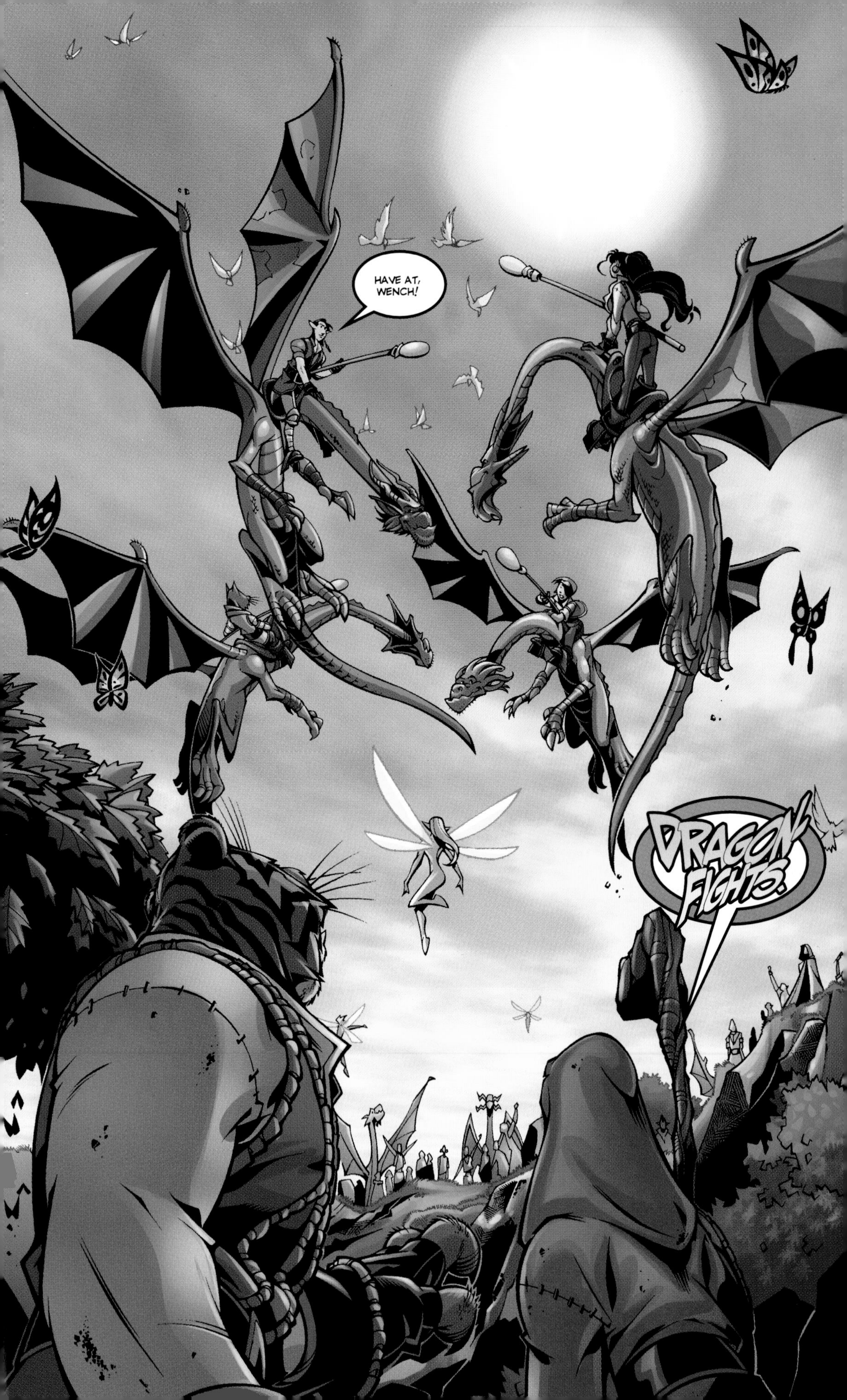
HAVE AT, WENCH!
DRAGON FIGHTS.

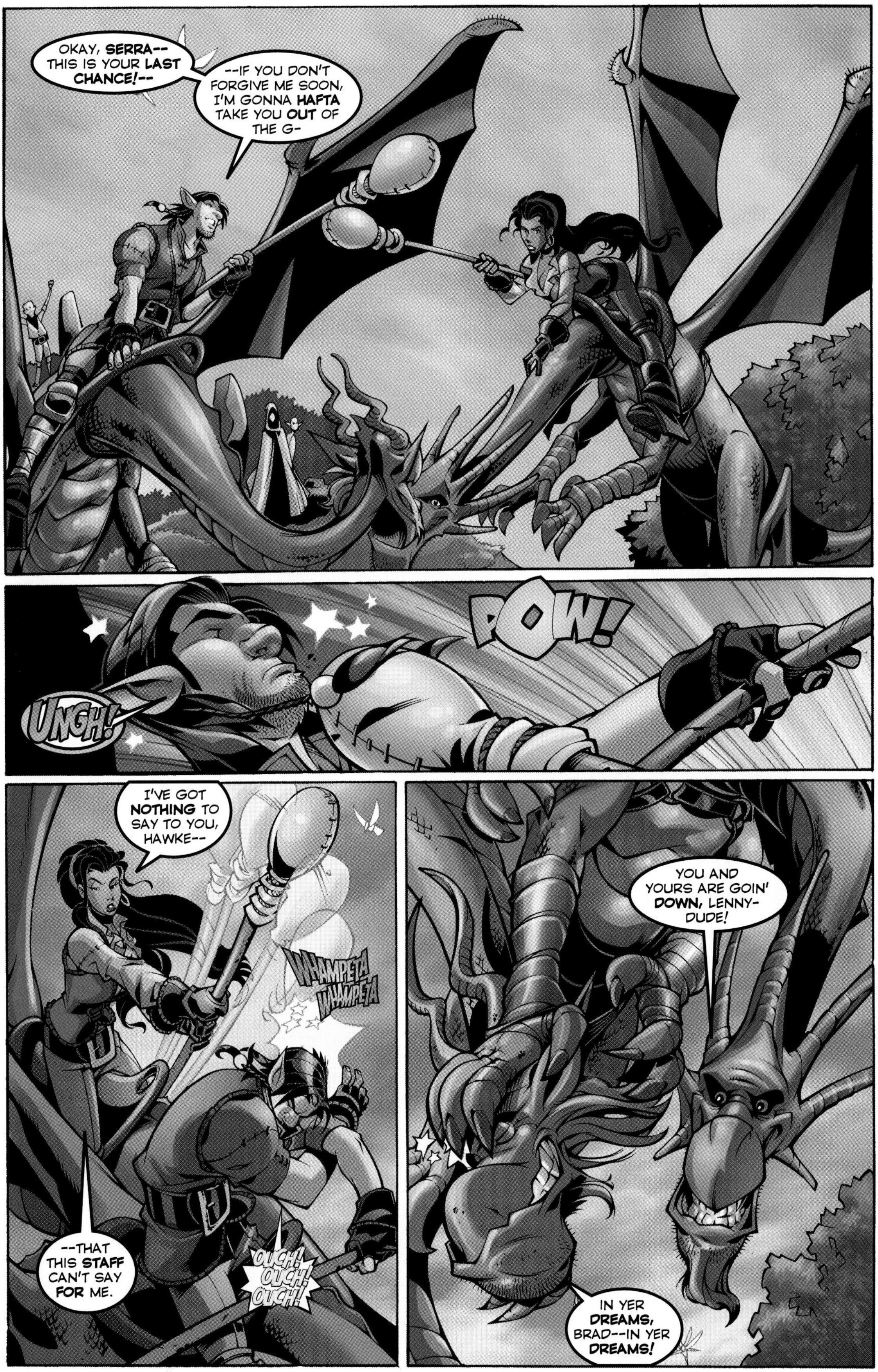
OKAY, SERRA-- THIS IS YOUR LAST CHANCE!--
--IF YOU DON'T FORGIVE ME SOON, I'M GONNA HAFTA TAKE YOU OUT OF THE G-
POW!
UNGH!
I'VE GOT NOTHING TO SAY TO YOU, HAWKE--
WHAMPETA WHAMPETA
--THAT THIS STAFF CAN'T SAY FOR ME.
OUCH! OUCH! OUCH!
YOU AND YOURS ARE GOIN' DOWN, LENNY-DUDE!
IN YER DREAMS, BRAD--IN YER DREAMS!

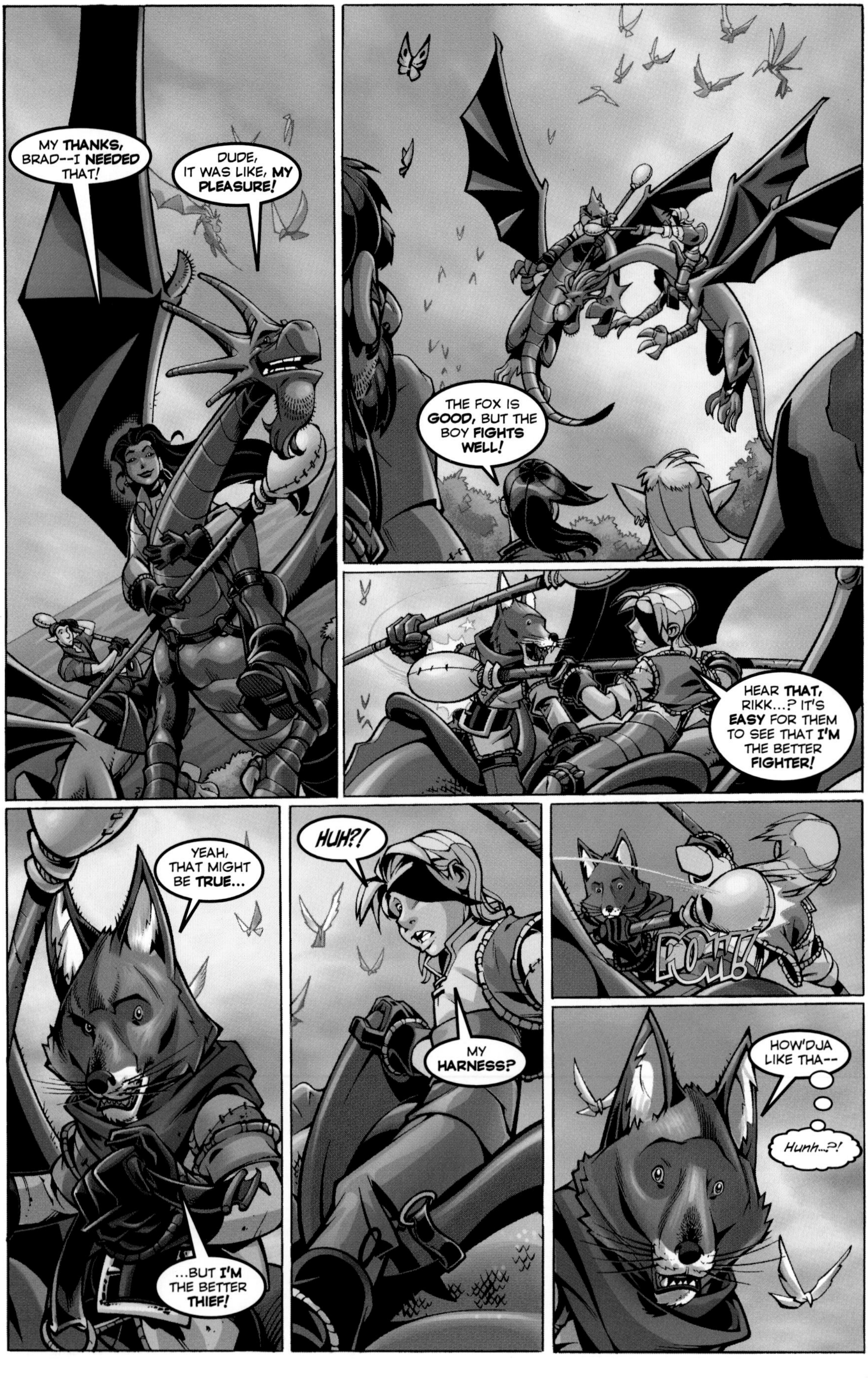

MY THANKS, BRAD--I NEEDED THAT!
DUDE, IT WAS LIKE, MY PLEASURE!
THE FOX IS GOOD, BUT THE BOY FIGHTS WELL!
HEAR THAT, RIKK...? IT'S EASY FOR THEM TO SEE THAT I'M THE BETTER FIGHTER!
YEAH, THAT MIGHT BE TRUE...
...BUT I'M THE BETTER THIEF!
HUH?!
MY HARNESS?
POW!
HOW'DJA LIKE THA--
Hunh...?!

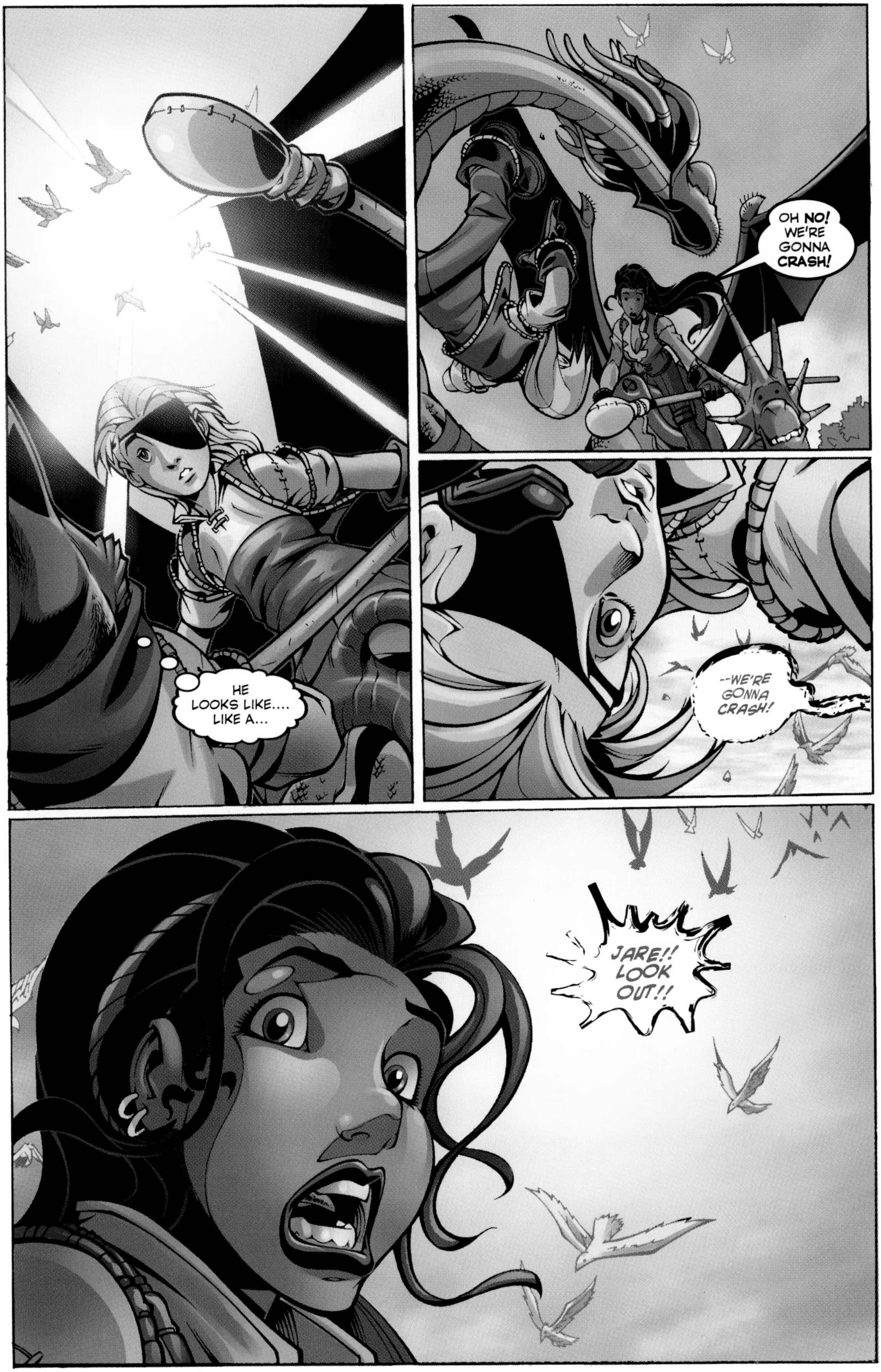
HE LOOKS LIKE.... LIKE A...
OH NO! WE'RE GONNA CRASH!
--WE'RE GONNA CRASH!
JARE!! LOOK OUT!!

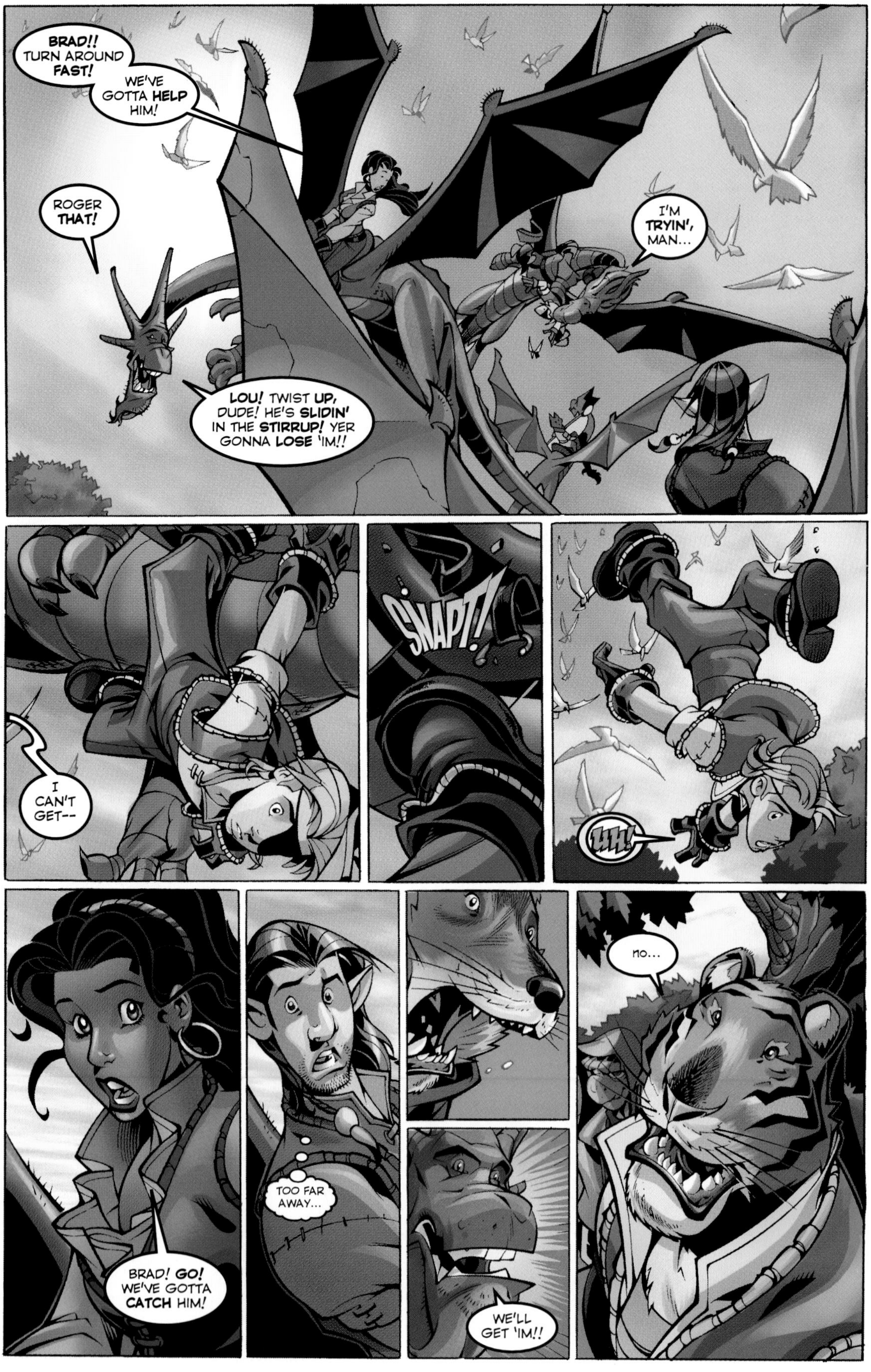
BRAD!! TURN AROUND FAST!
WE'VE GOTTA HELP HIM!
ROGER THAT!
LOU! TWIST UP, DUDE! HE'S SLIDIN' IN THE STIRRUP! YER GONNA LOSE 'IM!!
I'M TRYIN', MAN...
I CAN'T GET--
SNAPT!!
UH!
BRAD! GO! WE'VE GOTTA CATCH HIM!
TOO FAR AWAY...
WE'LL GET 'IM!!
no...

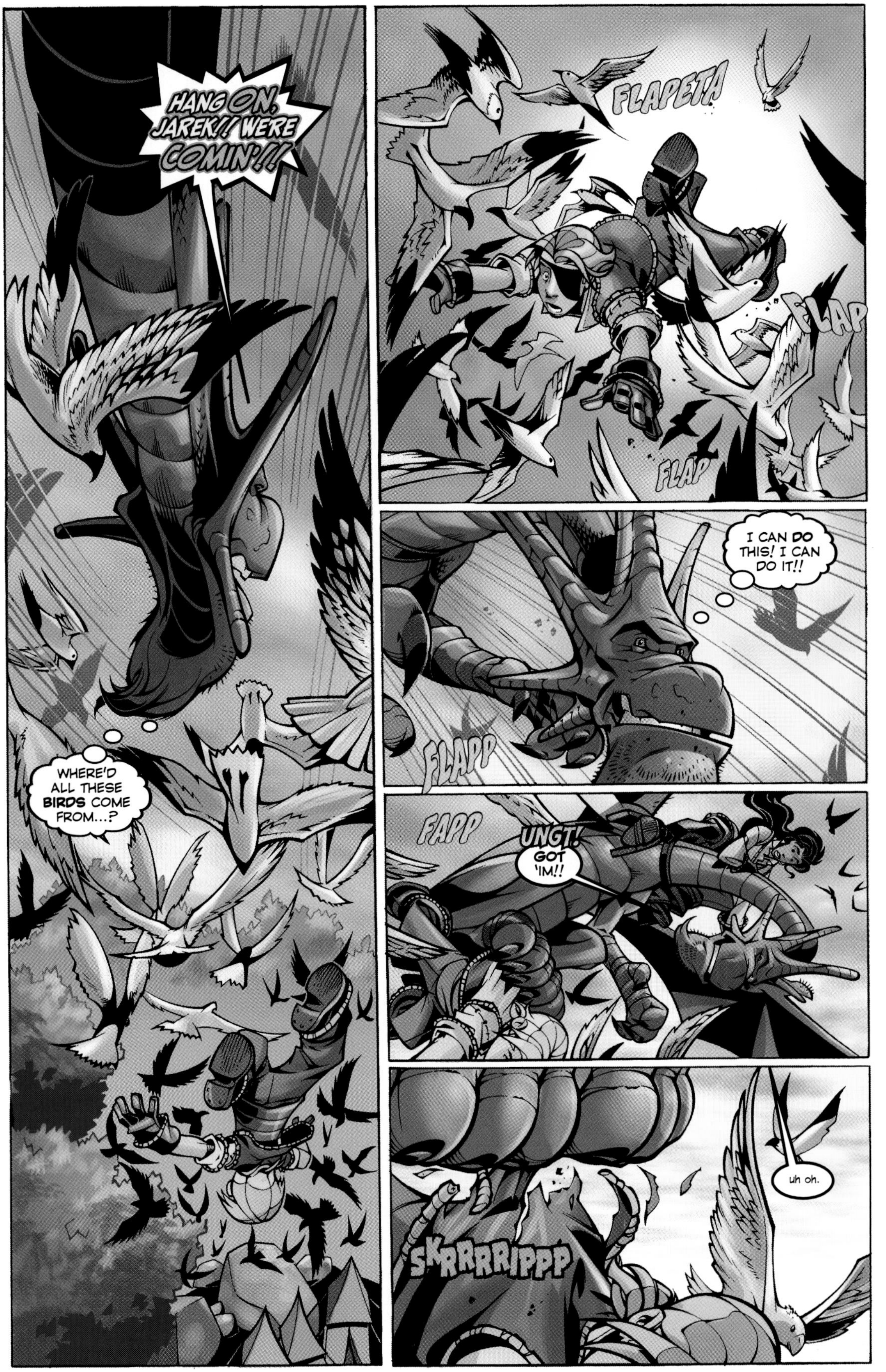
HANG ON, JAREK!! WE'RE COMIN'!!
WHERE'D ALL THESE BIRDS COME FROM...?
FLAPETA
FLAP
FLAP
I CAN DO THIS! I CAN DO IT!!
FLAPP
FAPP
UNGT! GOT 'IM!!
uh oh.
SKRRRRIPPP

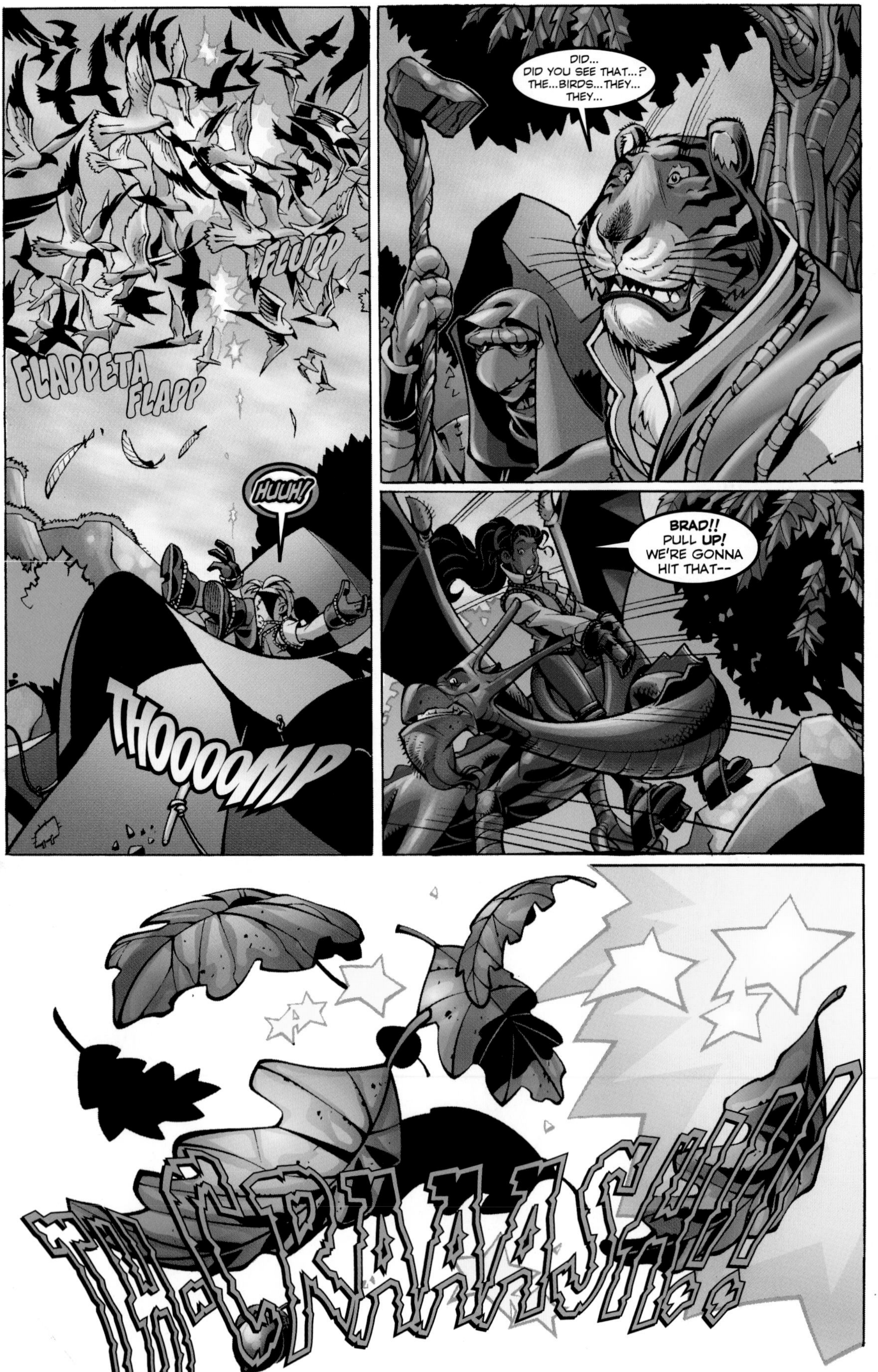

FLOPP
FLAPPETA FLAPP
DID... DID YOU SEE THAT...? THE...BIRDS...THEY... THEY...
HUUH!
THOOOOMP
BRAD!! PULL UP! WE'RE GONNA HIT THAT--
THRAAASH!!

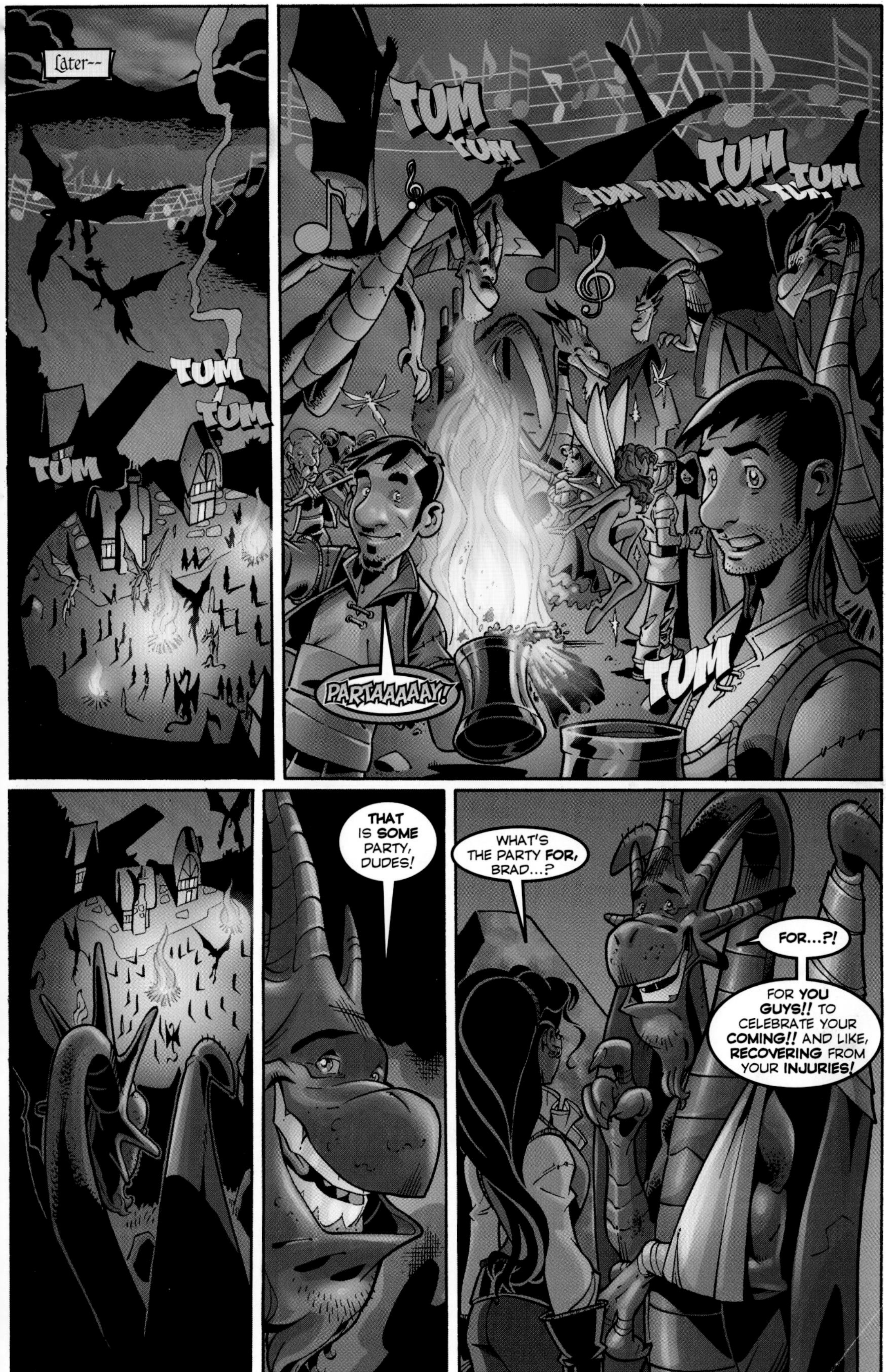
Later--
TUM
TUM
TUM
TUM
TUM
TUM TUM TUM TUM TUM TUM
PARTAAAAAY!!
TUM
THAT IS SOME PARTY, DUDES!
WHAT'S THE PARTY FOR, BRAD...?
FOR...?!
FOR YOU GUYS!! TO CELEBRATE YOUR COMING!! AND LIKE, RECOVERING FROM YOUR INJURIES!

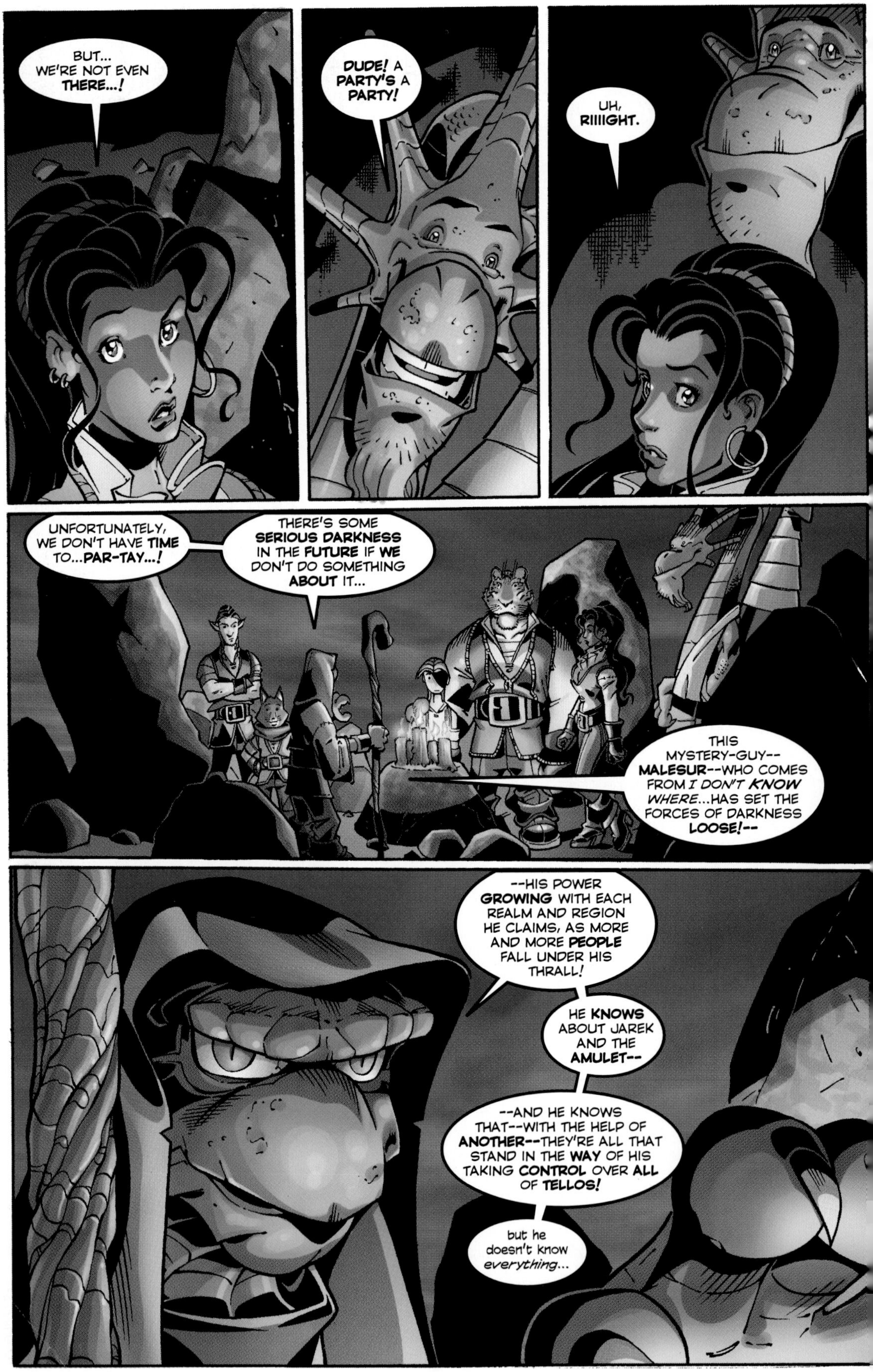
BUT... WE'RE NOT EVEN THERE...!
DUDE! A PARTY'S A PARTY!
UH, RIIIIGHT.
UNFORTUNATELY, WE DON'T HAVE TIME TO...PAR-TAY...!
THERE'S SOME SERIOUS DARKNESS IN THE FUTURE IF WE DON'T DO SOMETHING ABOUT IT...
THIS MYSTERY-GUY--MALESUR--WHO COMES FROM I DON'T KNOW WHERE...HAS SET THE FORCES OF DARKNESS LOOSE!--
--HIS POWER GROWING WITH EACH REALM AND REGION HE CLAIMS, AS MORE AND MORE PEOPLE FALL UNDER HIS THRALL!
HE KNOWS ABOUT JAREK AND THE AMULET--
--AND HE KNOWS THAT--WITH THE HELP OF ANOTHER--THEY'RE ALL THAT STAND IN THE WAY OF HIS TAKING CONTROL OVER ALL OF TELLOS!
but he doesn't know everything...

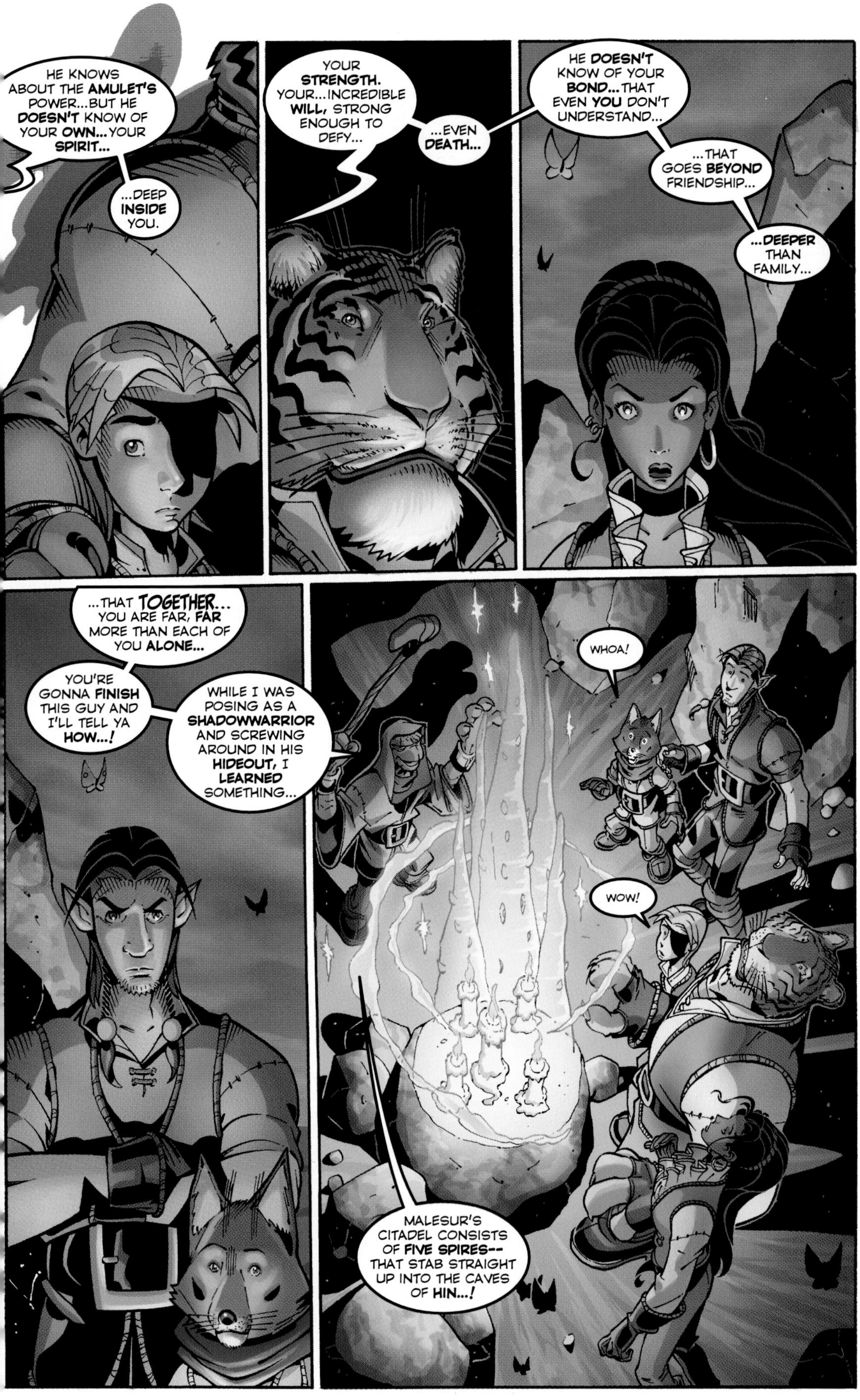
HE KNOWS ABOUT THE AMULET'S POWER...BUT HE DOESN'T KNOW OF YOUR OWN...YOUR SPIRIT...
...DEEP INSIDE YOU.
YOUR STRENGTH. YOUR...INCREDIBLE WILL, STRONG ENOUGH TO DEFY...
...EVEN DEATH...
HE DOESN'T KNOW OF YOUR BOND...THAT EVEN YOU DON'T UNDERSTAND...
...THAT GOES BEYOND FRIENDSHIP...
...DEEPER THAN FAMILY...
...THAT TOGETHER... YOU ARE FAR, FAR MORE THAN EACH OF YOU ALONE...
YOU'RE GONNA FINISH THIS GUY AND I'LL TELL YA HOW...!
WHILE I WAS POSING AS A SHADOWWARRIOR AND SCREWING AROUND IN HIS HIDEOUT, I LEARNED SOMETHING...
WHOA!
WOW!
MALESUR'S CITADEL CONSISTS OF FIVE SPIRES-- THAT STAB STRAIGHT UP INTO THE CAVES OF HIN...!

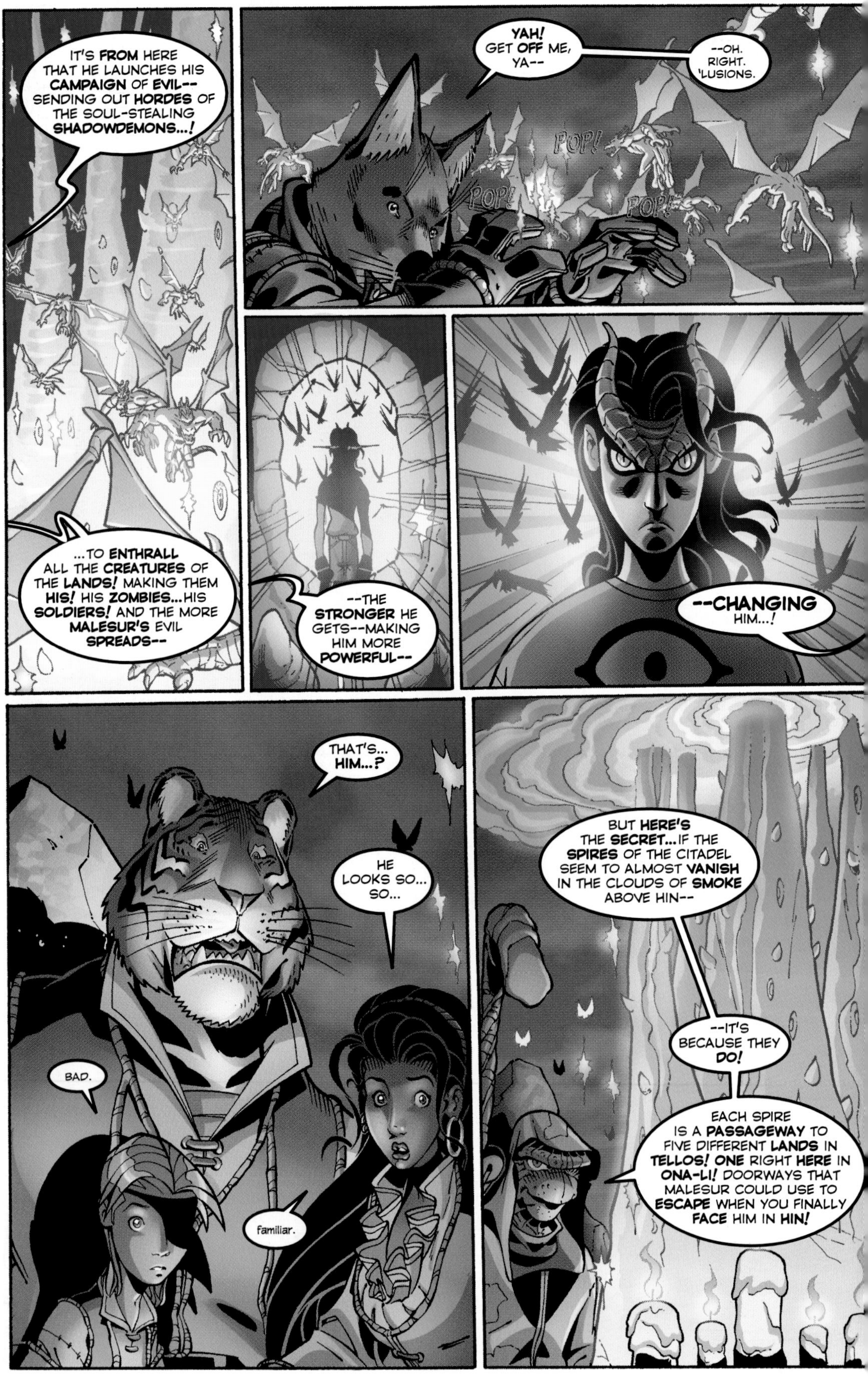
IT'S FROM HERE THAT HE LAUNCHES HIS CAMPAIGN OF EVIL-- SENDING OUT HORDES OF THE SOUL-STEALING SHADOWDEMONS...!
...TO ENTHRALL ALL THE CREATURES OF THE LANDS! MAKING THEM HIS! HIS ZOMBIES...HIS SOLDIERS! AND THE MORE MALESUR'S EVIL SPREADS--
YAH! GET OFF ME, YA--
--OH. RIGHT. 'LUSIONS.
POP!
POP!
POP!
--THE STRONGER HE GETS--MAKING HIM MORE POWERFUL--
--CHANGING HIM...!
THAT'S... HIM...?
HE LOOKS SO... SO...
BAD.
familiar.
BUT HERE'S THE SECRET...IF THE SPIRES OF THE CITADEL SEEM TO ALMOST VANISH IN THE CLOUDS OF SMOKE ABOVE HIN--
--IT'S BECAUSE THEY DO!
EACH SPIRE IS A PASSAGEWAY TO FIVE DIFFERENT LANDS IN TELLOS! ONE RIGHT HERE IN ONA-LI! DOORWAYS THAT MALESUR COULD USE TO ESCAPE WHEN YOU FINALLY FACE HIM IN HIN!

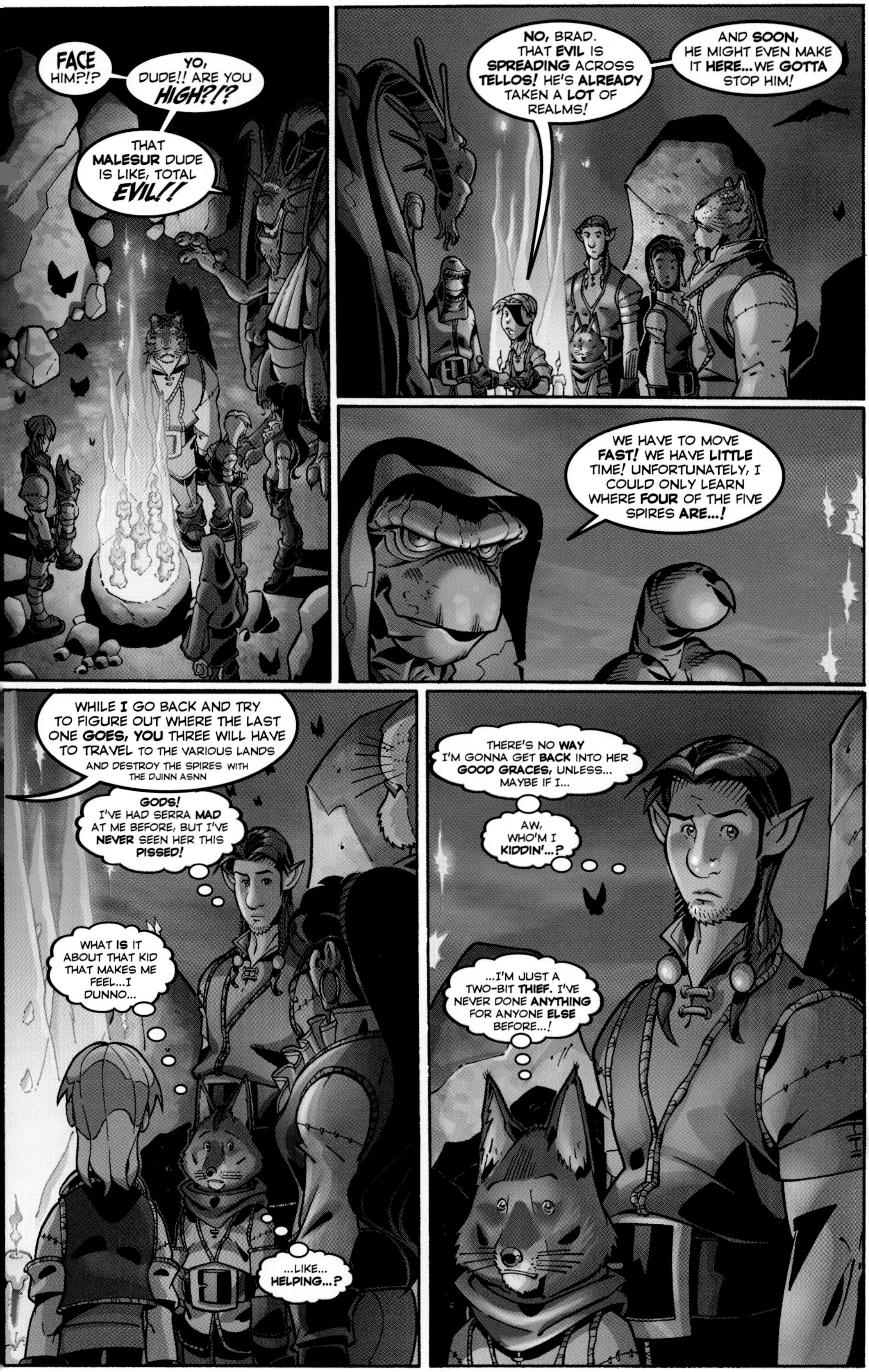
FACE HIM?!?
YO, DUDE!! ARE YOU HIGH?!?
THAT MALESUR DUDE IS LIKE, TOTAL EVIL!!
NO, BRAD. THAT EVIL IS SPREADING ACROSS TELLOS! HE'S ALREADY TAKEN A LOT OF REALMS!
AND SOON, HE MIGHT EVEN MAKE IT HERE...WE GOTTA STOP HIM!
WE HAVE TO MOVE FAST! WE HAVE LITTLE TIME! UNFORTUNATELY, I COULD ONLY LEARN WHERE FOUR OF THE FIVE SPIRES ARE...!
WHILE I GO BACK AND TRY TO FIGURE OUT WHERE THE LAST ONE GOES, YOU THREE WILL HAVE TO TRAVEL TO THE VARIOUS LANDS AND DESTROY THE SPIRES WITH THE DJINN ASNN
GODS! I'VE HAD SERRA MAD AT ME BEFORE, BUT I'VE NEVER SEEN HER THIS PISSED!
WHAT IS IT ABOUT THAT KID THAT MAKES ME FEEL...I DUNNO...
...LIKE... HELPING...?
THERE'S NO WAY I'M GONNA GET BACK INTO HER GOOD GRACES, UNLESS... MAYBE IF I...
AW, WHO'M I KIDDIN'...?
...I'M JUST A TWO-BIT THIEF. I'VE NEVER DONE ANYTHING FOR ANYONE ELSE BEFORE...!

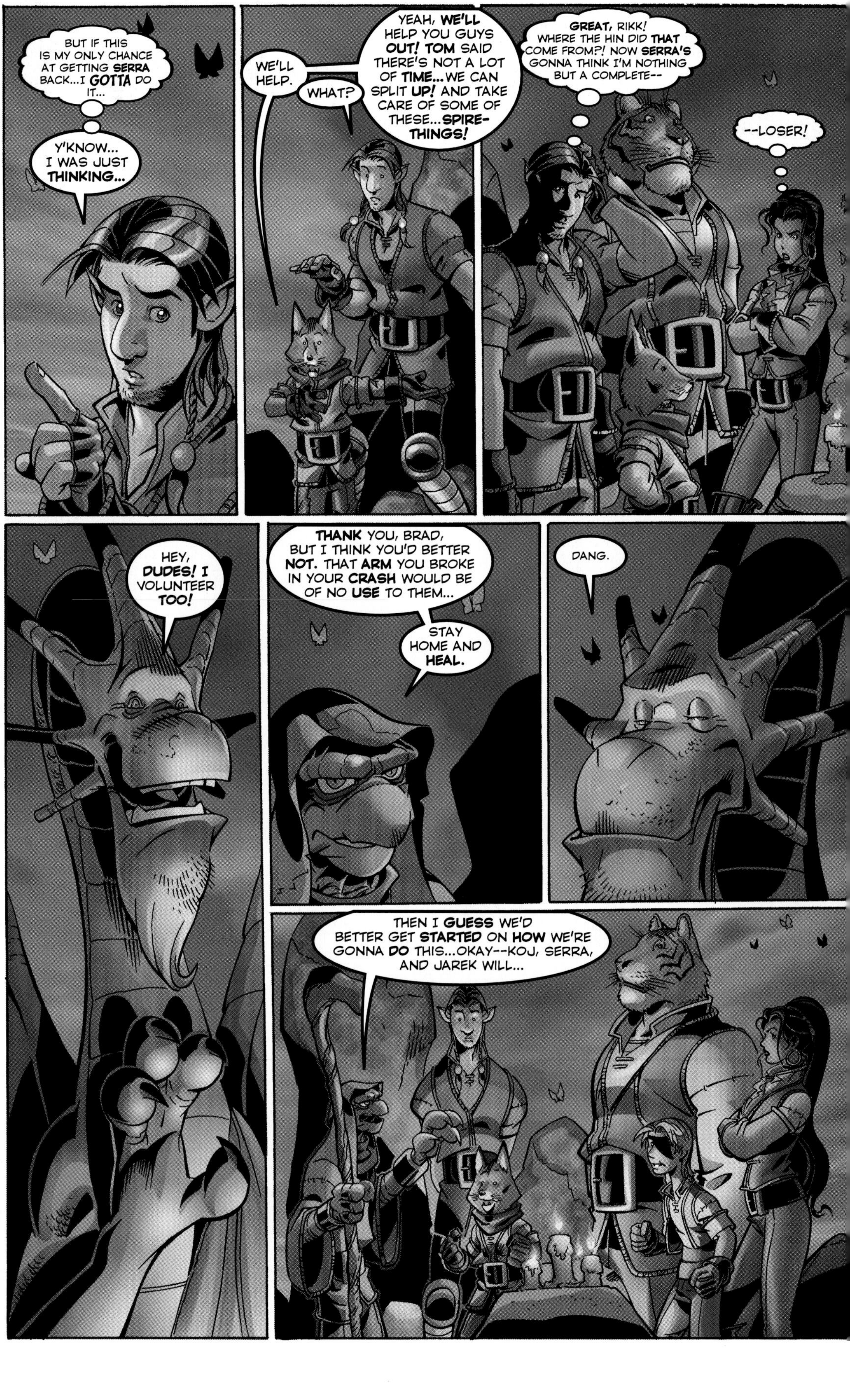
BUT IF THIS IS MY ONLY CHANCE AT GETTING SERRA BACK...I GOTTA DO IT...
Y'KNOW... I WAS JUST THINKING...
WE'LL HELP.
WHAT?
YEAH, WE'LL HELP YOU GUYS OUT! TOM SAID THERE'S NOT A LOT OF TIME...WE CAN SPLIT UP! AND TAKE CARE OF SOME OF THESE...SPIRE-THINGS!
GREAT, RIKK! WHERE THE HIN DID THAT COME FROM?! NOW SERRA'S GONNA THINK I'M NOTHING BUT A COMPLETE--
--LOSER!
HEY, DUDES! I VOLUNTEER TOO!
THANK YOU, BRAD, BUT I THINK YOU'D BETTER NOT. THAT ARM YOU BROKE IN YOUR CRASH WOULD BE OF NO USE TO THEM...
STAY HOME AND HEAL.
DANG.
THEN I GUESS WE'D BETTER GET STARTED ON HOW WE'RE GONNA DO THIS...OKAY--KOJ, SERRA, AND JAREK WILL...

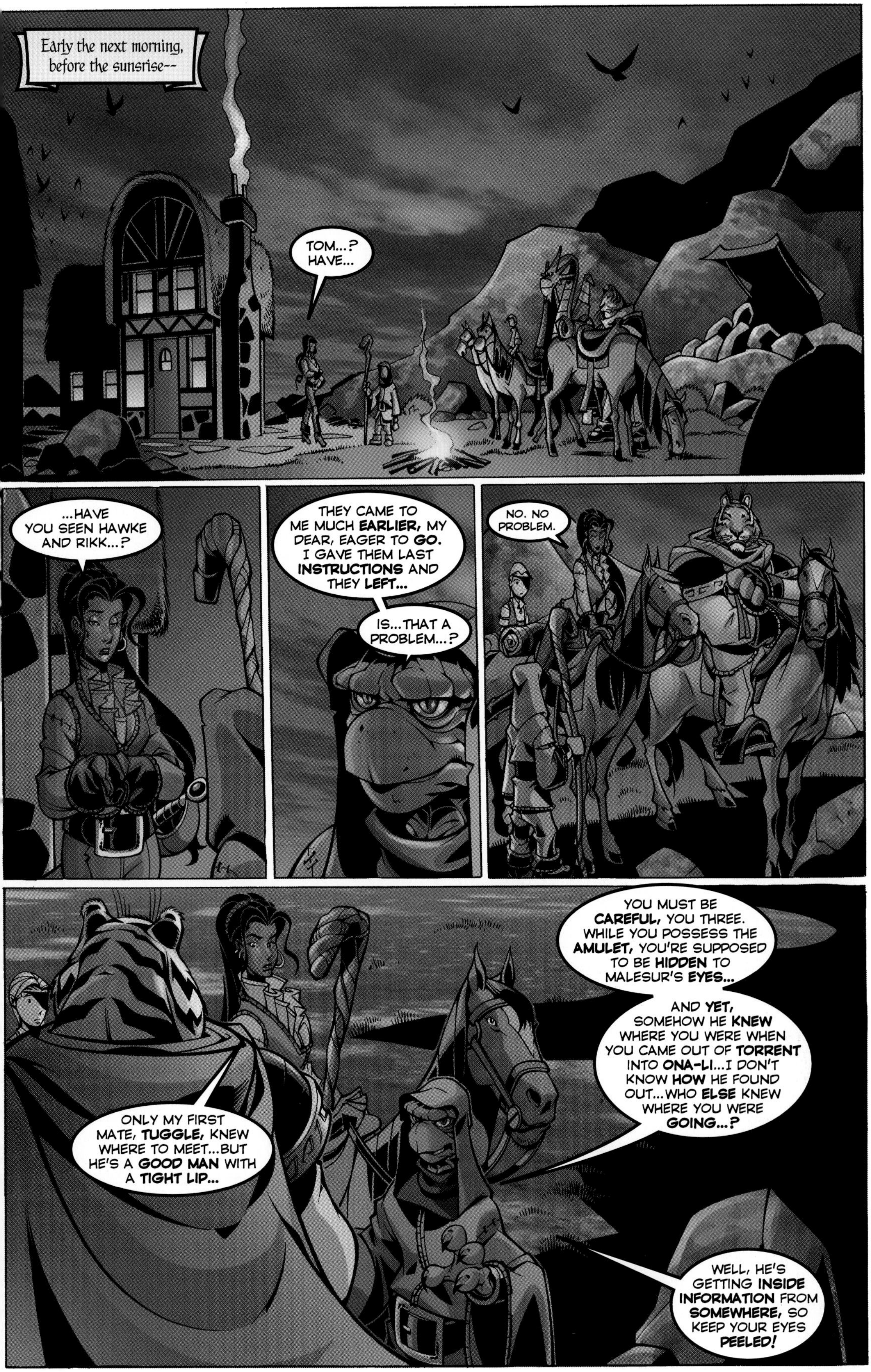
Early the next morning, before the sunsrise--
TOM...? HAVE...
...HAVE YOU SEEN HAWKE AND RIKK...?
THEY CAME TO ME MUCH EARLIER, MY DEAR, EAGER TO GO. I GAVE THEM LAST INSTRUCTIONS AND THEY LEFT...
IS...THAT A PROBLEM...?
NO. NO PROBLEM.
YOU MUST BE CAREFUL, YOU THREE. WHILE YOU POSSESS THE AMULET, YOU'RE SUPPOSED TO BE HIDDEN TO MALESUR'S EYES...
AND YET, SOMEHOW HE KNEW WHERE YOU WERE WHEN YOU CAME OUT OF TORRENT INTO ONA-LI...I DON'T KNOW HOW HE FOUND OUT...WHO ELSE KNEW WHERE YOU WERE GOING...?
ONLY MY FIRST MATE, TUGGLE, KNEW WHERE TO MEET...BUT HE'S A GOOD MAN WITH A TIGHT LIP...
WELL, HE'S GETTING INSIDE INFORMATION FROM SOMEWHERE, SO KEEP YOUR EYES PEELED!

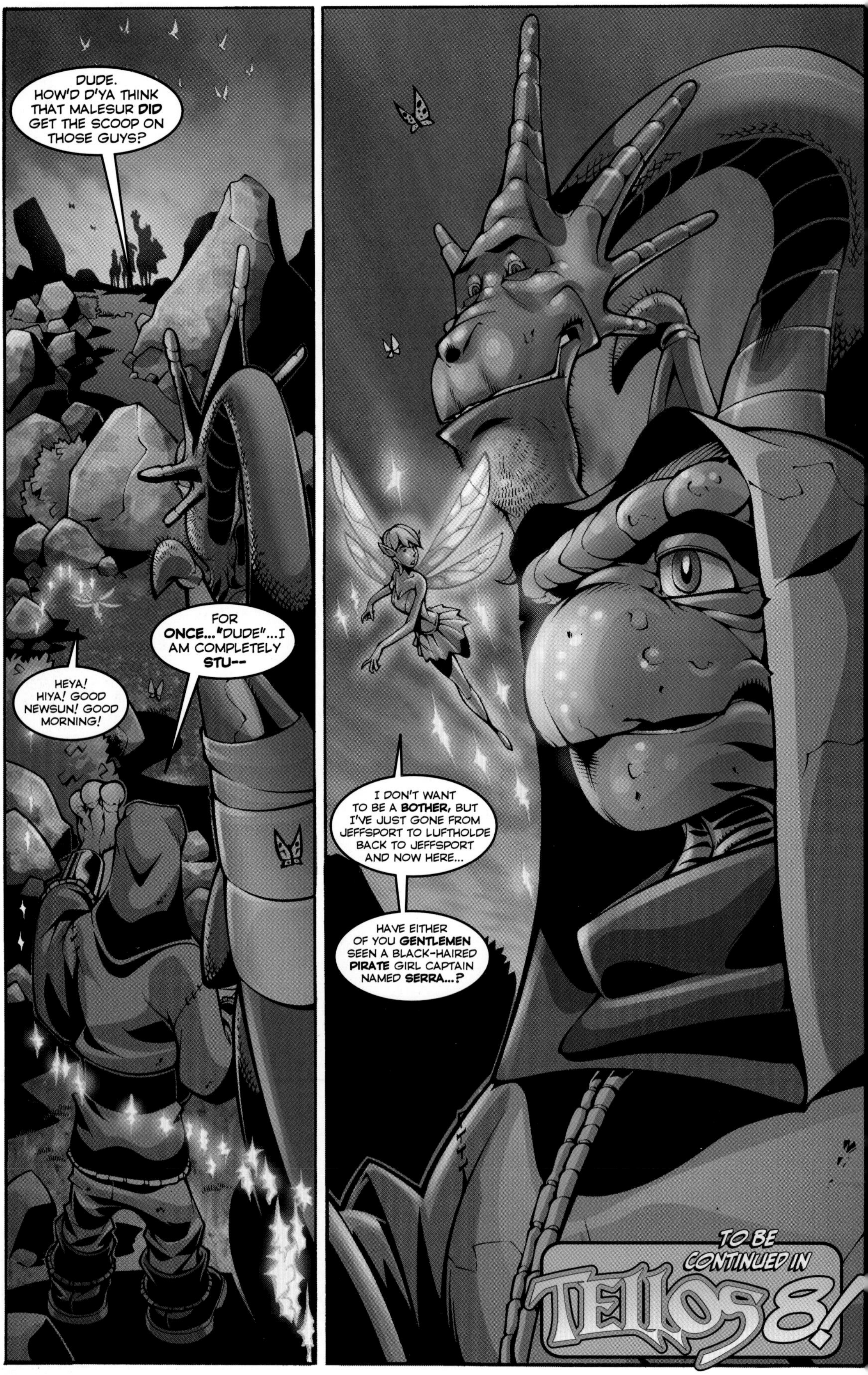
DUDE. HOW'D D'YA THINK THAT MALESUR DID GET THE SCOOP ON THOSE GUYS?
FOR ONCE..."DUDE"...I AM COMPLETELY STU--
HEYA! HIYA! GOOD NEWSUN! GOOD MORNING!
I DON'T WANT TO BE A BOTHER, BUT I'VE JUST GONE FROM JEFFSPORT TO LUFTHOLDE BACK TO JEFFSPORT AND NOW HERE...
HAVE EITHER OF YOU GENTLEMEN SEEN A BLACK-HAIRED PIRATE GIRL CAPTAIN NAMED SERRA...?
TO BE CONTINUED IN
TELLOS 8!

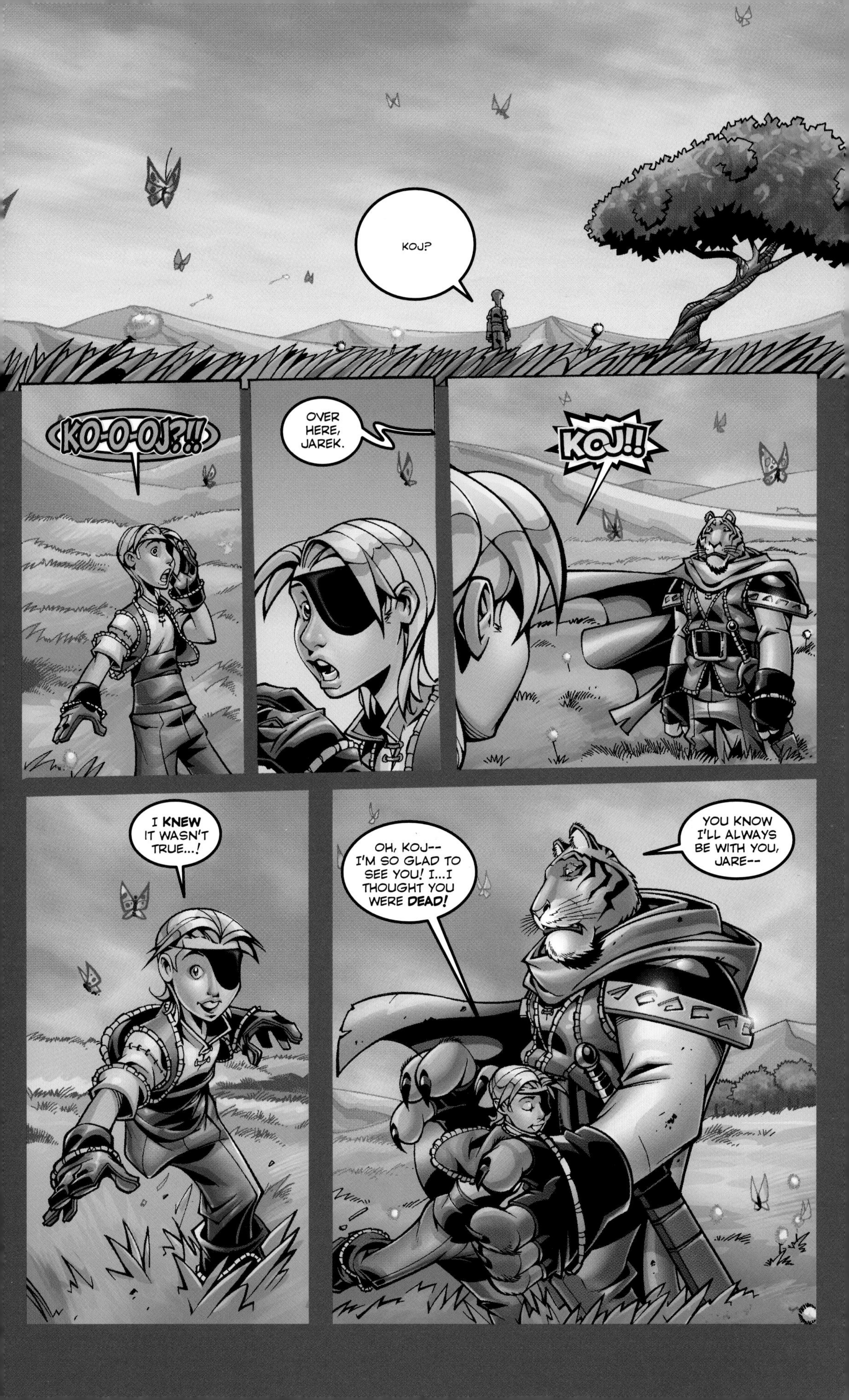
KOJ?
KO-O-OJ?!!
OVER HERE, JAREK.
KOJ!!
I KNEW IT WASN'T TRUE...!
OH, KOJ-- I'M SO GLAD TO SEE YOU! I...I THOUGHT YOU WERE DEAD!
YOU KNOW I'LL ALWAYS BE WITH YOU, JARE--

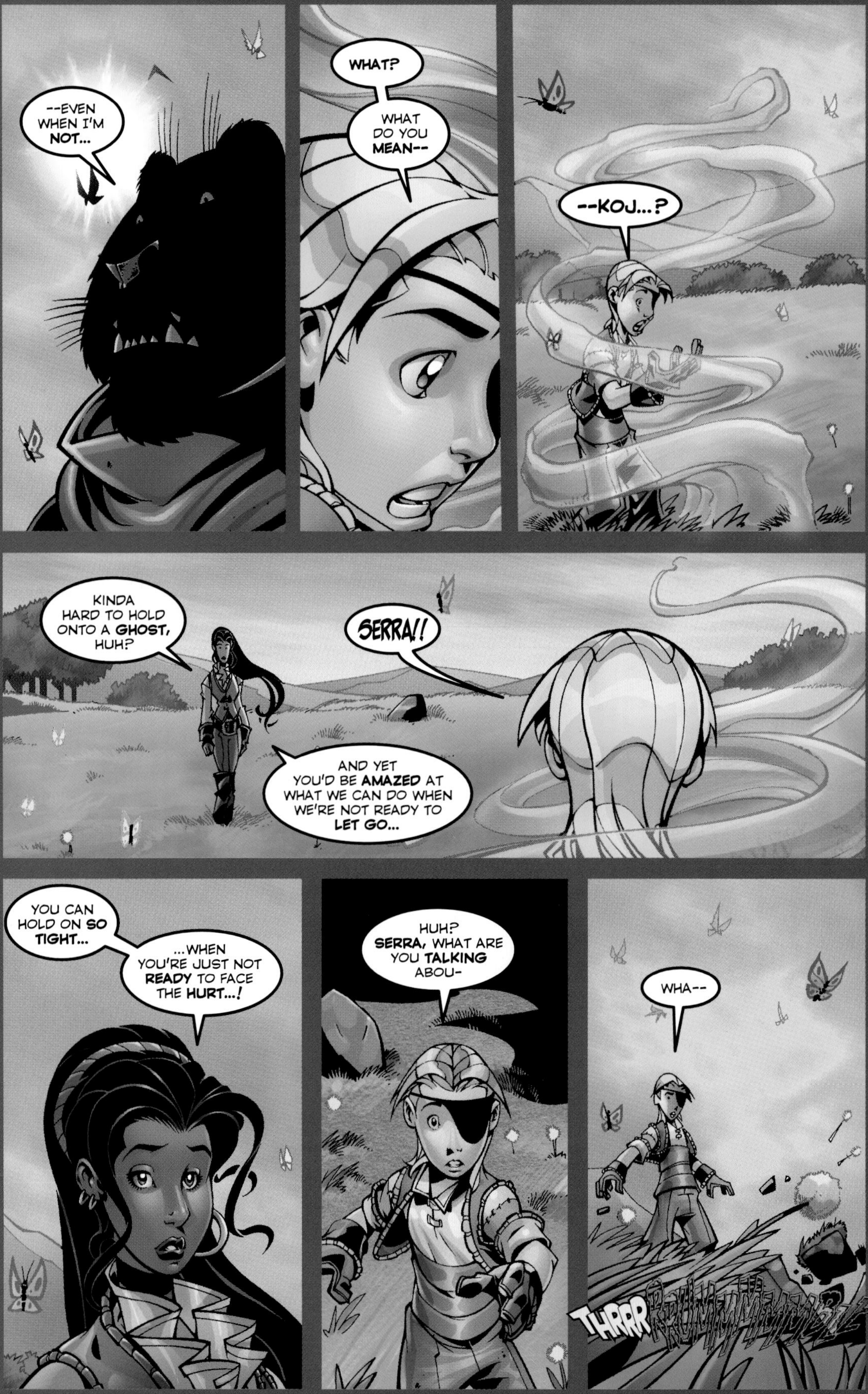
--EVEN WHEN I'M NOT...
WHAT?
WHAT DO YOU MEAN--
--KOJ...?
KINDA HARD TO HOLD ONTO A GHOST, HUH?
SERRA!!
AND YET YOU'D BE AMAZED AT WHAT WE CAN DO WHEN WE'RE NOT READY TO LET GO...
YOU CAN HOLD ON SO TIGHT...
...WHEN YOU'RE JUST NOT READY TO FACE THE HURT...!
HUH? SERRA, WHAT ARE YOU TALKING ABOU-
WHA--
THRRR

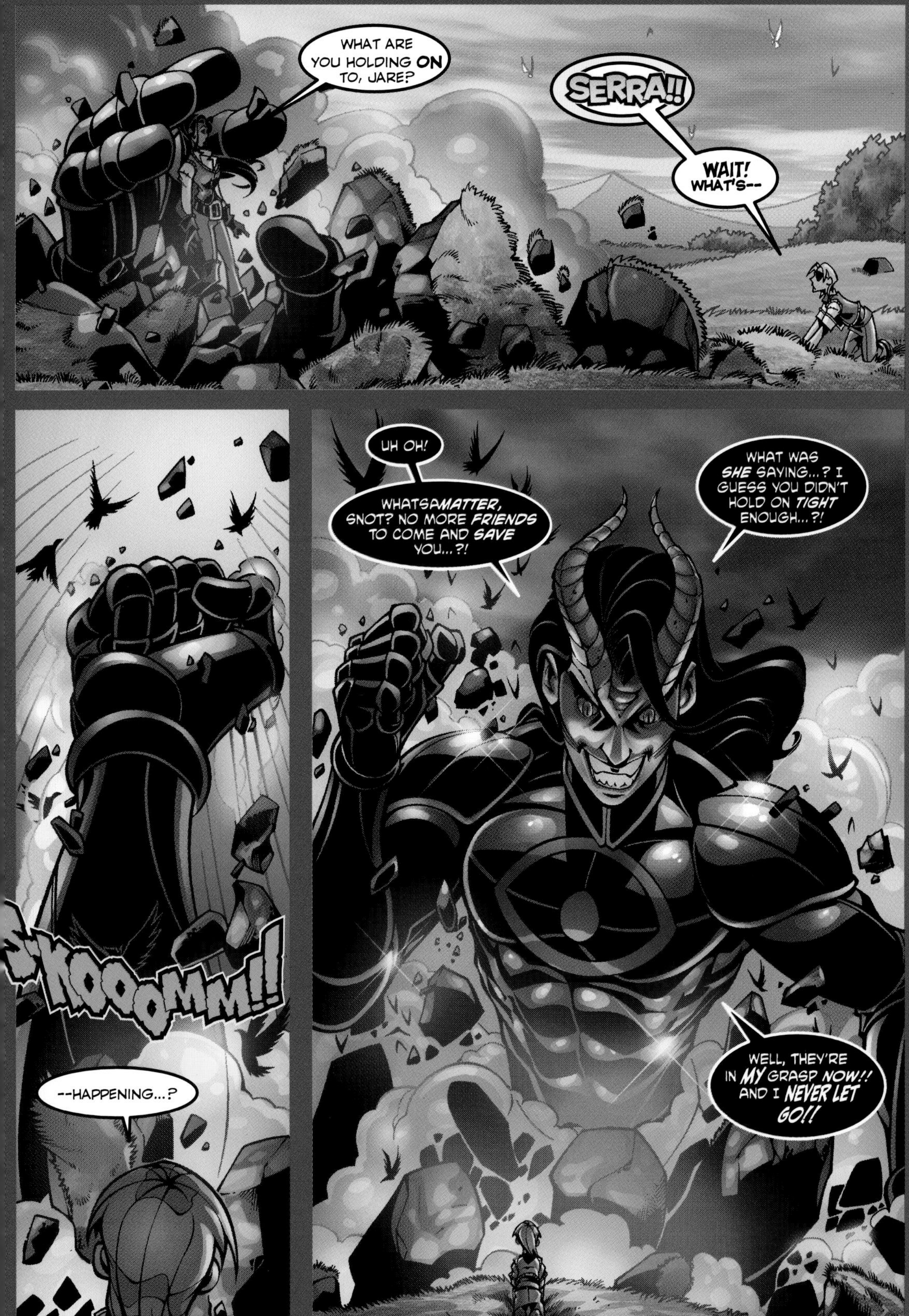
WHAT ARE YOU HOLDING ON TO, JARE?
SERRA!!
WAIT! WHAT'S--
KHOOOMM!!
--HAPPENING...?
UH OH!
WHATSAMATTER, SNOT? NO MORE FRIENDS TO COME AND SAVE YOU...?!
WHAT WAS SHE SAYING...? I GUESS YOU DIDN'T HOLD ON TIGHT ENOUGH...?!
WELL, THEY'RE IN MY GRASP NOW!! AND I NEVER LET GO!!

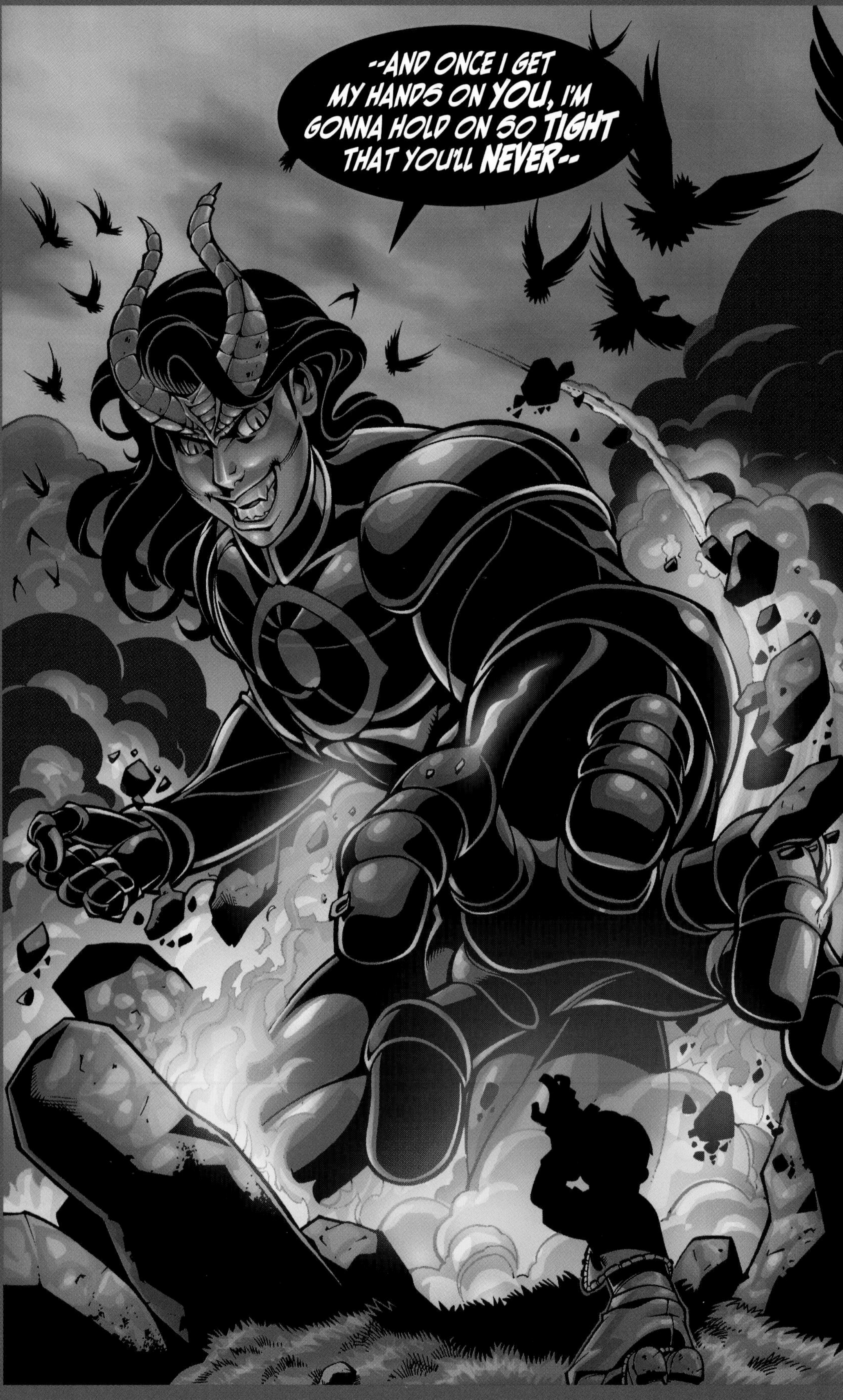
--AND ONCE I GET MY HANDS ON YOU, I'M GONNA HOLD ON SO TIGHT THAT YOU'LL NEVER--

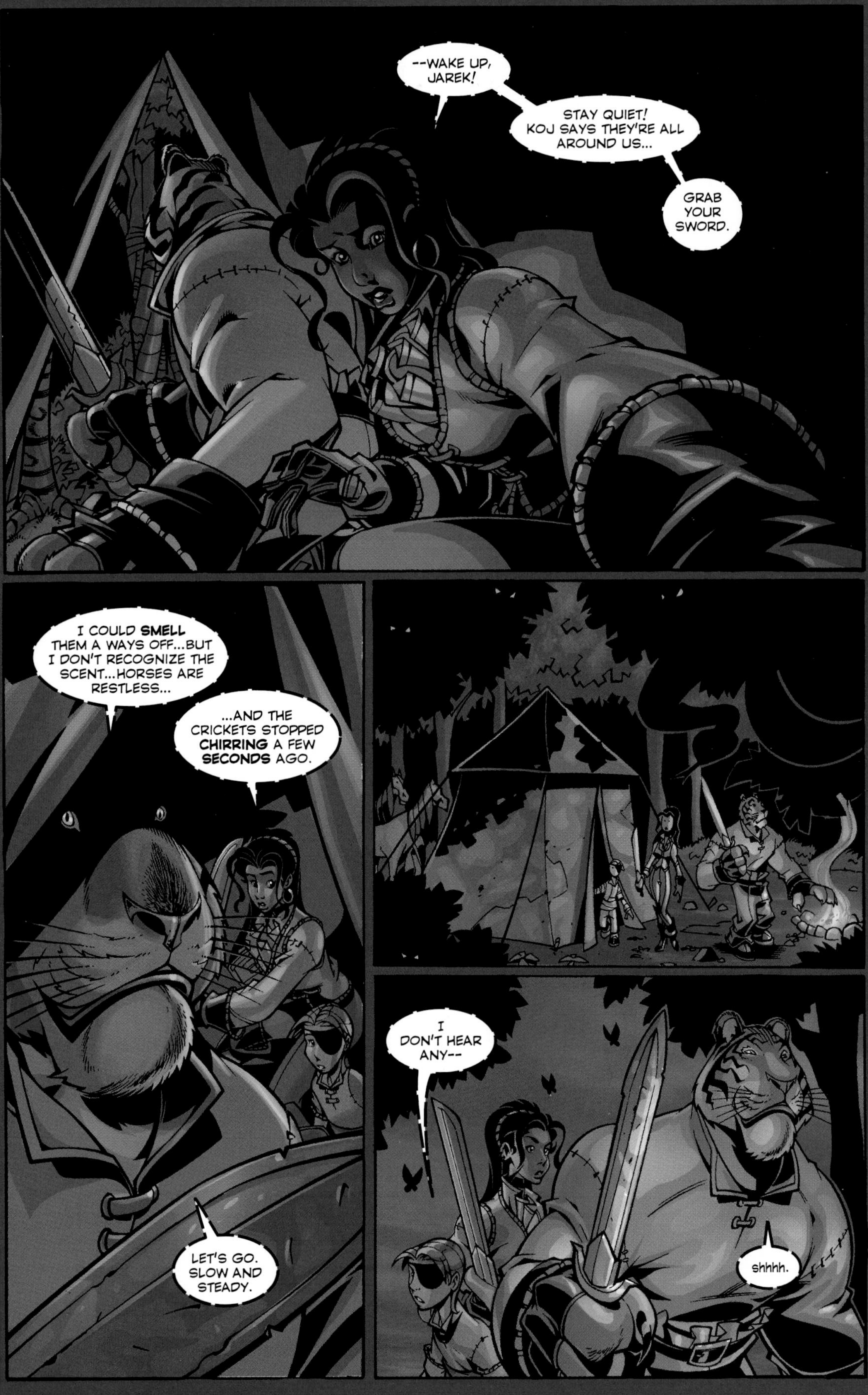
--WAKE UP, JAREK!
STAY QUIET! KOJ SAYS THEY'RE ALL AROUND US...
GRAB YOUR SWORD.
I COULD **SMELL** THEM A WAYS OFF...BUT I DON'T RECOGNIZE THE SCENT...HORSES ARE RESTLESS...
...AND THE CRICKETS STOPPED **CHIRRING** A FEW **SECONDS** AGO.
LET'S GO. SLOW AND STEADY.
I DON'T HEAR ANY--
shhhh.

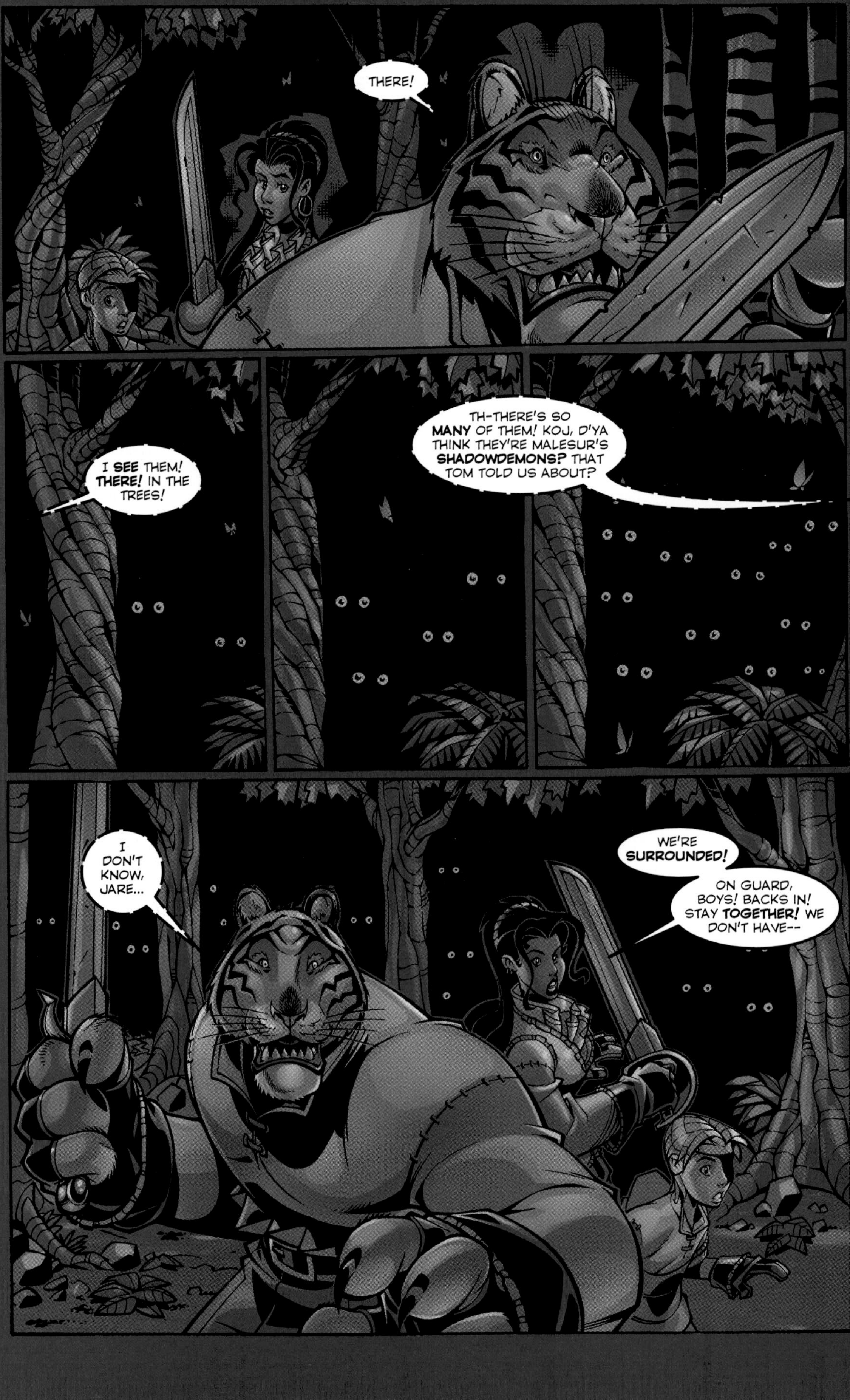
THERE!
I SEE THEM! THERE! IN THE TREES!
TH-THERE'S SO MANY OF THEM! KOJ, D'YA THINK THEY'RE MALESUR'S SHADOWDEMONS? THAT TOM TOLD US ABOUT?
I DON'T KNOW, JARE...
WE'RE SURROUNDED!
ON GUARD, BOYS! BACKS IN! STAY TOGETHER! WE DON'T HAVE--

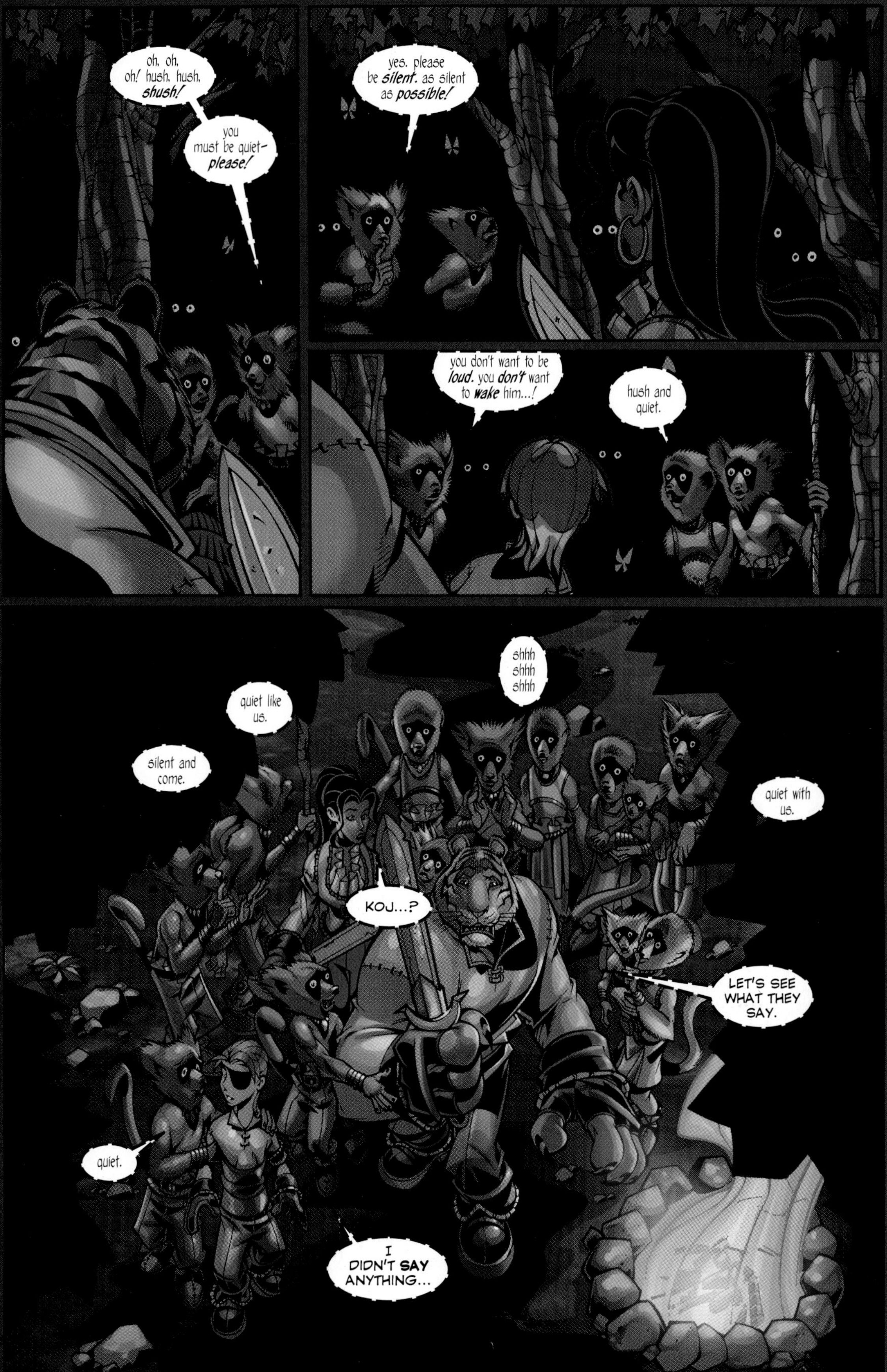
oh, oh, oh! hush, hush, shush!
you must be quiet- please!
yes. please be silent. as silent as possible!
you don't want to be loud. you don't want to wake him...!
hush and quiet.
quiet like us.
shhh shhh shhh
silent and come.
quiet with us.
KOJ...?
LET'S SEE WHAT THEY SAY.
quiet.
I DIDN'T SAY ANYTHING...

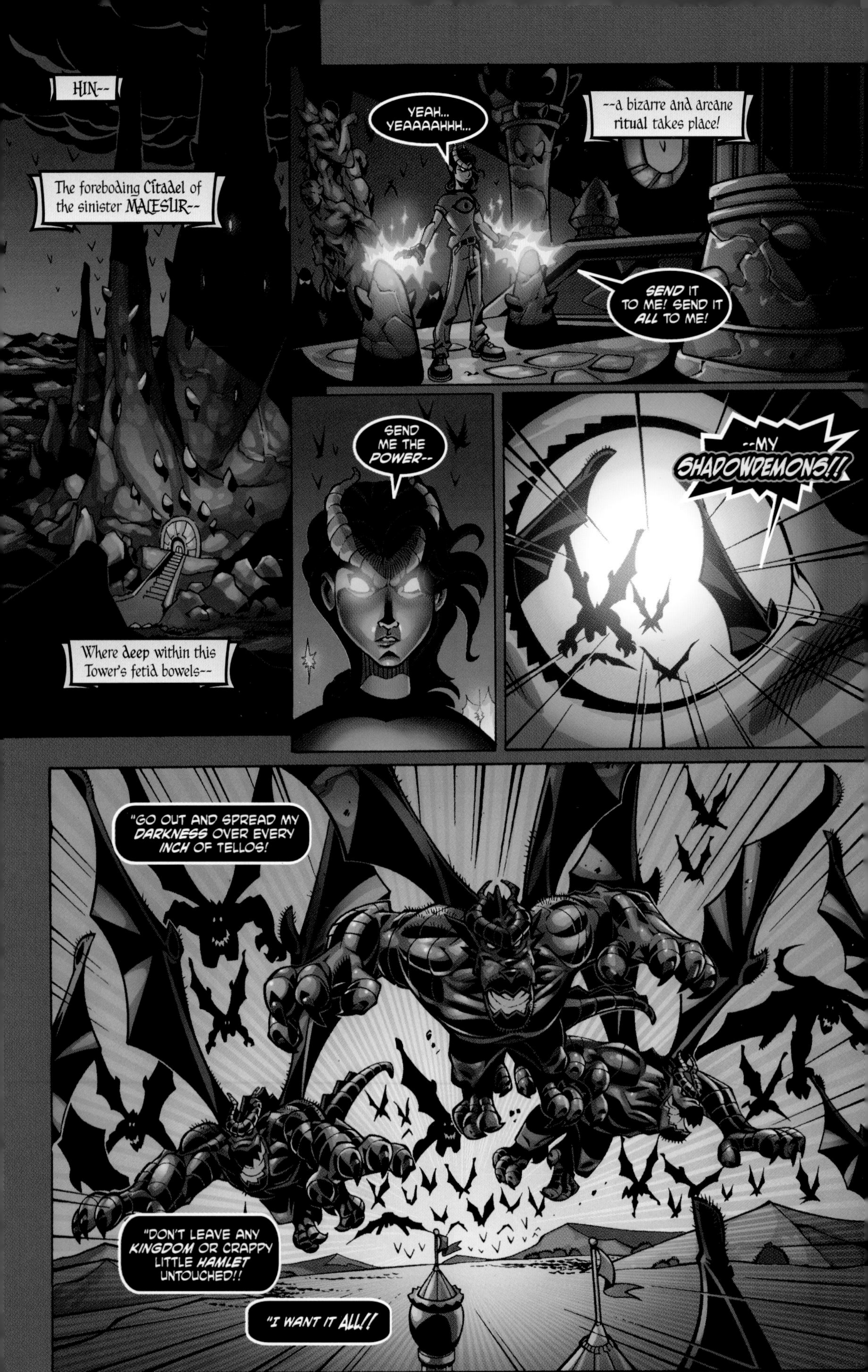
HIN--
The foreboding Citadel of the sinister MALESUR--
Where deep within this Tower's fetid bowels--
--a bizarre and arcane ritual takes place!
YEAH... YEAAAAAHHH...
SEND IT TO ME! SEND IT ALL TO ME!
SEND ME THE POWER--
--MY SHADOWDEMONS!!
"GO OUT AND SPREAD MY DARKNESS OVER EVERY INCH OF TELLOS!
"DON'T LEAVE ANY KINGDOM OR CRAPPY LITTLE HAMLET UNTOUCHED!!
"I WANT IT ALL!!

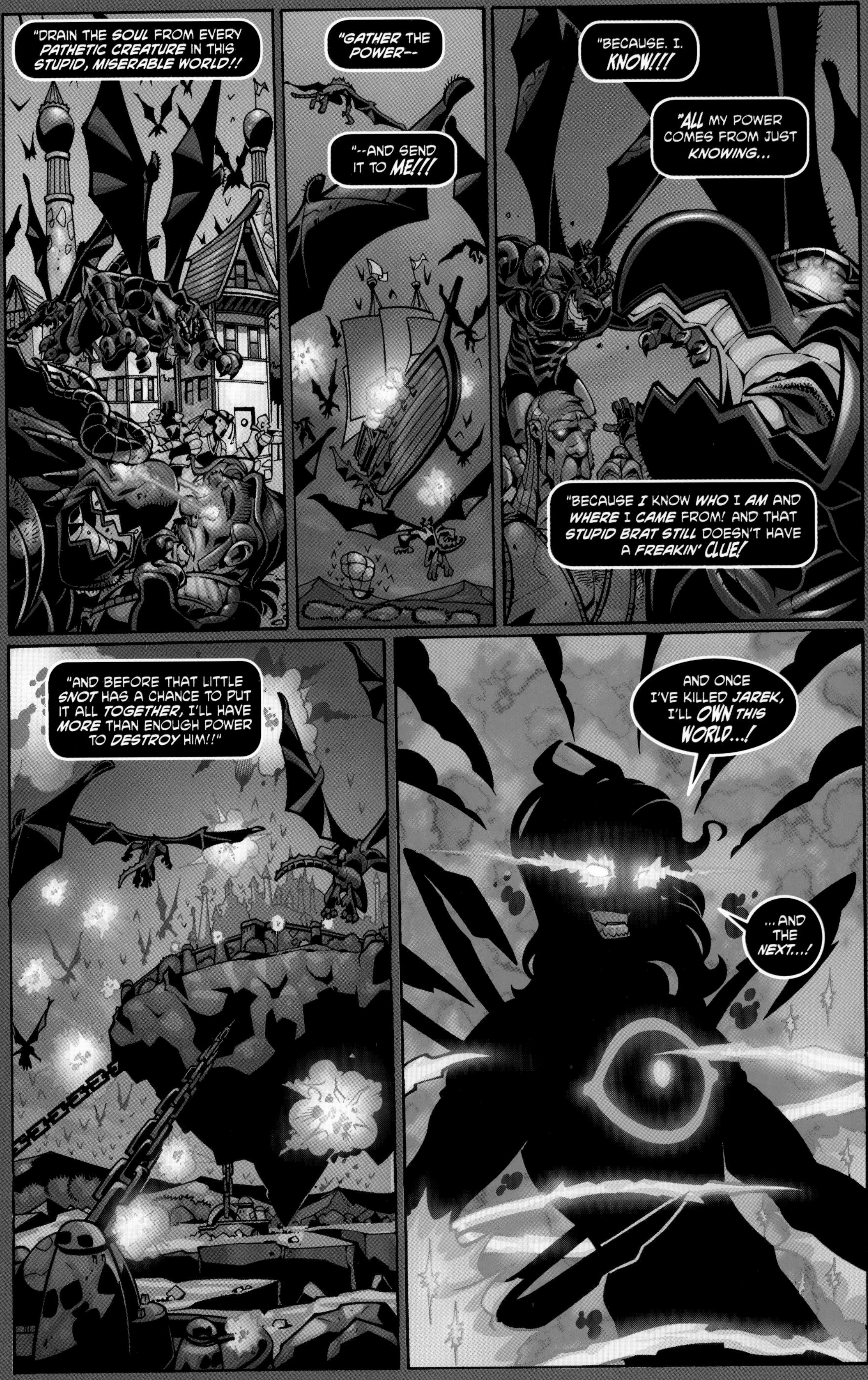
"DRAIN THE SOUL FROM EVERY PATHETIC CREATURE IN THIS STUPID, MISERABLE WORLD!!
"GATHER THE POWER--
"--AND SEND IT TO ME!!!
"BECAUSE. I. KNOW!!!
"ALL MY POWER COMES FROM JUST KNOWING...
"BECAUSE I KNOW WHO I AM AND WHERE I CAME FROM! AND THAT STUPID BRAT STILL DOESN'T HAVE A FREAKIN' CLUE!
"AND BEFORE THAT LITTLE SNOT HAS A CHANCE TO PUT IT ALL TOGETHER, I'LL HAVE MORE THAN ENOUGH POWER TO DESTROY HIM!!"
AND ONCE I'VE KILLED JAREK, I'LL OWN THIS WORLD...!
...AND THE NEXT...!

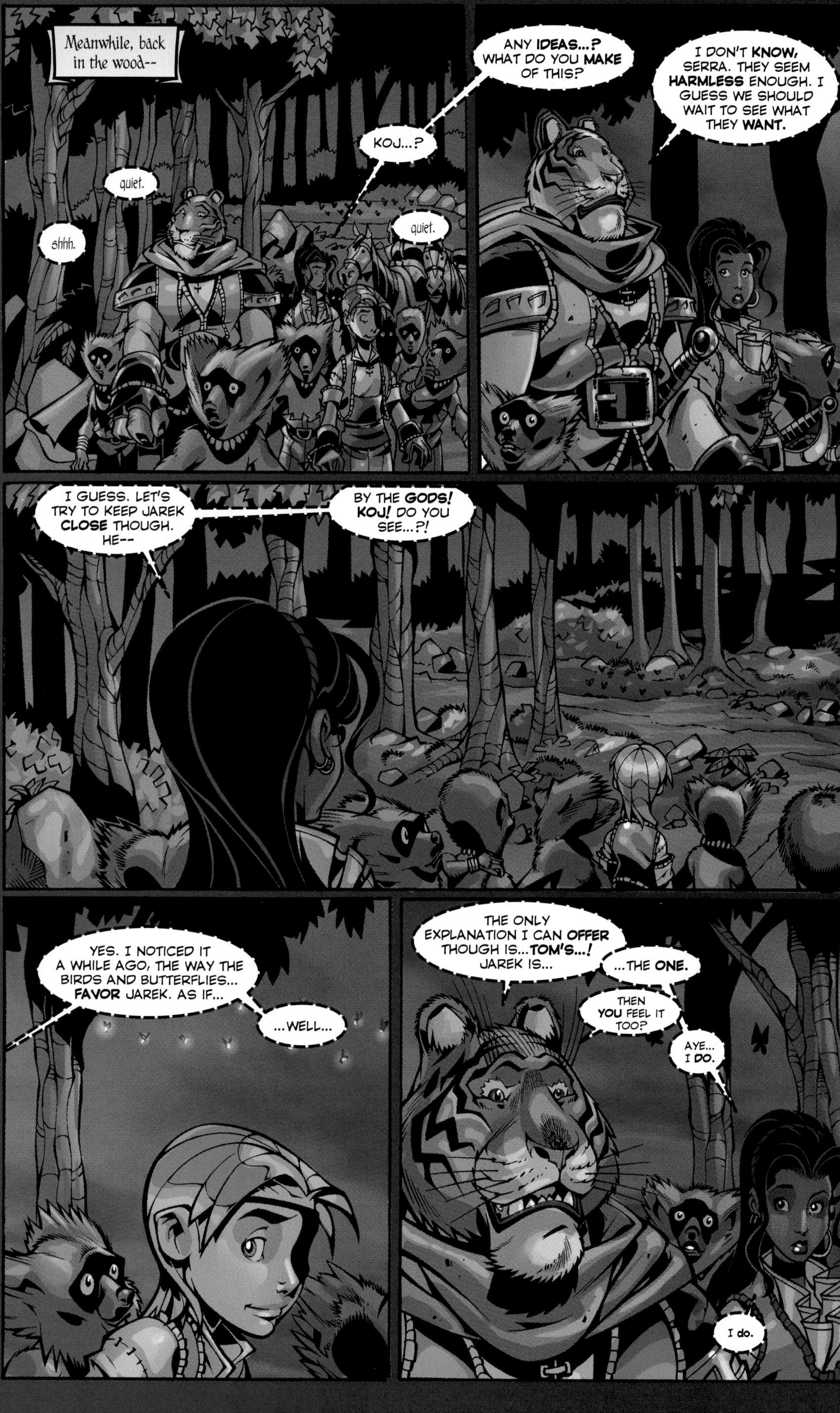

Meanwhile, back in the wood--
quiet.
shhh.
KOJ...?
quiet.
ANY IDEAS...? WHAT DO YOU MAKE OF THIS?
I DON'T KNOW, SERRA. THEY SEEM HARMLESS ENOUGH. I GUESS WE SHOULD WAIT TO SEE WHAT THEY WANT.
I GUESS. LET'S TRY TO KEEP JAREK CLOSE THOUGH. HE--
BY THE GODS! KOJ! DO YOU SEE...?!
YES. I NOTICED IT A WHILE AGO, THE WAY THE BIRDS AND BUTTERFLIES... FAVOR JAREK. AS IF...
...WELL...
THE ONLY EXPLANATION I CAN OFFER THOUGH IS...TOM'S...! JAREK IS...
...THE ONE.
THEN YOU FEEL IT TOO?
AYE... I DO.
I do.

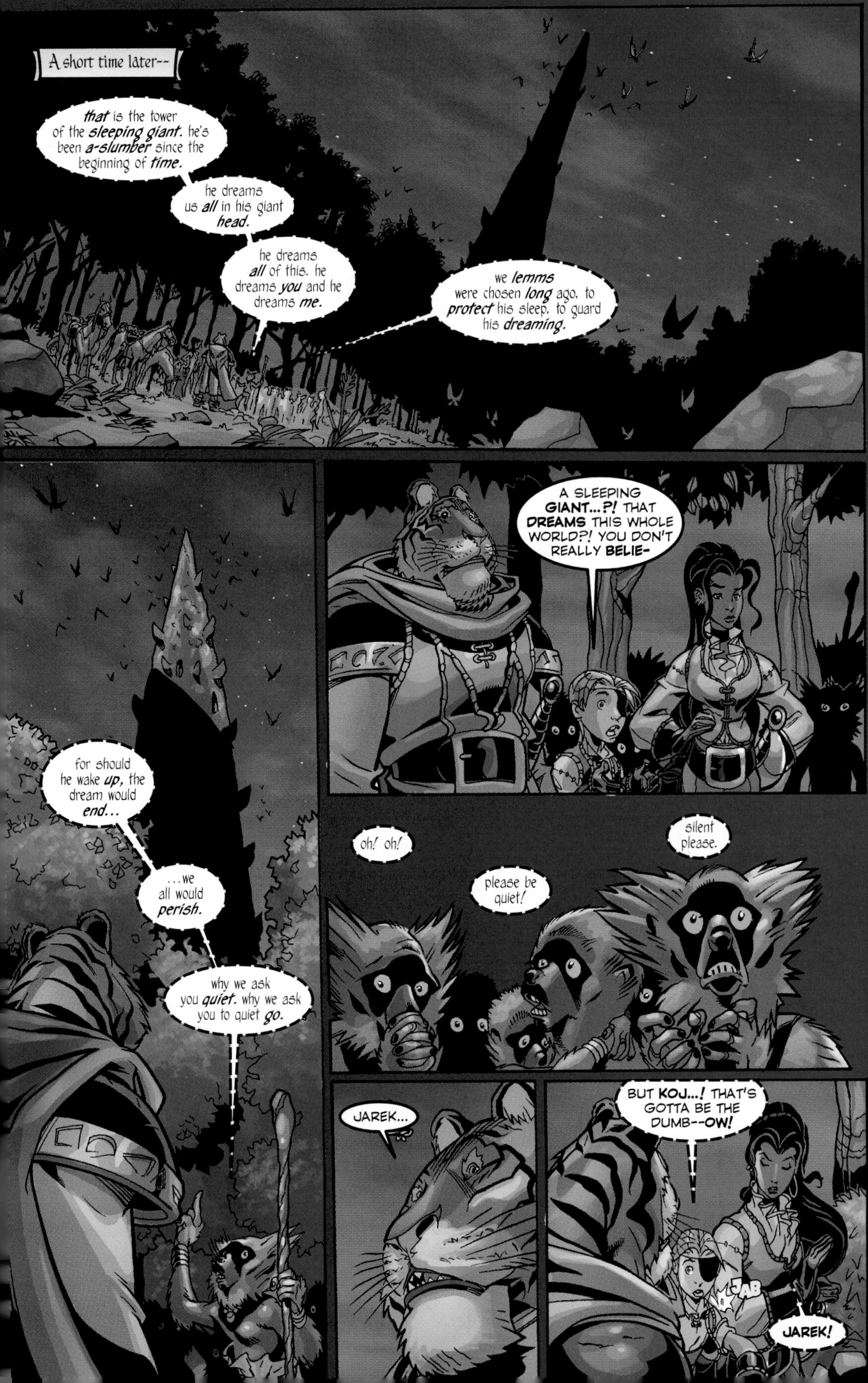
A short time later--
that is the tower of the sleeping giant. he's been a-slumber since the beginning of time.
he dreams us all in his giant head.
he dreams all of this. he dreams you and he dreams me.
we lemms were chosen long ago, to protect his sleep, to guard his dreaming.
for should he wake up, the dream would end...
...we all would perish.
why we ask you quiet. why we ask you to quiet go.
A SLEEPING GIANT...?! THAT DREAMS THIS WHOLE WORLD?! YOU DON'T REALLY BELIE-
oh! oh!
please be quiet!
silent please.
JAREK...
BUT KOJ...! THAT'S GOTTA BE THE DUMB--OW!
JAB
JAREK!

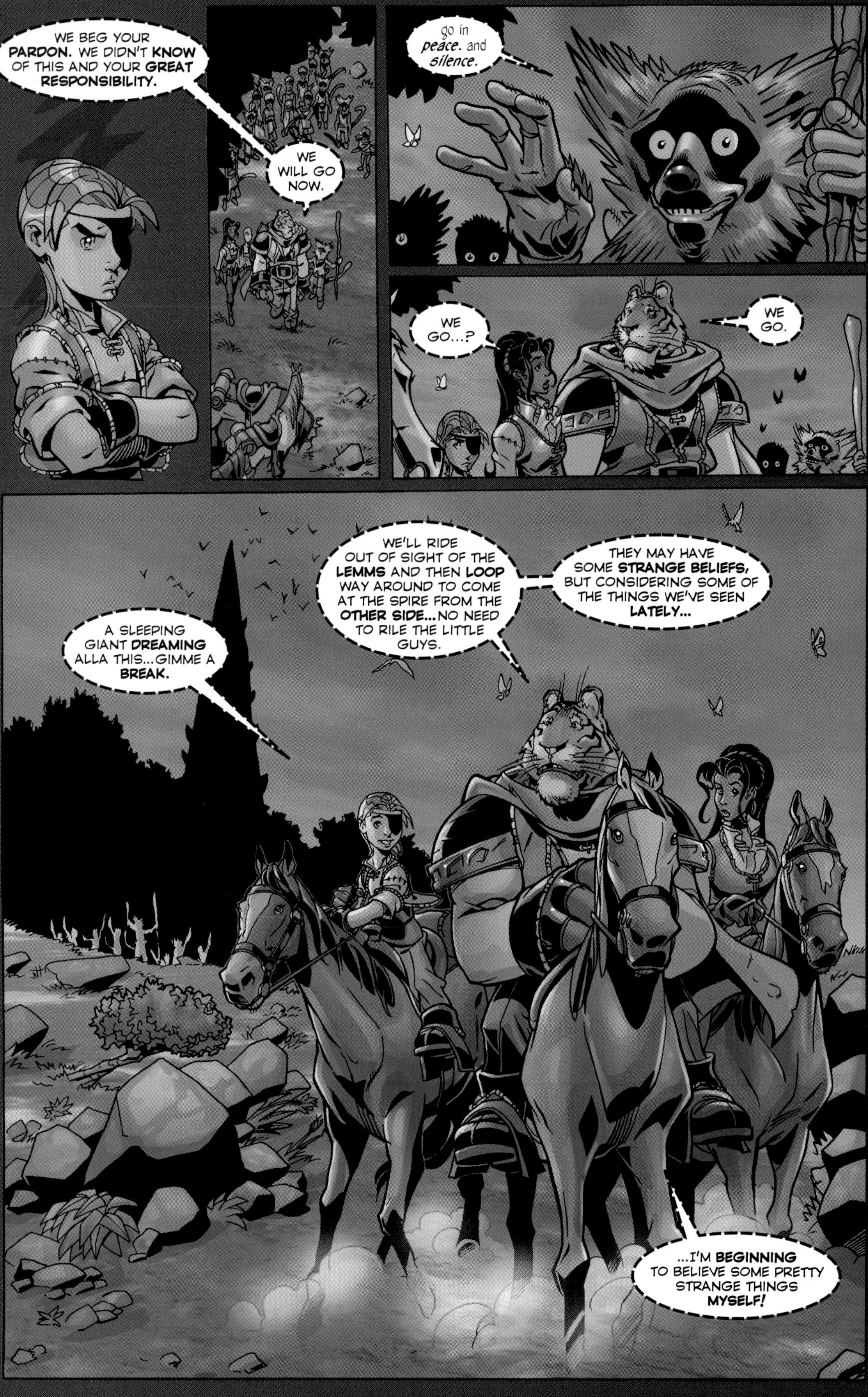
WE BEG YOUR PARDON. WE DIDN'T KNOW OF THIS AND YOUR GREAT RESPONSIBILITY.
WE WILL GO NOW.
go in peace. and silence.
WE GO...?
WE GO.
A SLEEPING GIANT DREAMING ALLA THIS...GIMME A BREAK.
WE'LL RIDE OUT OF SIGHT OF THE LEMMS AND THEN LOOP WAY AROUND TO COME AT THE SPIRE FROM THE OTHER SIDE...NO NEED TO RILE THE LITTLE GUYS.
THEY MAY HAVE SOME STRANGE BELIEFS, BUT CONSIDERING SOME OF THE THINGS WE'VE SEEN LATELY...
...I'M BEGINNING TO BELIEVE SOME PRETTY STRANGE THINGS MYSELF!

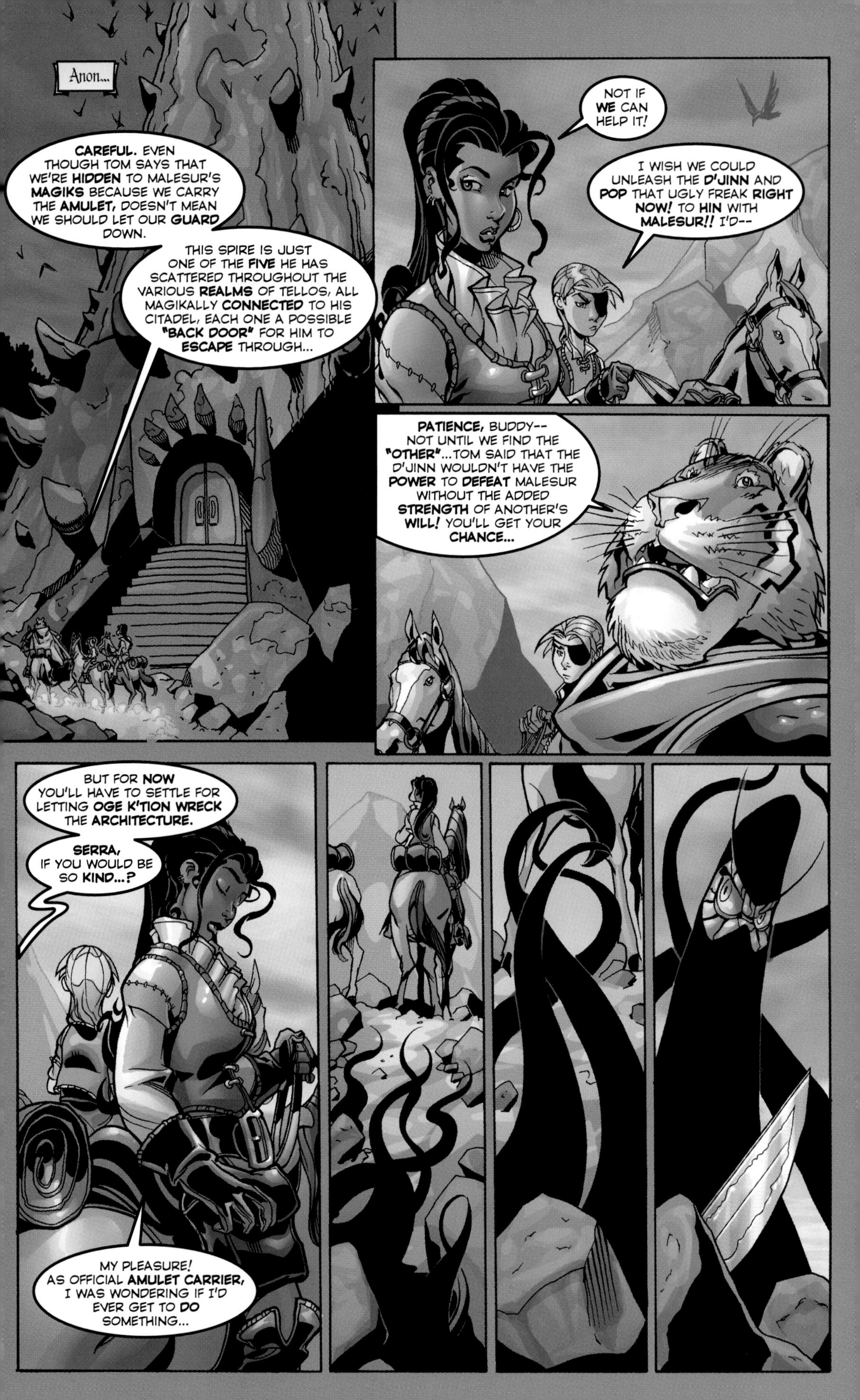

Anon...
CAREFUL. EVEN THOUGH TOM SAYS THAT WE'RE HIDDEN TO MALESUR'S MAGIKS BECAUSE WE CARRY THE AMULET, DOESN'T MEAN WE SHOULD LET OUR GUARD DOWN.
THIS SPIRE IS JUST ONE OF THE FIVE HE HAS SCATTERED THROUGHOUT THE VARIOUS REALMS OF TELLOS, ALL MAGIKALLY CONNECTED TO HIS CITADEL, EACH ONE A POSSIBLE "BACK DOOR" FOR HIM TO ESCAPE THROUGH...
NOT IF WE CAN HELP IT!
I WISH WE COULD UNLEASH THE D'JINN AND POP THAT UGLY FREAK RIGHT NOW! TO HIN WITH MALESUR!! I'D--
PATIENCE, BUDDY-- NOT UNTIL WE FIND THE "OTHER"...TOM SAID THAT THE D'JINN WOULDN'T HAVE THE POWER TO DEFEAT MALESUR WITHOUT THE ADDED STRENGTH OF ANOTHER'S WILL! YOU'LL GET YOUR CHANCE...
BUT FOR NOW YOU'LL HAVE TO SETTLE FOR LETTING OGE K'TION WRECK THE ARCHITECTURE.
SERRA, IF YOU WOULD BE SO KIND...?
MY PLEASURE! AS OFFICIAL AMULET CARRIER, I WAS WONDERING IF I'D EVER GET TO DO SOMETHING...

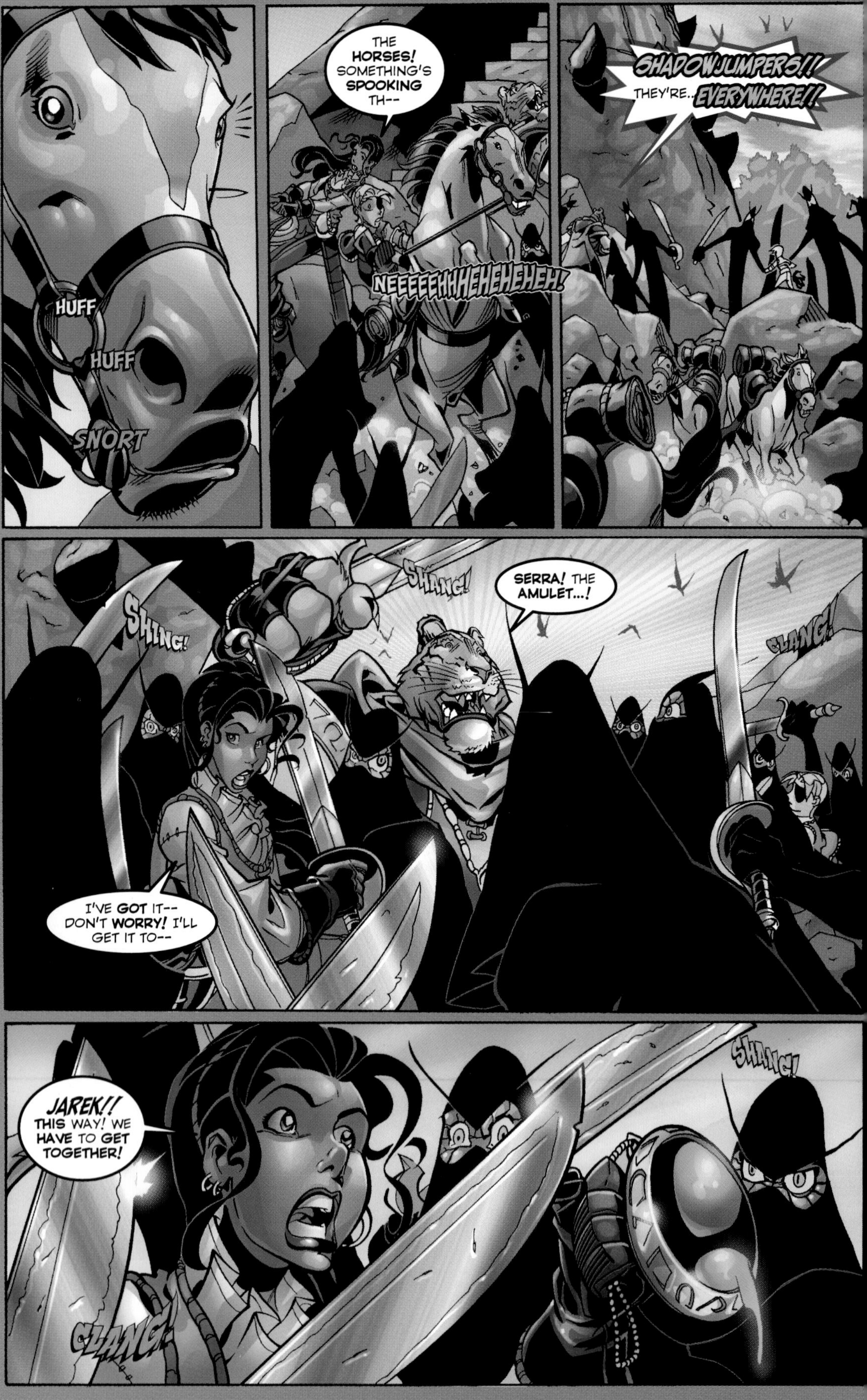
HUFF
HUFF
SNORT
THE HORSES! SOMETHING'S SPOOKING TH--
NEEEEEHHHEHEHEHEH!
SHADOWJUMPERS!!
THEY'RE...EVERYWHERE!!
SHING!
SHANG!
SERRA! THE AMULET...!
CLANG!
I'VE GOT IT-- DON'T WORRY! I'LL GET IT TO--
JAREK!! THIS WAY! WE HAVE TO GET TOGETHER!
SHANG!
CLANG!

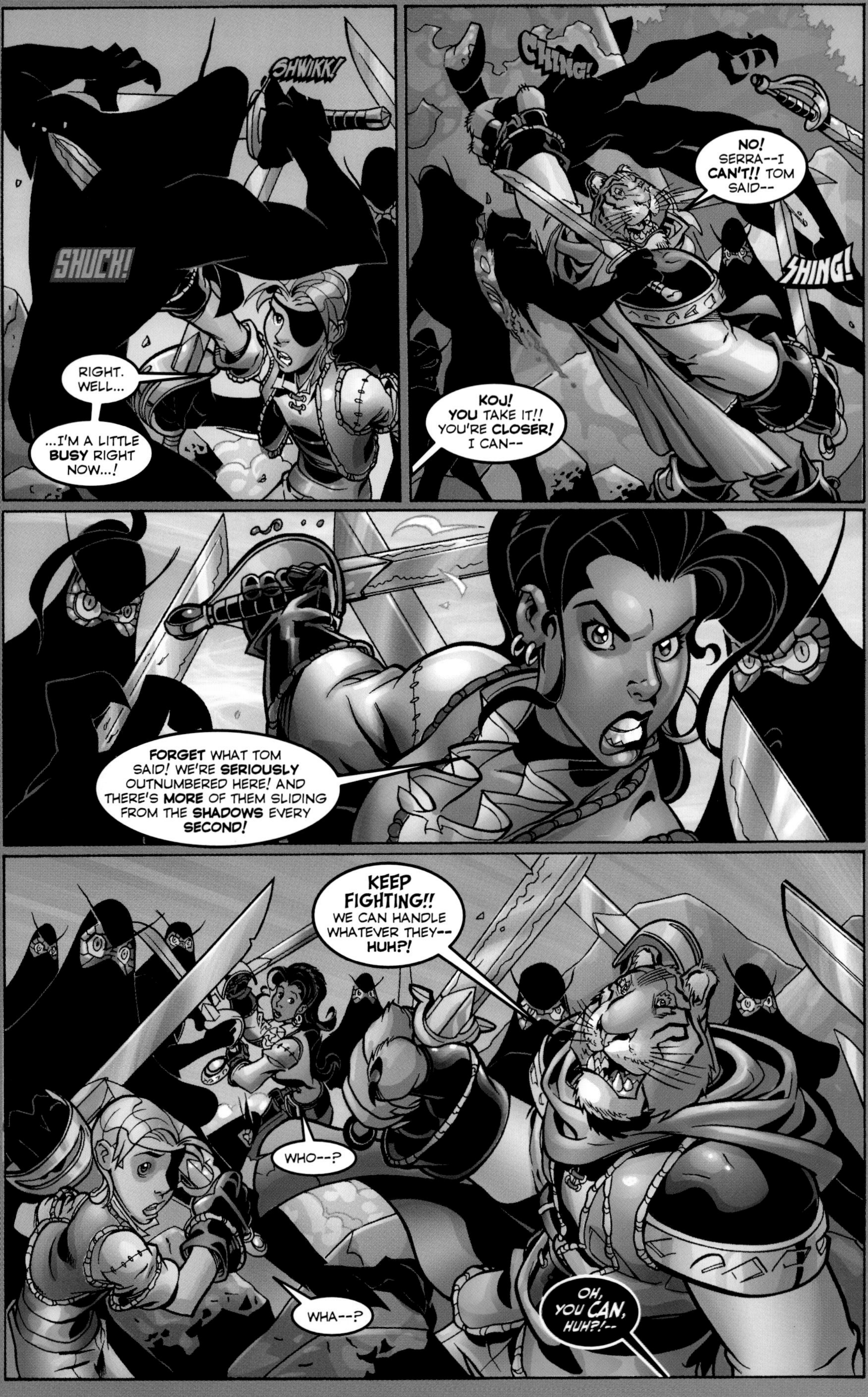
SHWIKK!
SHUCK!
RIGHT. WELL...
...I'M A LITTLE BUSY RIGHT NOW...!
CHING!
NO! SERRA--I CAN'T!! TOM SAID--
SHING!
KOJ! YOU TAKE IT!! YOU'RE CLOSER! I CAN--
FORGET WHAT TOM SAID! WE'RE SERIOUSLY OUTNUMBERED HERE! AND THERE'S MORE OF THEM SLIDING FROM THE SHADOWS EVERY SECOND!
KEEP FIGHTING!! WE CAN HANDLE WHATEVER THEY-- HUH?!
WHO--?
WHA--?
OH, YOU CAN, HUH?!--

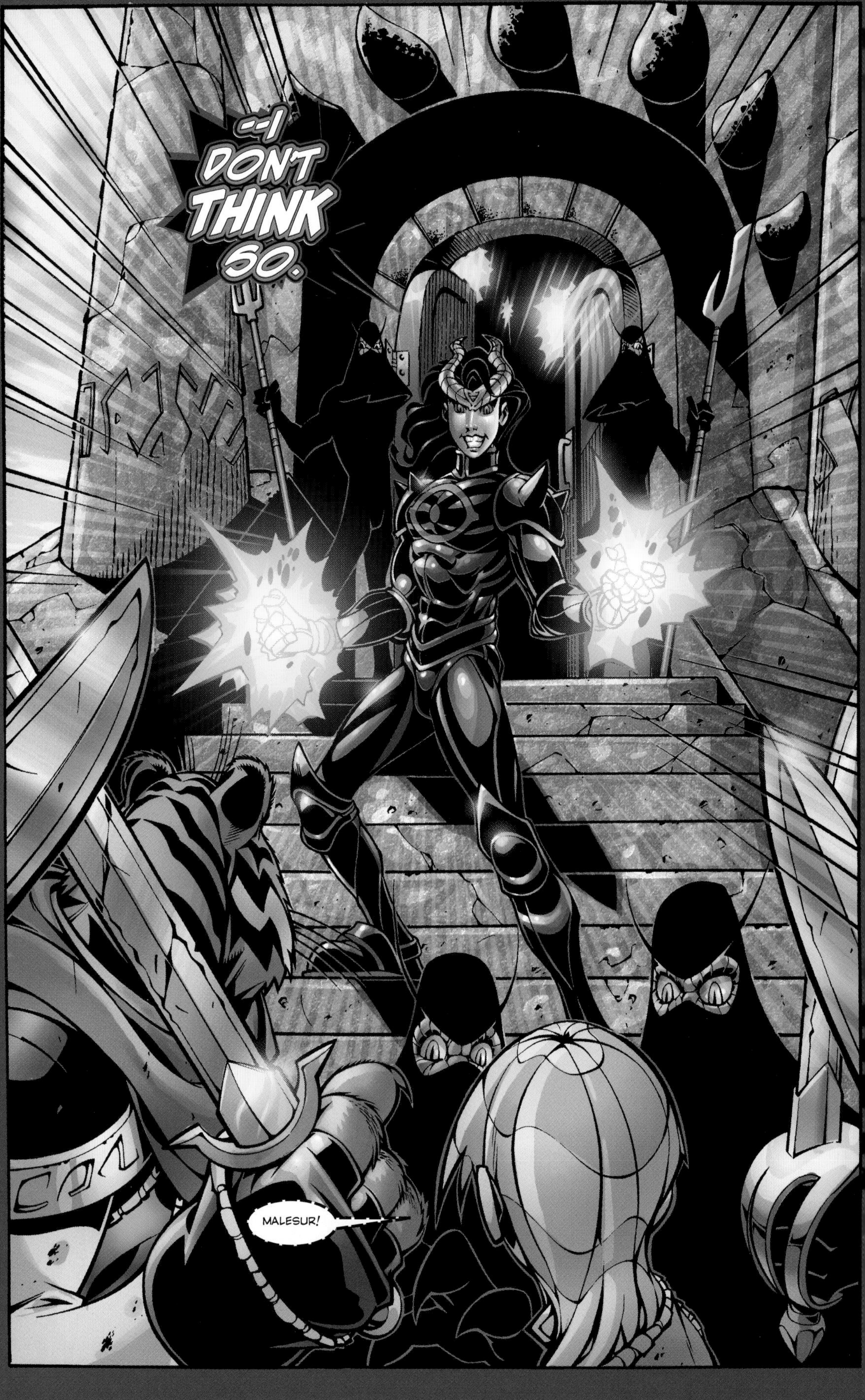
--I DON'T THINK SO.
MALESUR!

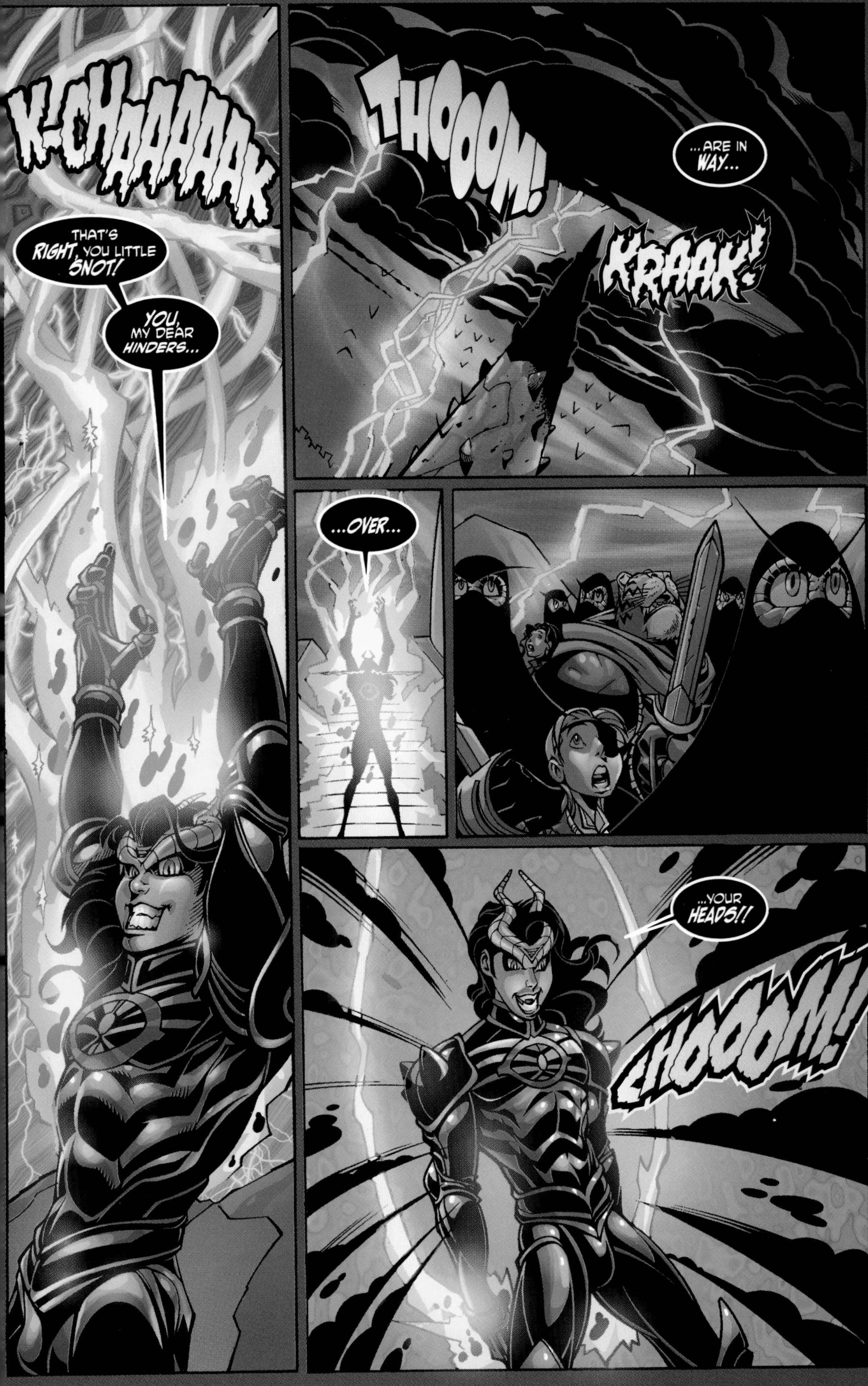
K-CHAAAAAK
THAT'S RIGHT, YOU LITTLE SNOT!
YOU, MY DEAR HINDERS...
THOOOM!
...ARE IN WAY...
KRAAK!
...OVER...
...YOUR HEADS!!
CHOOOM!

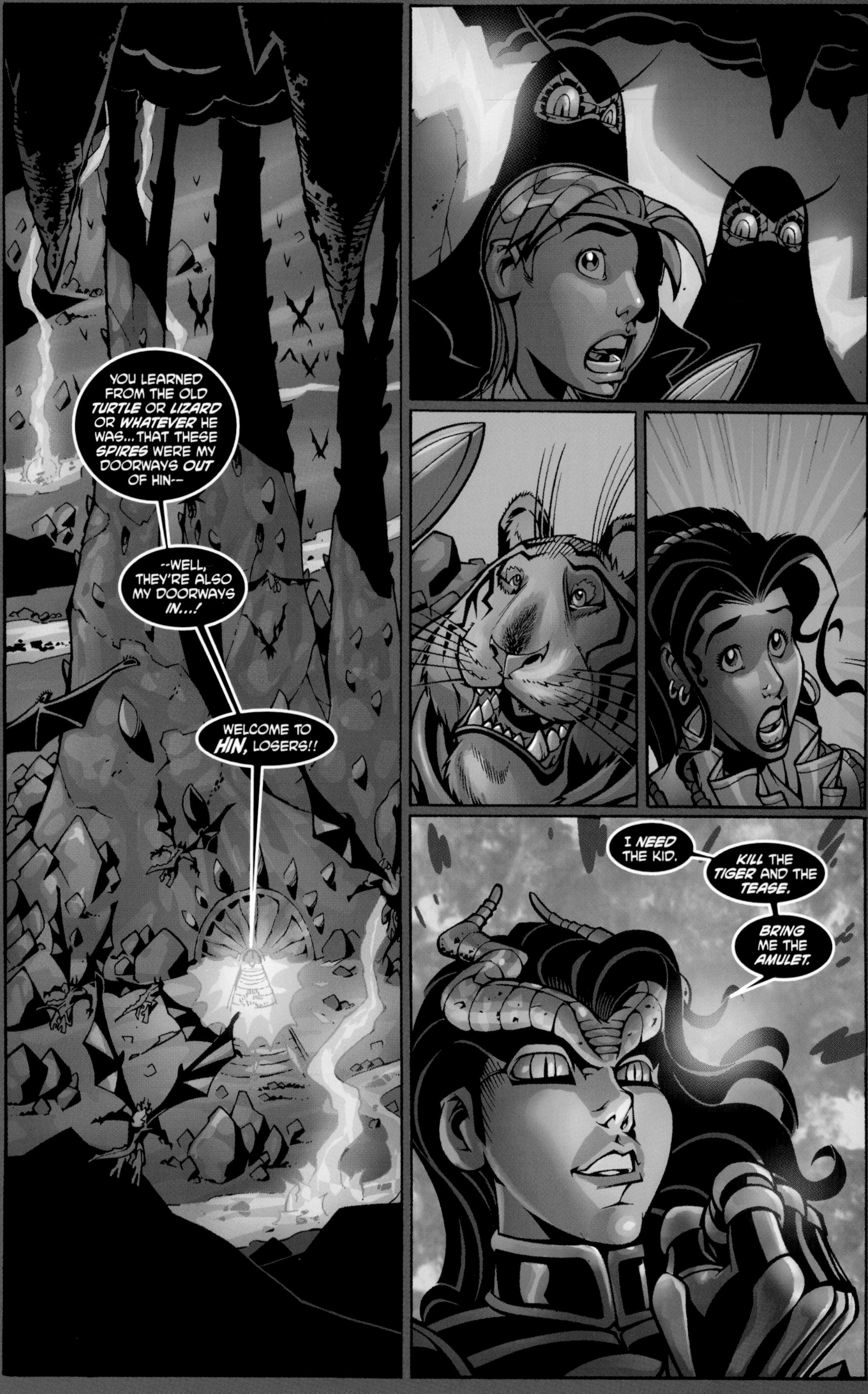
YOU LEARNED FROM THE OLD TURTLE OR LIZARD OR WHATEVER HE WAS...THAT THESE SPIRES WERE MY DOORWAYS OUT OF HIN--
--WELL, THEY'RE ALSO MY DOORWAYS IN...!
WELCOME TO HIN, LOSERS!!
I NEED THE KID.
KILL THE TIGER AND THE TEASE.
BRING ME THE AMULET.

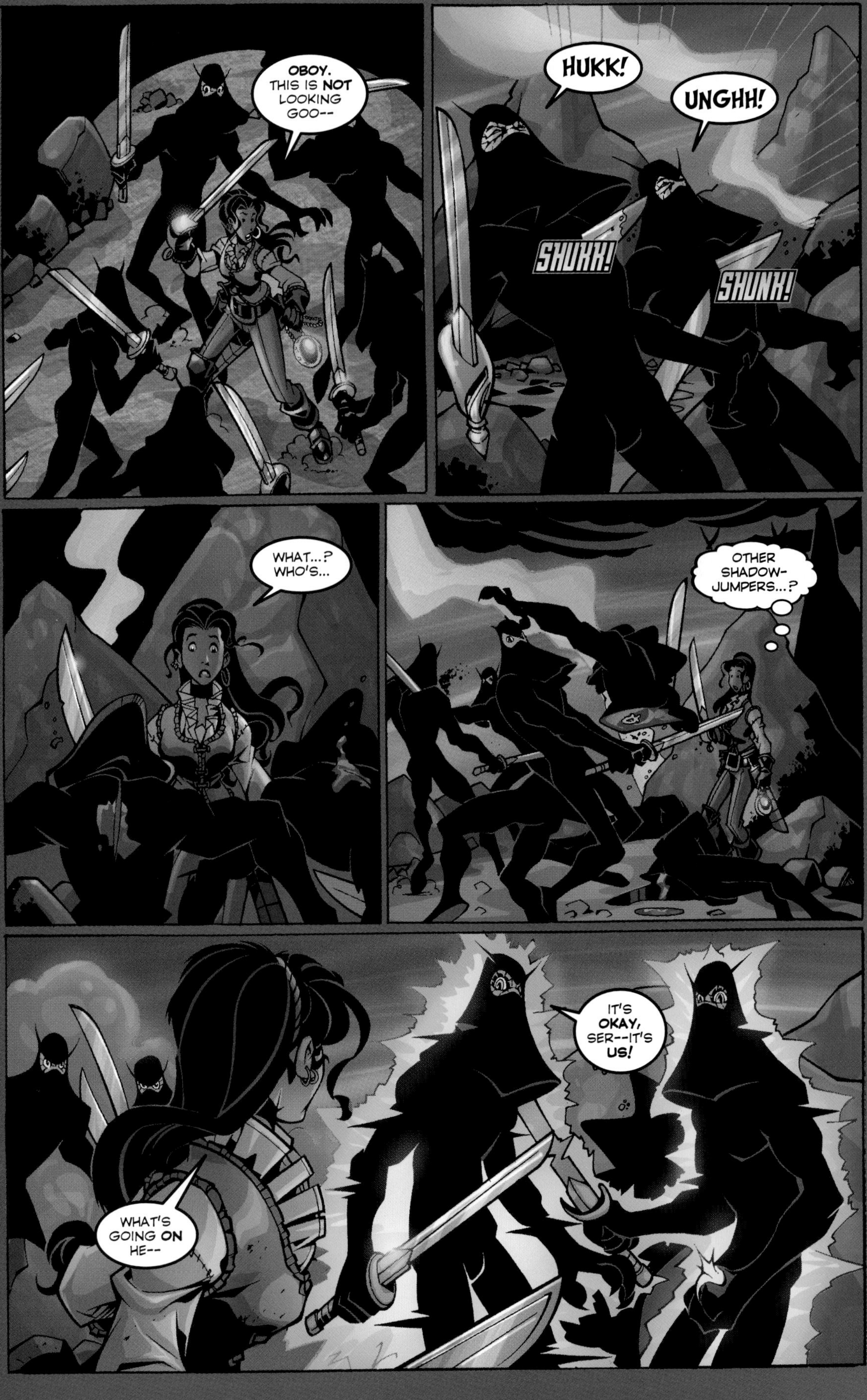
OBOY. THIS IS NOT LOOKING GOO--
HUKK!
UNGHH!
SHUKK!
SHUNK!
WHAT...? WHO'S...
OTHER SHADOW-JUMPERS...?
IT'S OKAY, SER--IT'S US!
WHAT'S GOING ON HE--

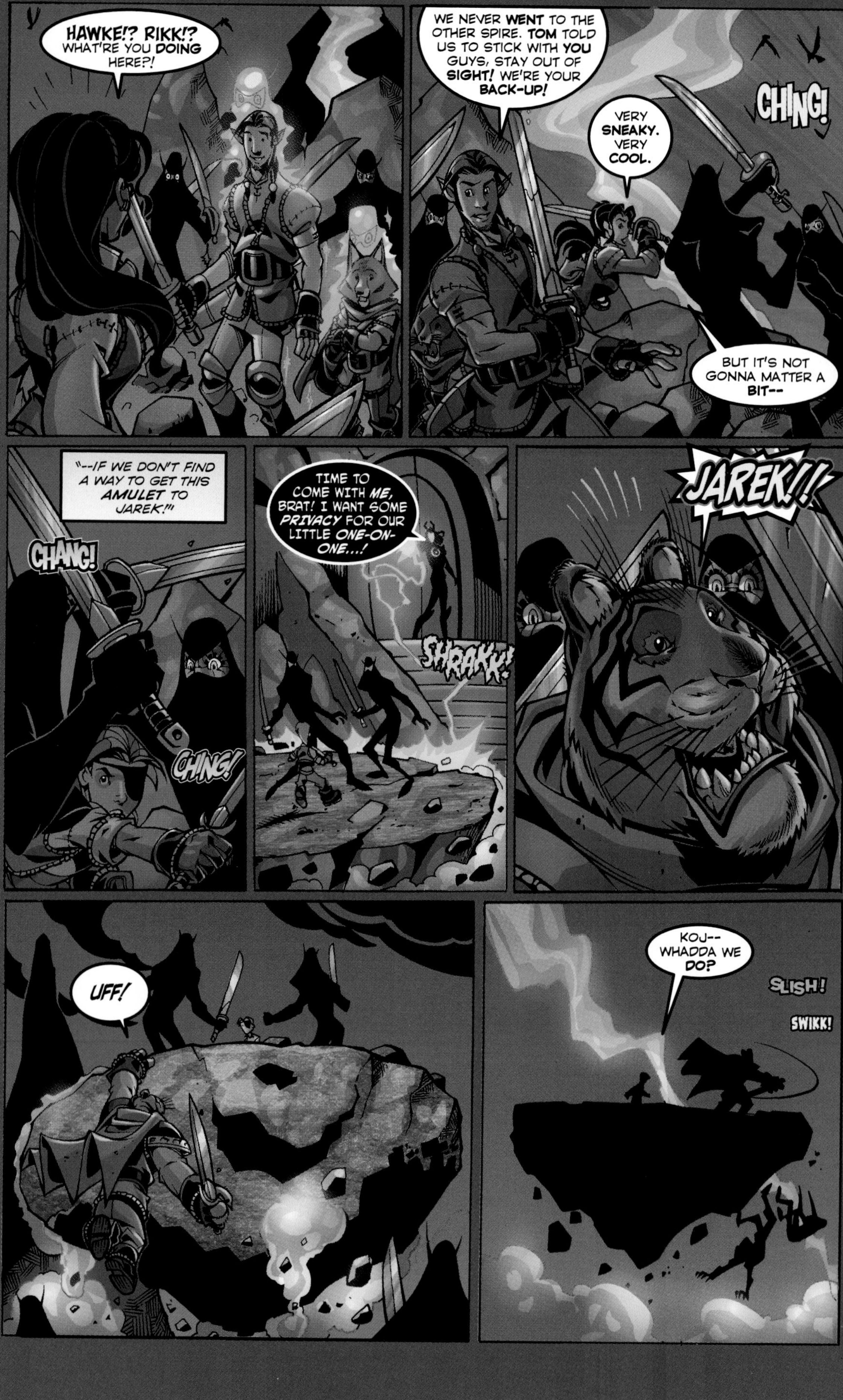
HAWKE!? RIKK!? WHAT'RE YOU DOING HERE?!
WE NEVER WENT TO THE OTHER SPIRE. TOM TOLD US TO STICK WITH YOU GUYS, STAY OUT OF SIGHT! WE'RE YOUR BACK-UP!
VERY SNEAKY. VERY COOL.
CHING!
BUT IT'S NOT GONNA MATTER A BIT--
"--IF WE DON'T FIND A WAY TO GET THIS AMULET TO JAREK!"
CHANG!
CHING!
TIME TO COME WITH ME, BRAT! I WANT SOME PRIVACY FOR OUR LITTLE ONE-ON-ONE...!
SHRAKK!
JAREK!!
UFF!
KOJ-- WHADDA WE DO?
SLISH!
SWIKK!

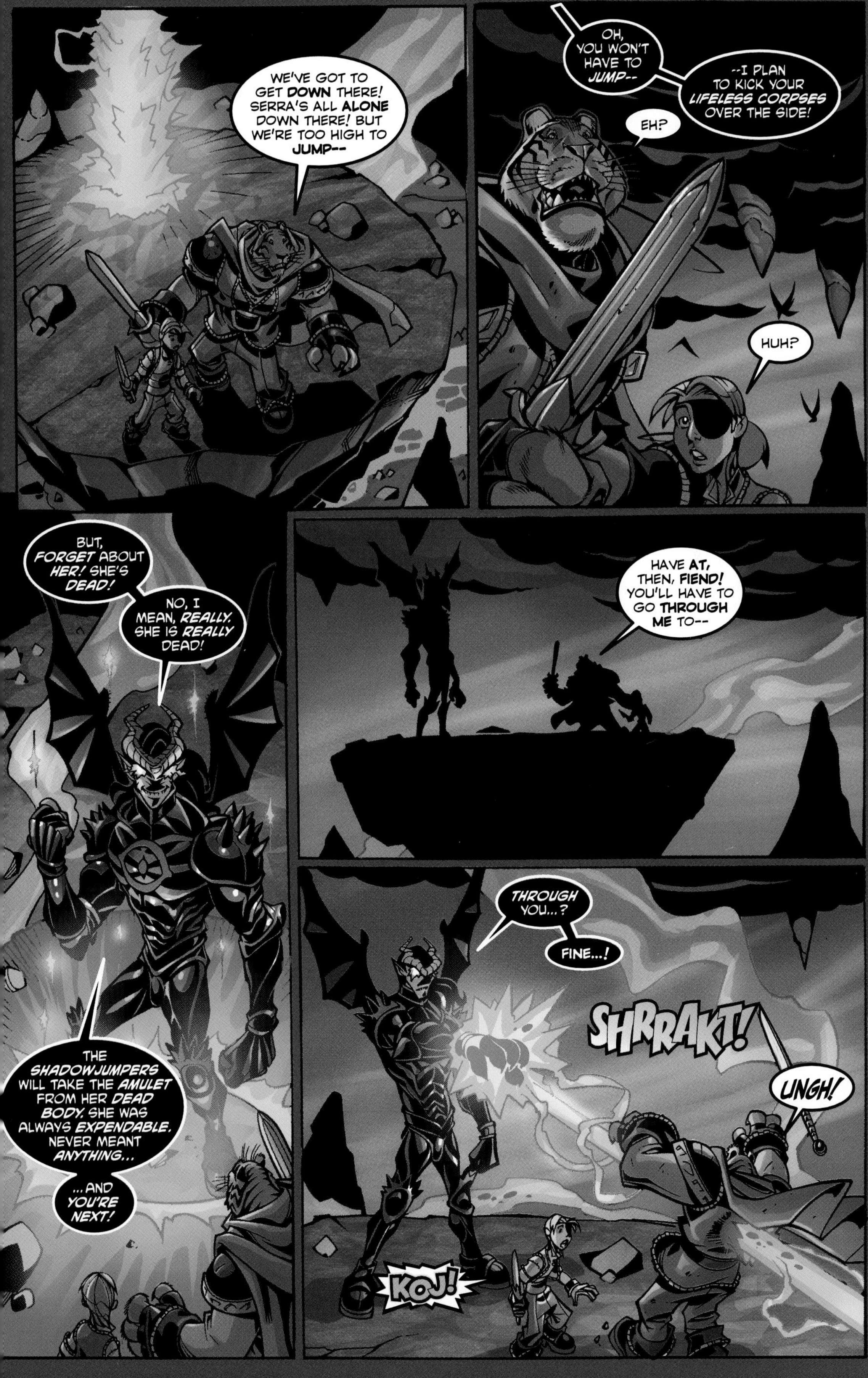

WE'VE GOT TO GET **DOWN** THERE! SERRA'S ALL **ALONE** DOWN THERE! BUT WE'RE TOO HIGH TO **JUMP--**
OH, YOU WON'T HAVE TO *JUMP--*
--I PLAN TO KICK YOUR *LIFELESS CORPSES* OVER THE SIDE!
EH?
HUH?
BUT, *FORGET* ABOUT *HER!* SHE'S *DEAD!*
NO, I MEAN, *REALLY.* SHE IS *REALLY* DEAD!
THE *SHADOWJUMPERS* WILL TAKE THE *AMULET* FROM HER *DEAD BODY.* SHE WAS ALWAYS *EXPENDABLE.* NEVER MEANT *ANYTHING...*
...AND *YOU'RE NEXT!*
HAVE **AT,** THEN, **FIEND!** YOU'LL HAVE TO GO **THROUGH ME** TO--
THROUGH YOU...?
FINE...!
SHRRAKT!
UNGH!
KOJ!

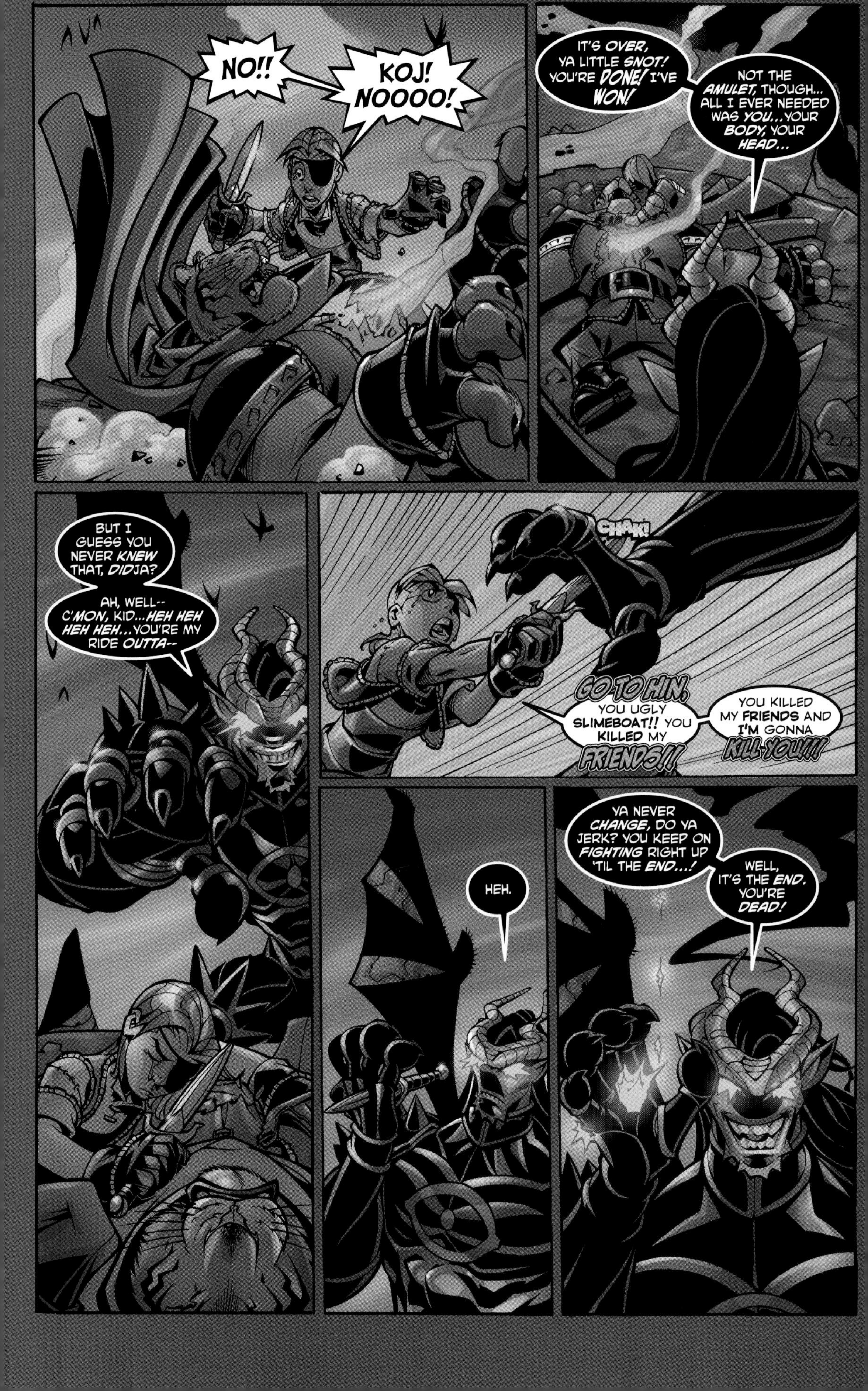
NO!!
KOJ! NOOOO!
IT'S OVER, YA LITTLE SNOT! YOU'RE DONE! I'VE WON!
NOT THE AMULET, THOUGH... ALL I EVER NEEDED WAS YOU...YOUR BODY, YOUR HEAD...
BUT I GUESS YOU NEVER KNEW THAT, DIDJA?
AH, WELL-- C'MON, KID...HEH HEH HEH HEH...YOU'RE MY RIDE OUTTA--
CHAK!
GO TO HIN, YOU UGLY SLIMEBOAT!! YOU KILLED MY FRIENDS!!
YOU KILLED MY FRIENDS AND I'M GONNA KILL YOU!!!
HEH.
YA NEVER CHANGE, DO YA JERK? YOU KEEP ON FIGHTING RIGHT UP 'TIL THE END...!
WELL, IT'S THE END. YOU'RE DEAD!

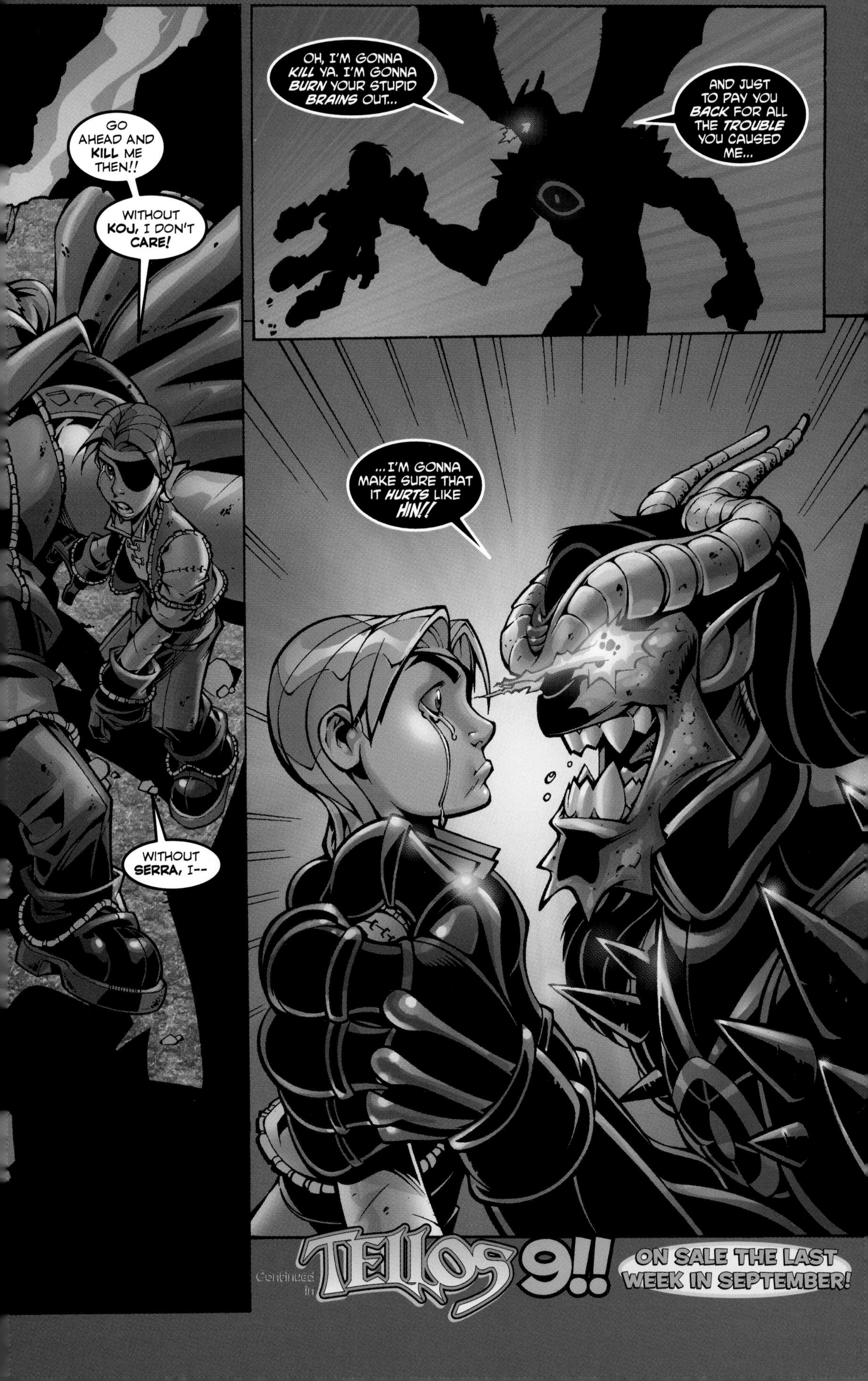
GO AHEAD AND KILL ME THEN!!
WITHOUT KOJ, I DON'T CARE!
WITHOUT SERRA, I--
OH, I'M GONNA KILL YA. I'M GONNA BURN YOUR STUPID BRAINS OUT...
AND JUST TO PAY YOU BACK FOR ALL THE TROUBLE YOU CAUSED ME...
...I'M GONNA MAKE SURE THAT IT HURTS LIKE HIN!!

Continued in TELLOS 9!! ON SALE THE LAST WEEK IN SEPTEMBER!

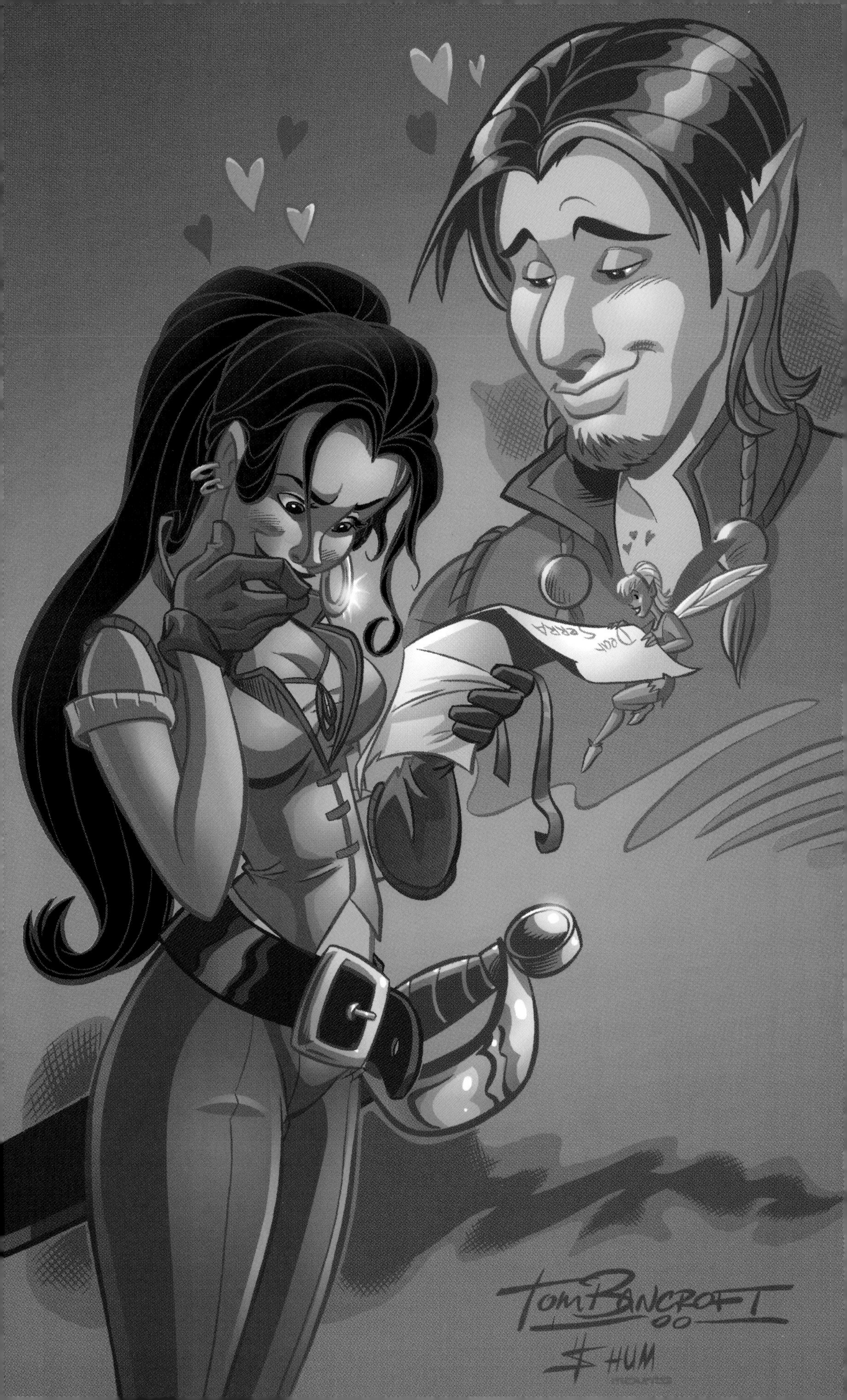

Dear Serra
Tom Bancroft 00
$ HUM

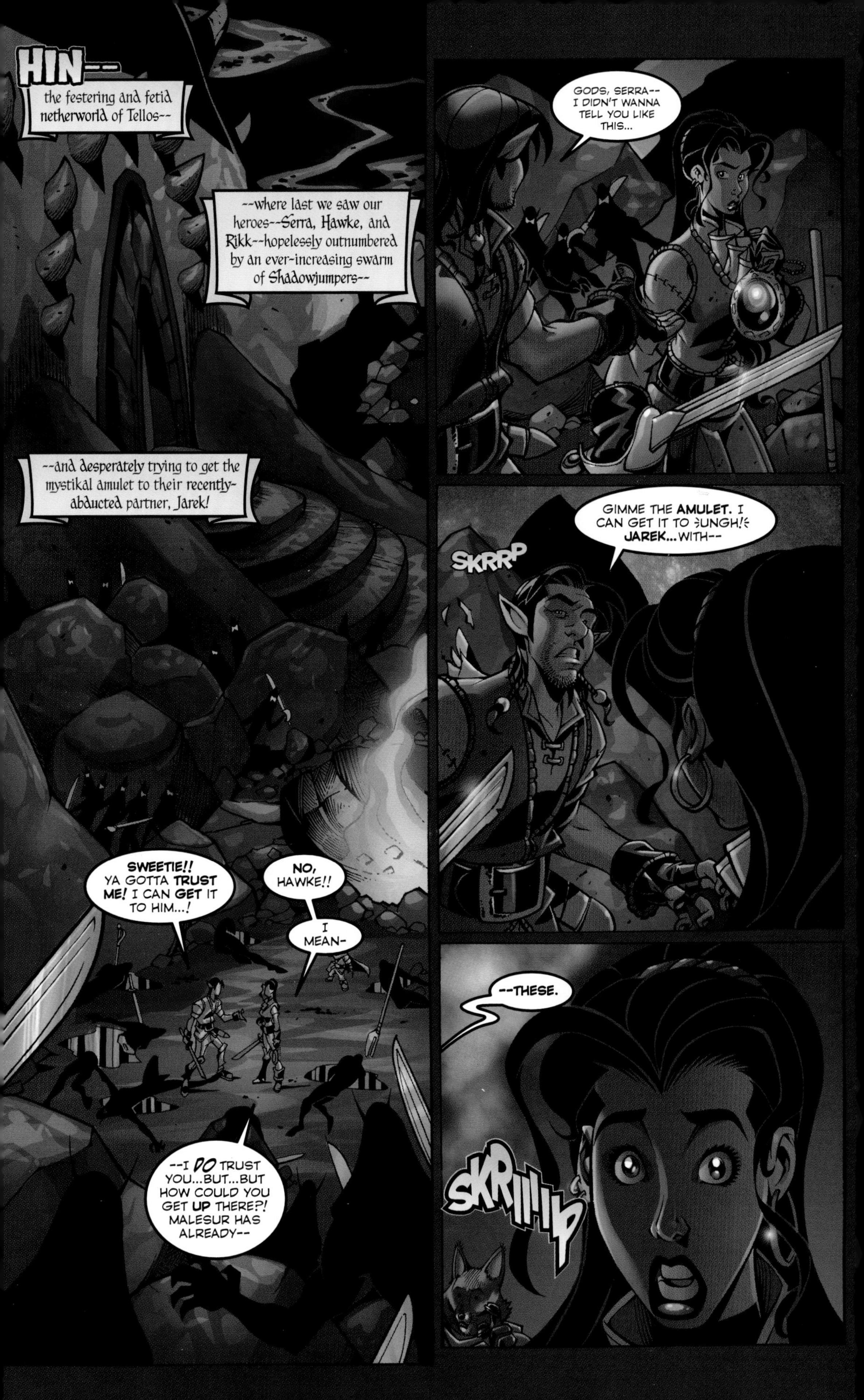
HIN--
the festering and fetid netherworld of Tellos--
--where last we saw our heroes--Serra, Hawke, and Rikk--hopelessly outnumbered by an ever-increasing swarm of Shadowjumpers--
--and desperately trying to get the mystikal amulet to their recently-abducted partner, Jarek!
SWEETIE!! YA GOTTA TRUST ME! I CAN GET IT TO HIM...!
NO, HAWKE!!
I MEAN-
--I DO TRUST YOU...BUT...BUT HOW COULD YOU GET UP THERE?! MALESUR HAS ALREADY--
GODS, SERRA-- I DIDN'T WANNA TELL YOU LIKE THIS...
GIMME THE AMULET. I CAN GET IT TO UNGH! JAREK...WITH--
SKRRP
--THESE.
SKRIIIIIP

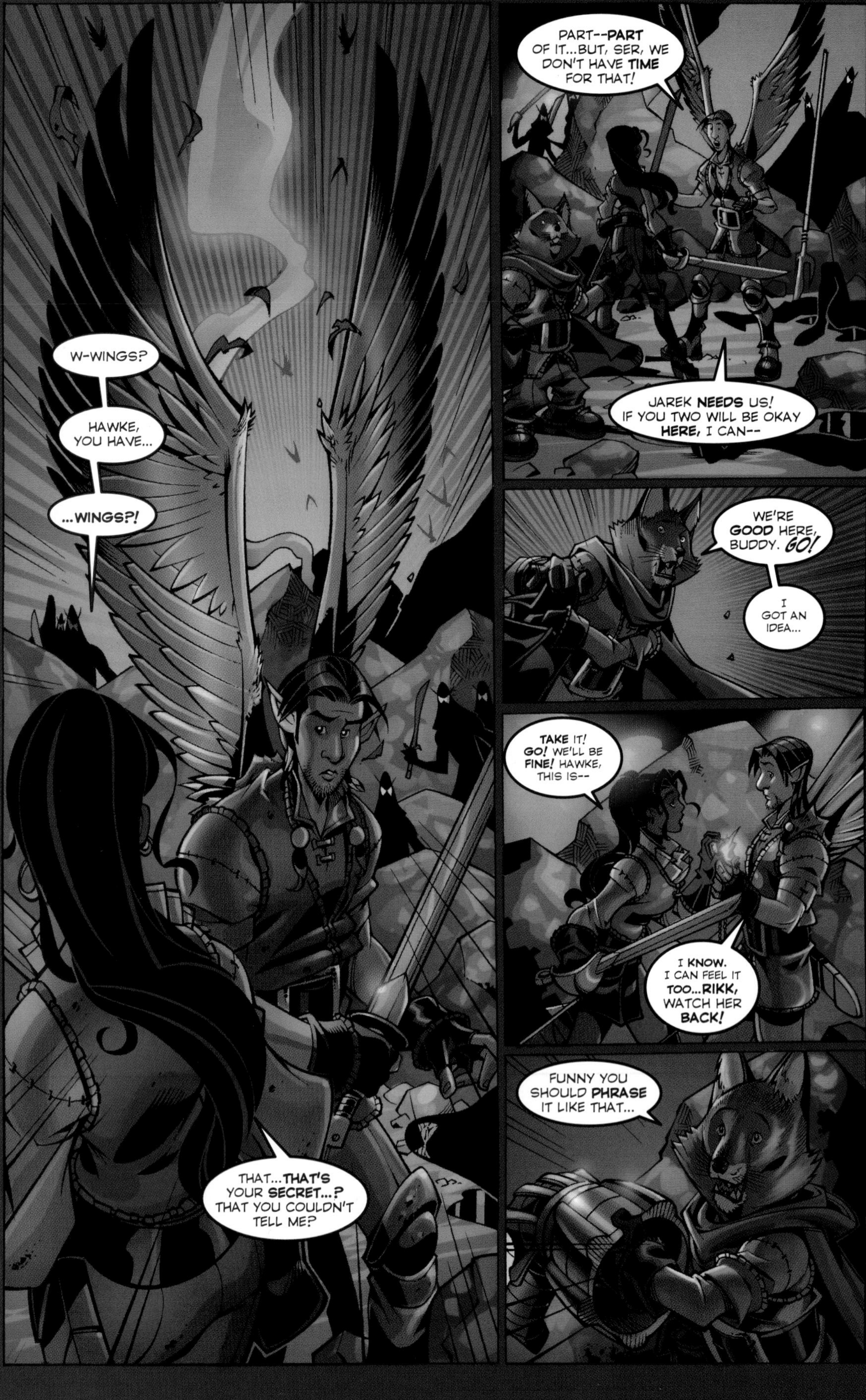
W-WINGS?
HAWKE, YOU HAVE...
...WINGS?!
THAT...THAT'S YOUR SECRET...? THAT YOU COULDN'T TELL ME?
PART--PART OF IT...BUT, SER, WE DON'T HAVE TIME FOR THAT!
JAREK NEEDS US! IF YOU TWO WILL BE OKAY HERE, I CAN--
WE'RE GOOD HERE, BUDDY. GO!
I GOT AN IDEA...
TAKE IT! GO! WE'LL BE FINE! HAWKE, THIS IS--
I KNOW. I CAN FEEL IT TOO...RIKK, WATCH HER BACK!
FUNNY YOU SHOULD PHRASE IT LIKE THAT...

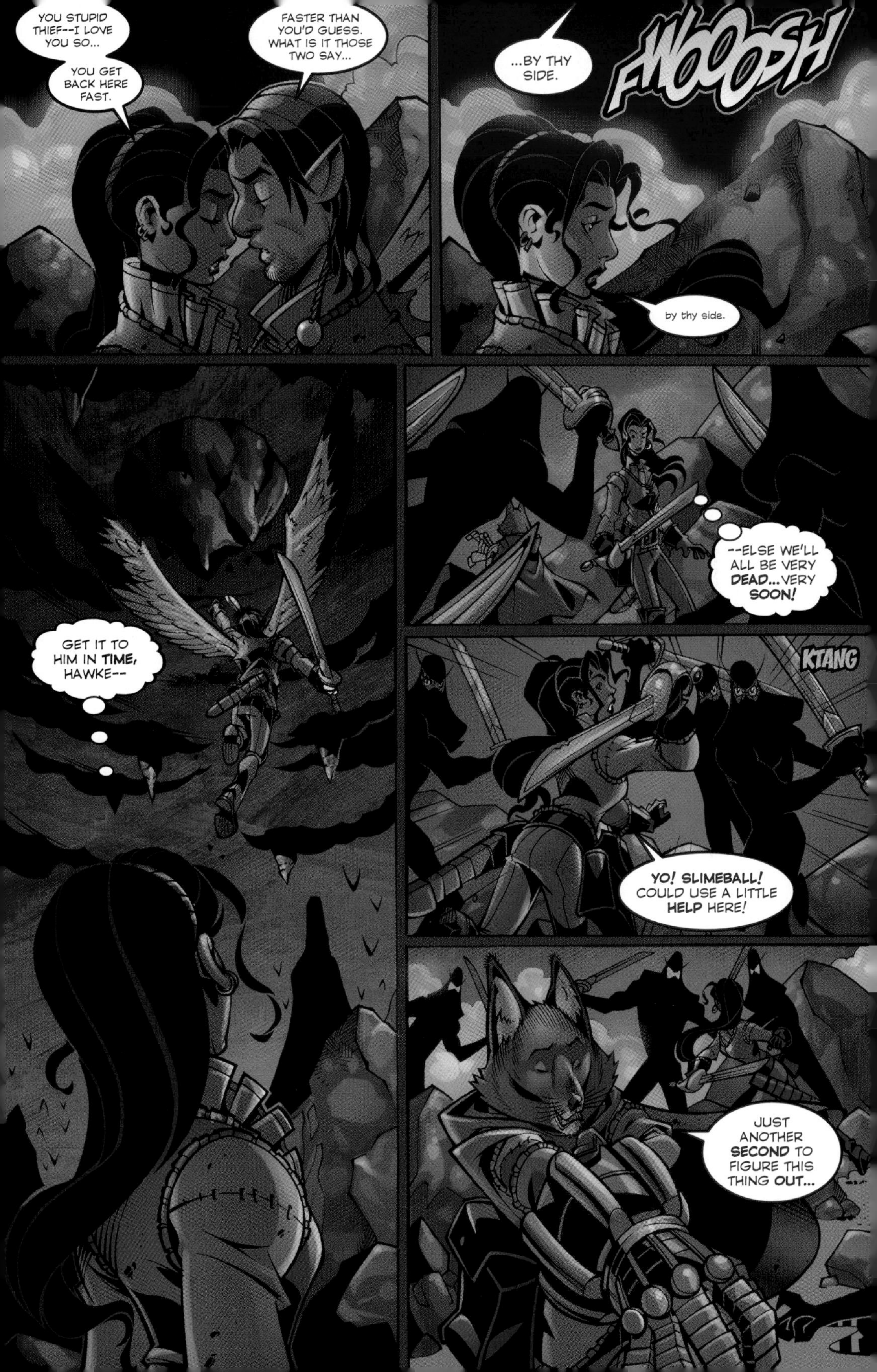

YOU STUPID THIEF--I LOVE YOU SO...
YOU GET BACK HERE FAST.
FASTER THAN YOU'D GUESS. WHAT IS IT THOSE TWO SAY...
...BY THY SIDE.
FWOOOSH
by thy side.
GET IT TO HIM IN TIME, HAWKE--
--ELSE WE'LL ALL BE VERY DEAD...VERY SOON!
KTANG
YO! SLIMEBALL! COULD USE A LITTLE HELP HERE!
JUST ANOTHER SECOND TO FIGURE THIS THING OUT...

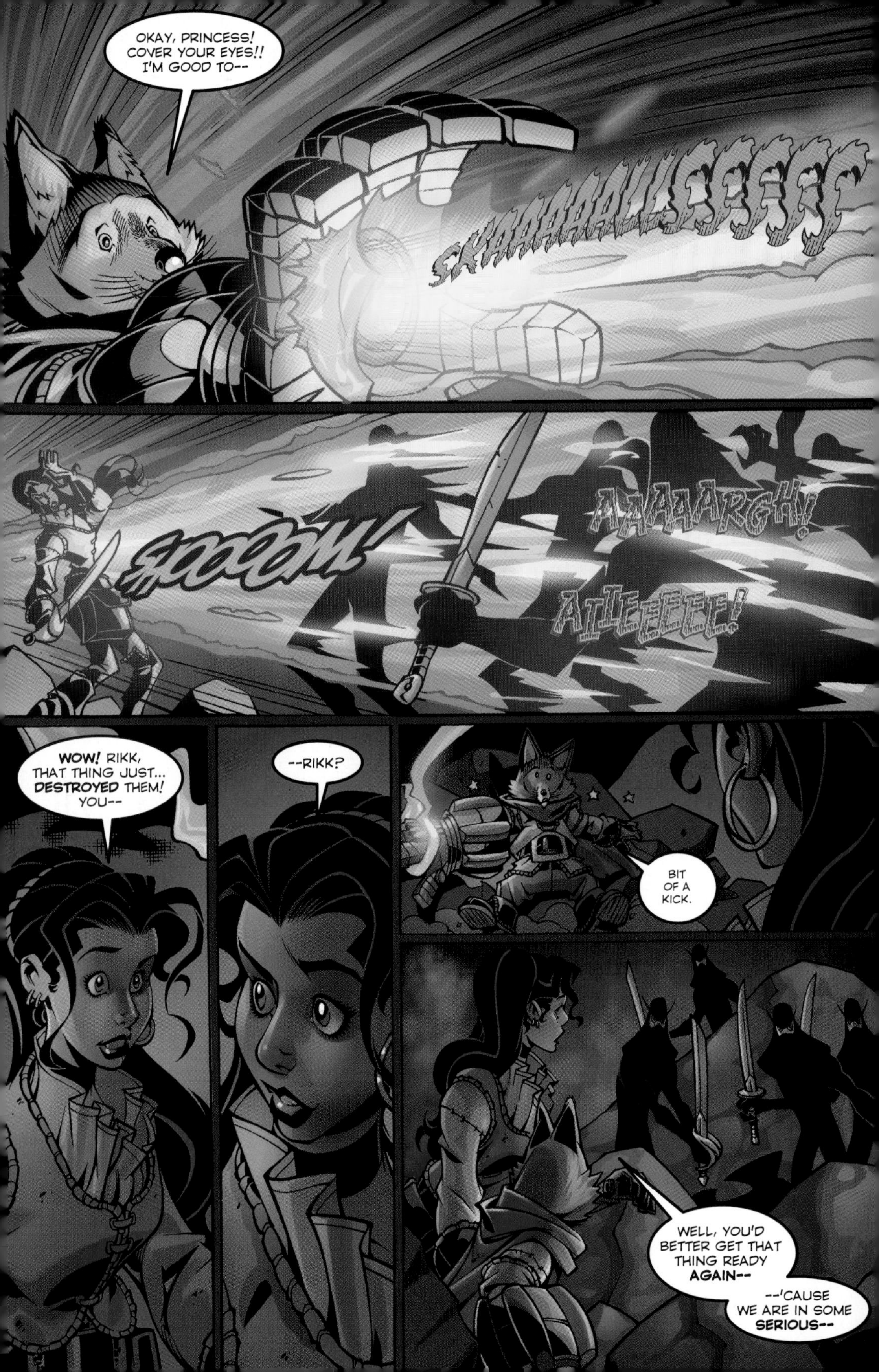
OKAY, PRINCESS! COVER YOUR EYES!! I'M GOOD TO--
SKRAAAAAAUUSSSSSS
SHOOOOM!
AAAAARGH!
AIIEEEEE!
WOW! RIKK, THAT THING JUST... DESTROYED THEM! YOU--
--RIKK?
BIT OF A KICK.
WELL, YOU'D BETTER GET THAT THING READY AGAIN--
--'CAUSE WE ARE IN SOME SERIOUS--

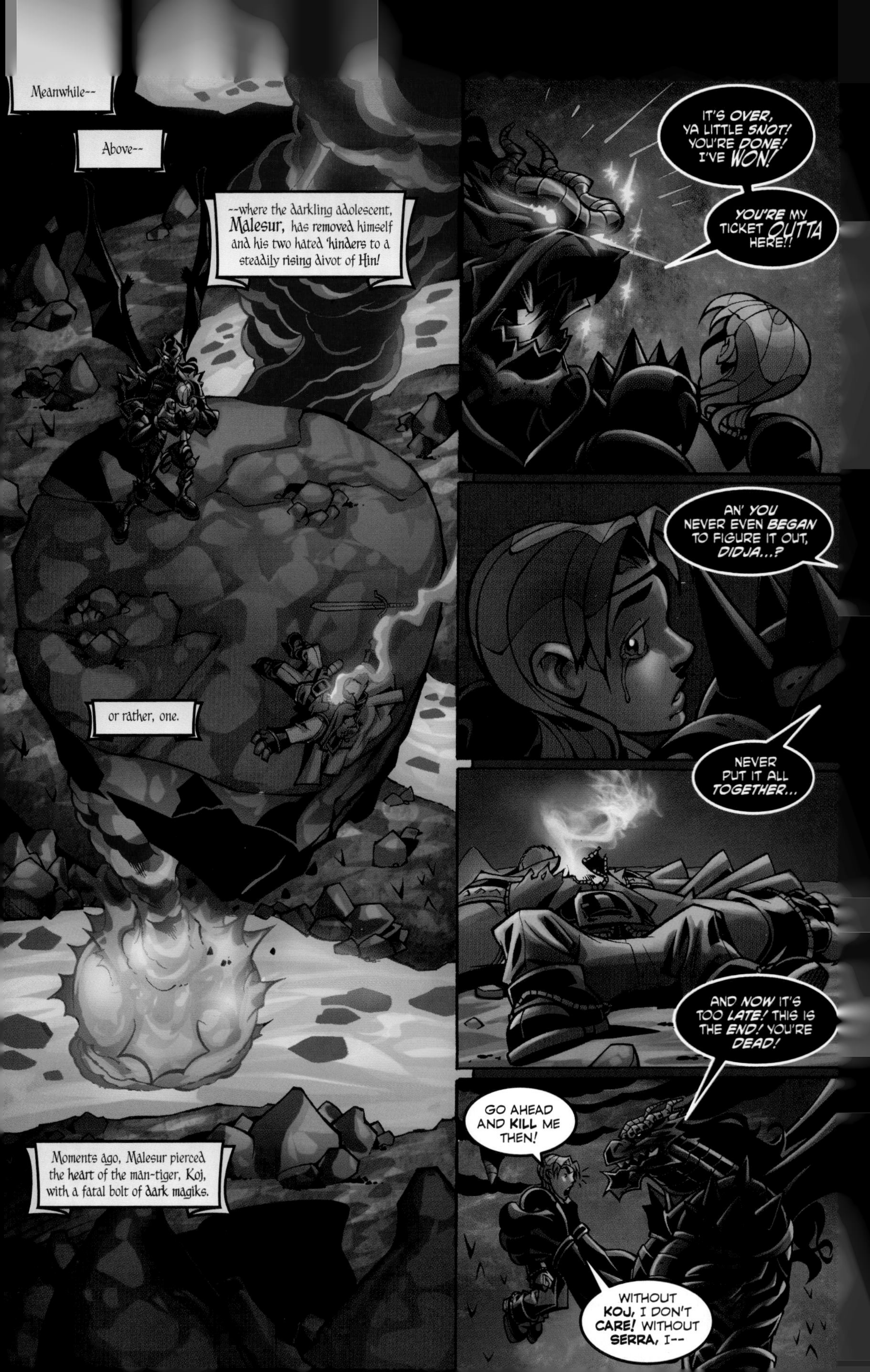
Meanwhile--
Above--
--where the darkling adolescent, Malesur, has removed himself and his two hated 'hinders to a steadily rising divot of Hin!
or rather, one.
Moments ago, Malesur pierced the heart of the man-tiger, Koj, with a fatal bolt of dark magiks.
IT'S OVER, YA LITTLE SNOT! YOU'RE DONE! I'VE WON!
YOU'RE MY TICKET OUTTA HERE!!
AN' YOU NEVER EVEN BEGAN TO FIGURE IT OUT, DIDJA...?
NEVER PUT IT ALL TOGETHER...
AND NOW IT'S TOO LATE! THIS IS THE END! YOU'RE DEAD!
GO AHEAD AND KILL ME THEN!
WITHOUT KOJ, I DON'T CARE! WITHOUT SERRA, I--

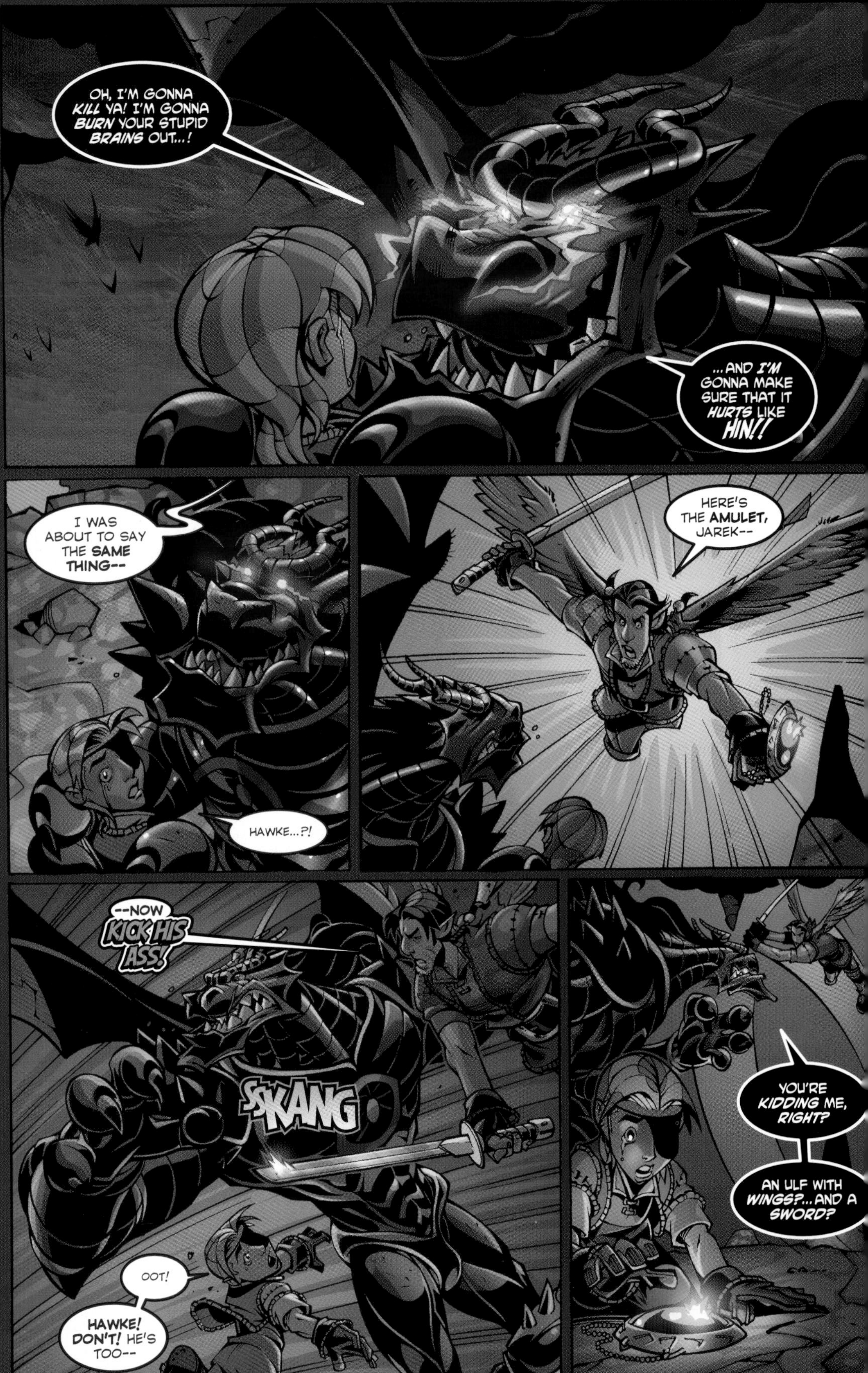
OH, I'M GONNA KILL YA! I'M GONNA BURN YOUR STUPID BRAINS OUT...!
...AND I'M GONNA MAKE SURE THAT IT HURTS LIKE HIN!!
I WAS ABOUT TO SAY THE SAME THING--
HAWKE...?!
HERE'S THE AMULET, JAREK--
--NOW KICK HIS ASS!
SSKANG
OOT!
HAWKE! DON'T! HE'S TOO--
YOU'RE KIDDING ME, RIGHT?
AN ULF WITH WINGS?...AND A SWORD?

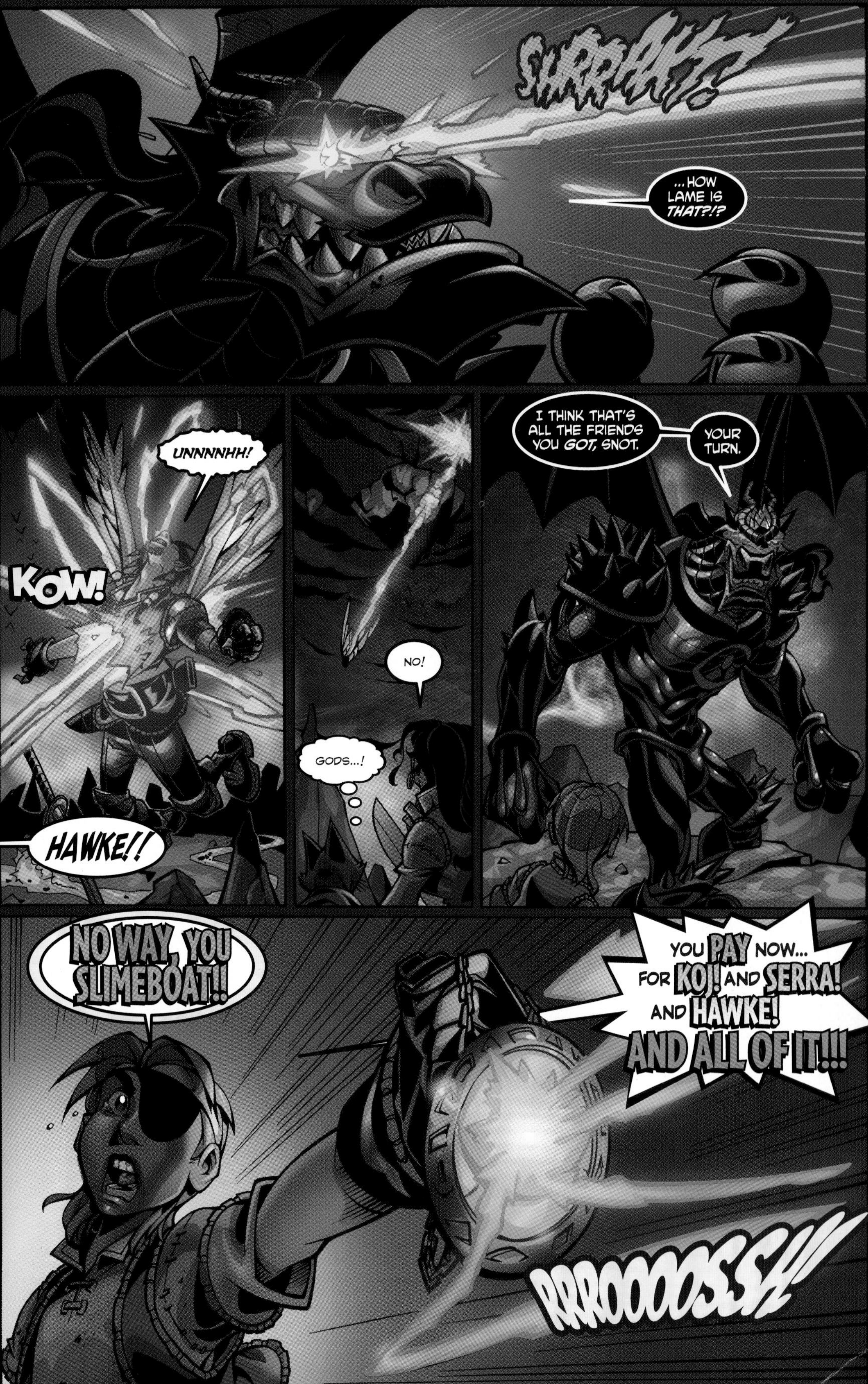

SHRRAAKT!
...HOW LAME IS THAT?!?
KOW!
UNNNNHH!
HAWKE!!
NO!
GODS...!
I THINK THAT'S ALL THE FRIENDS YOU GOT, SNOT.
YOUR TURN.
NO WAY, YOU SLIMEBOAT!!
YOU PAY NOW... FOR KOJ! AND SERRA! AND HAWKE! AND ALL OF IT!!!
RRROOOOOSSH!

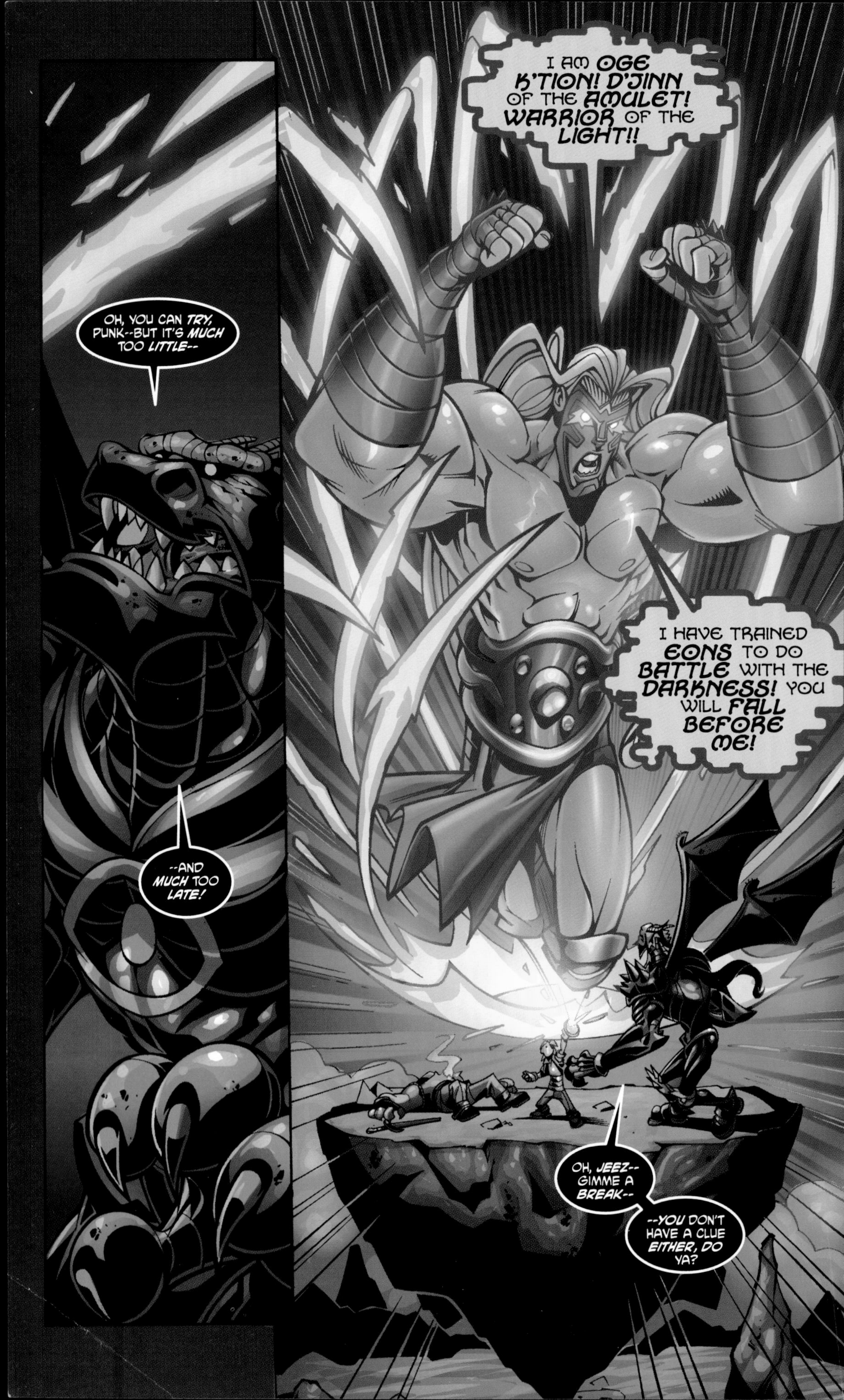
I AM OGE K'TION! D'JINN OF THE AMULET! WARRIOR OF THE LIGHT!!
OH, YOU CAN TRY, PUNK--BUT IT'S MUCH TOO LITTLE--
I HAVE TRAINED EONS TO DO BATTLE WITH THE DARKNESS! YOU WILL FALL BEFORE ME!
--AND MUCH TOO LATE!
OH, JEEZ-- GIMME A BREAK--
--YOU DON'T HAVE A CLUE EITHER, DO YA?

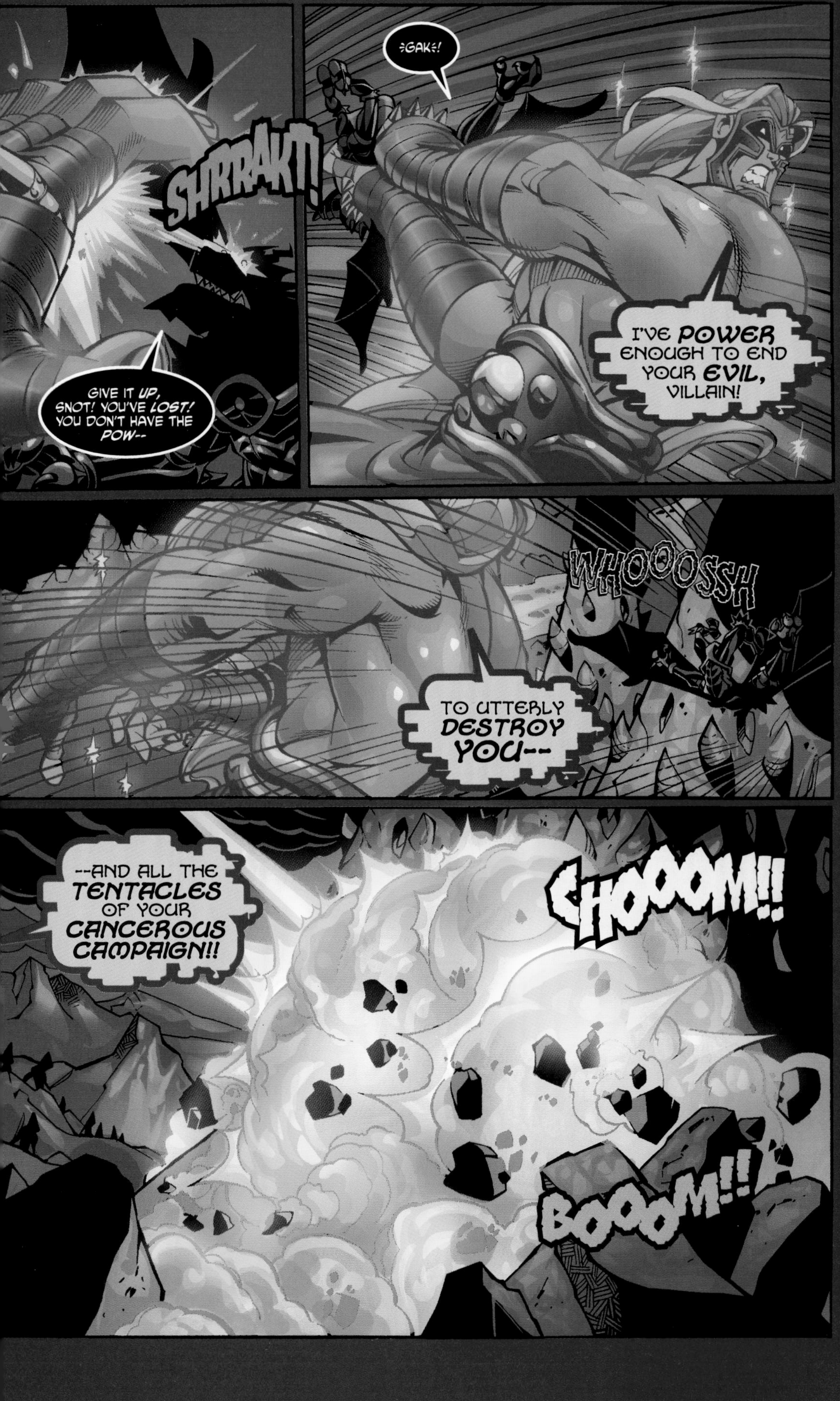
SHRRAKT!
GIVE IT UP, SNOT! YOU'VE LOST! YOU DON'T HAVE THE POW--
GAK!
I'VE POWER ENOUGH TO END YOUR EVIL, VILLAIN!
WHOOOOSSH
TO UTTERLY DESTROY YOU--
--AND ALL THE TENTACLES OF YOUR CANCEROUS CAMPAIGN!!
CHOOOM!!
BOOOM!!

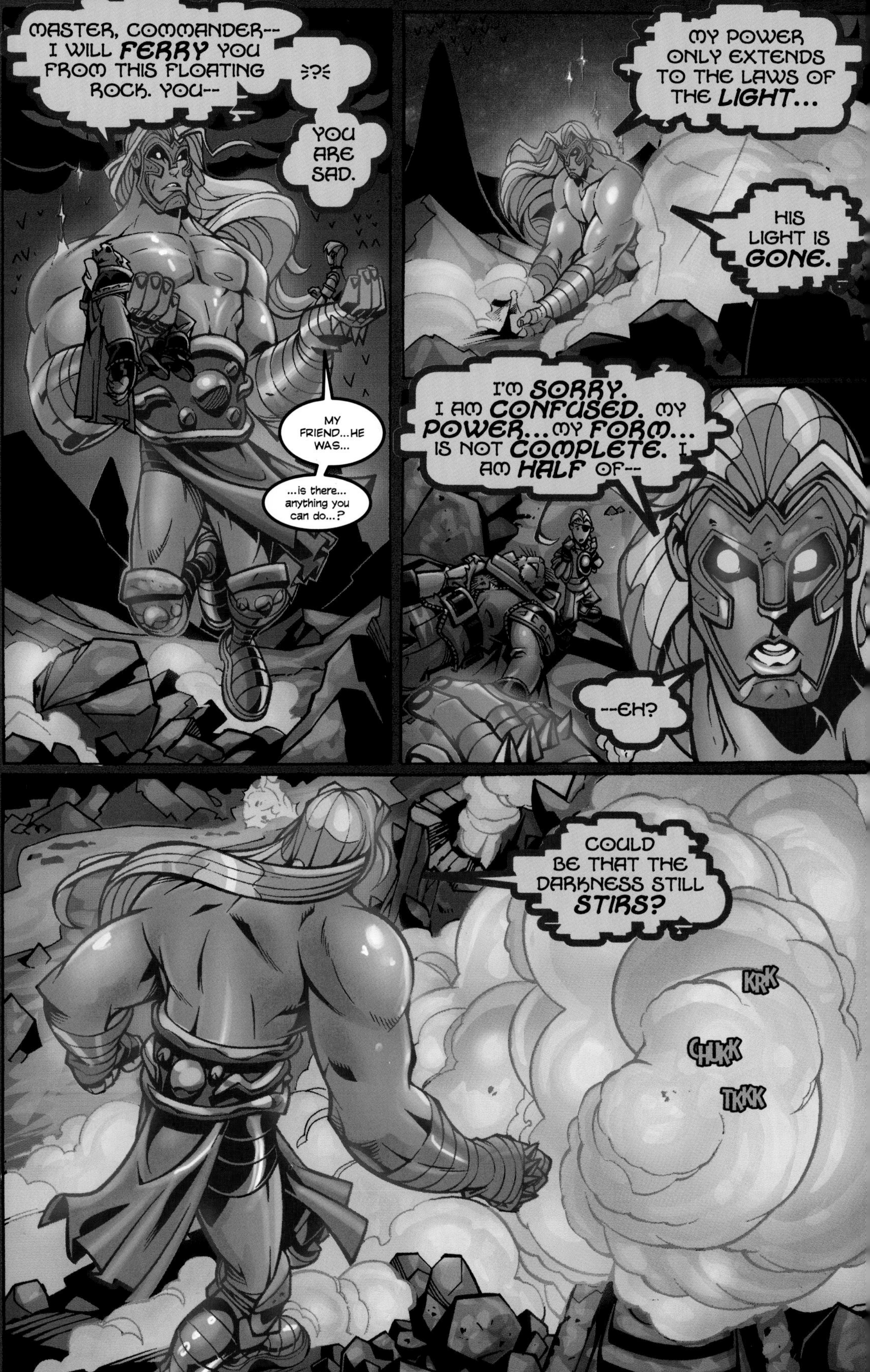
MASTER, COMMANDER-- I WILL FERRY YOU FROM THIS FLOATING ROCK. YOU--
YOU ARE SAD.
MY FRIEND...HE WAS...
...is there... anything you can do...?
MY POWER ONLY EXTENDS TO THE LAWS OF THE LIGHT...
HIS LIGHT IS GONE.
I'M SORRY. I AM CONFUSED. MY POWER...MY FORM... IS NOT COMPLETE. I AM HALF OF--
--EH?
COULD BE THAT THE DARKNESS STILL STIRS?
KRK
CHUKK
TKKK

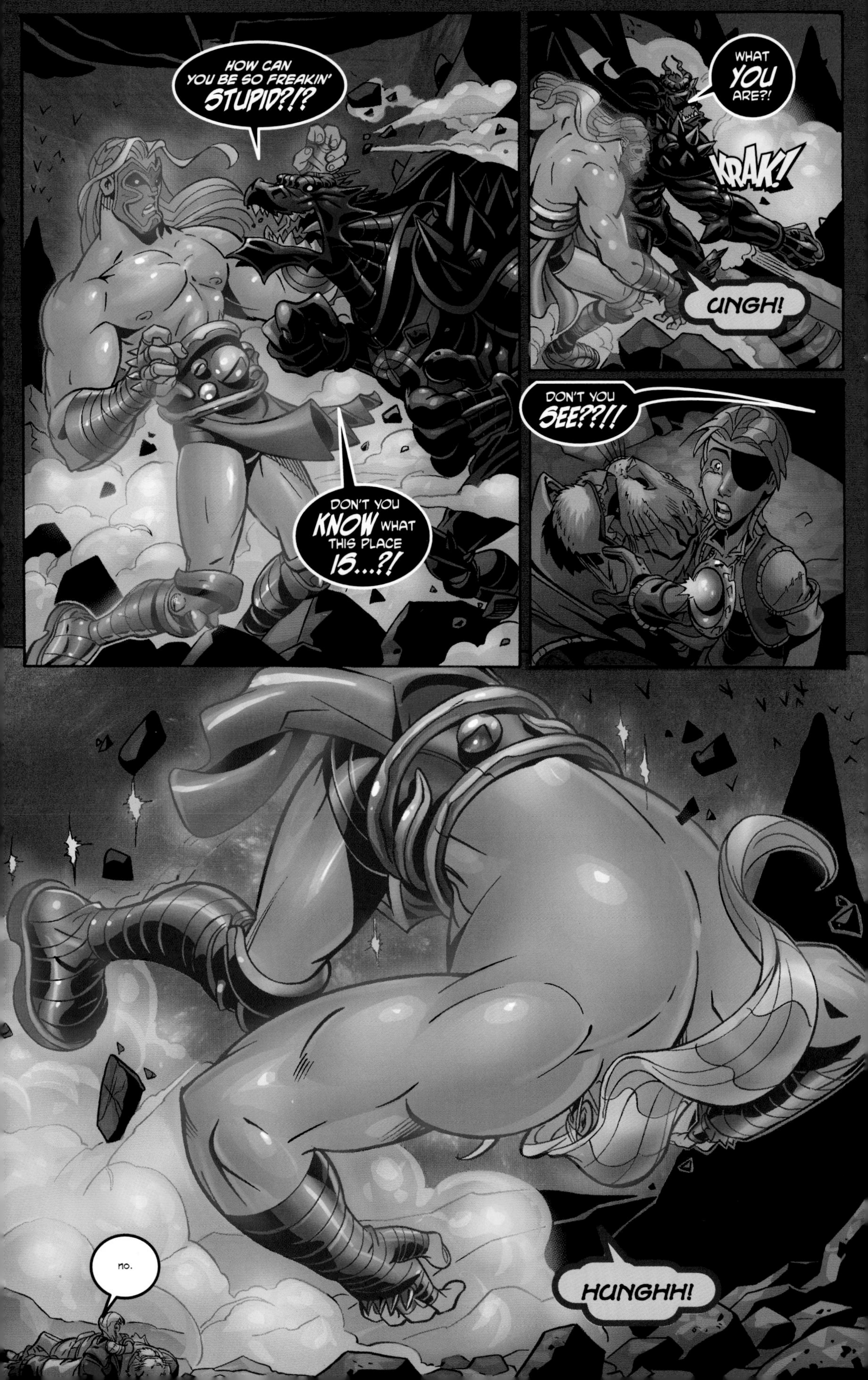
HOW CAN YOU BE SO FREAKIN' STUPID?!?
WHAT YOU ARE?!
KRAK!
UNGH!
DON'T YOU KNOW WHAT THIS PLACE IS...?!
DON'T YOU SEE??!!
no.
HUNGHH!

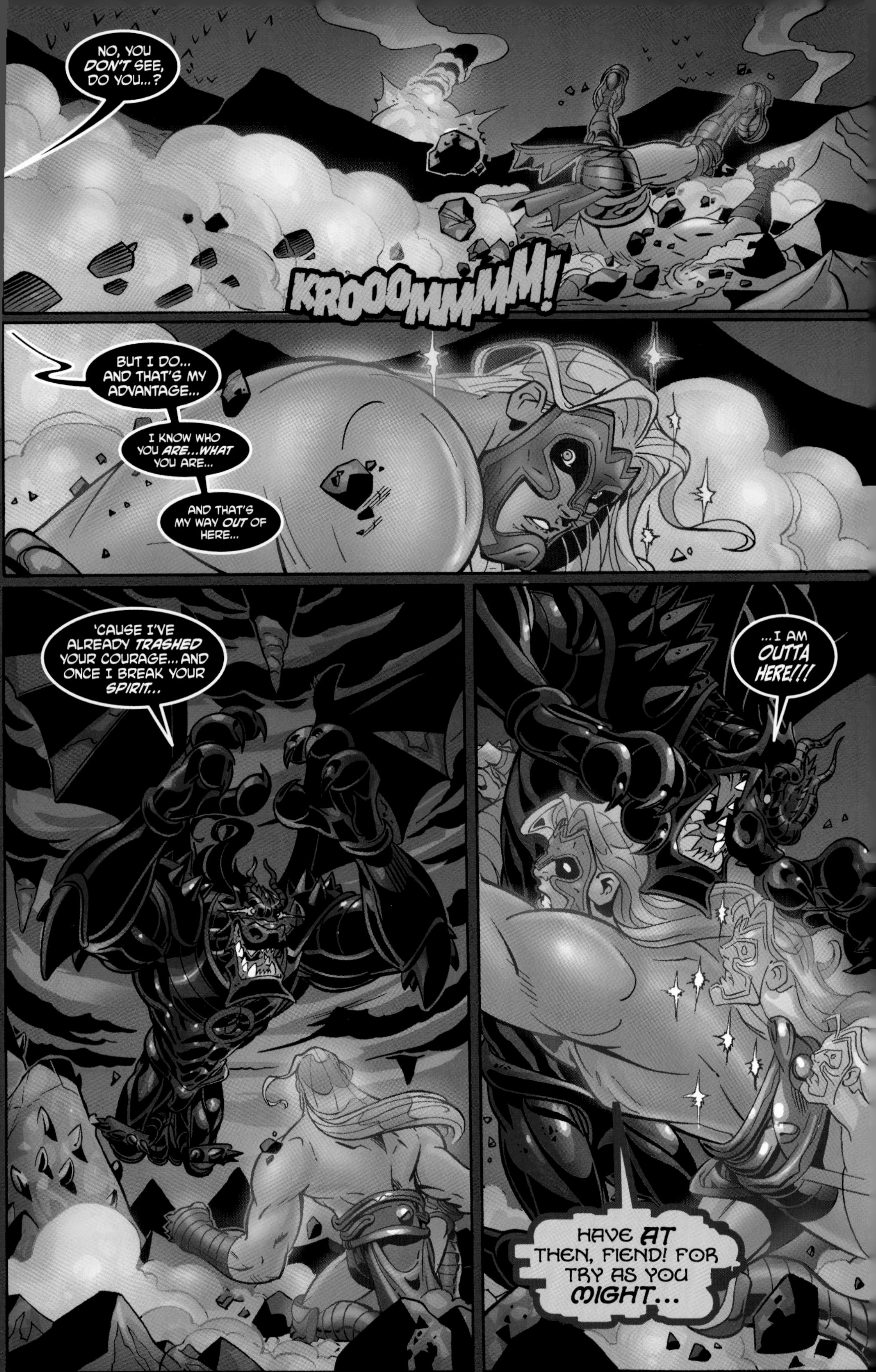
NO, YOU DON'T SEE, DO YOU...?
KROOOMMMMM!
BUT I DO... AND THAT'S MY ADVANTAGE...
I KNOW WHO YOU ARE...WHAT YOU ARE...
AND THAT'S MY WAY OUT OF HERE...
'CAUSE I'VE ALREADY TRASHED YOUR COURAGE...AND ONCE I BREAK YOUR SPIRIT...
...I AM OUTTA HERE!!!
HAVE AT THEN, FIEND! FOR TRY AS YOU MIGHT...

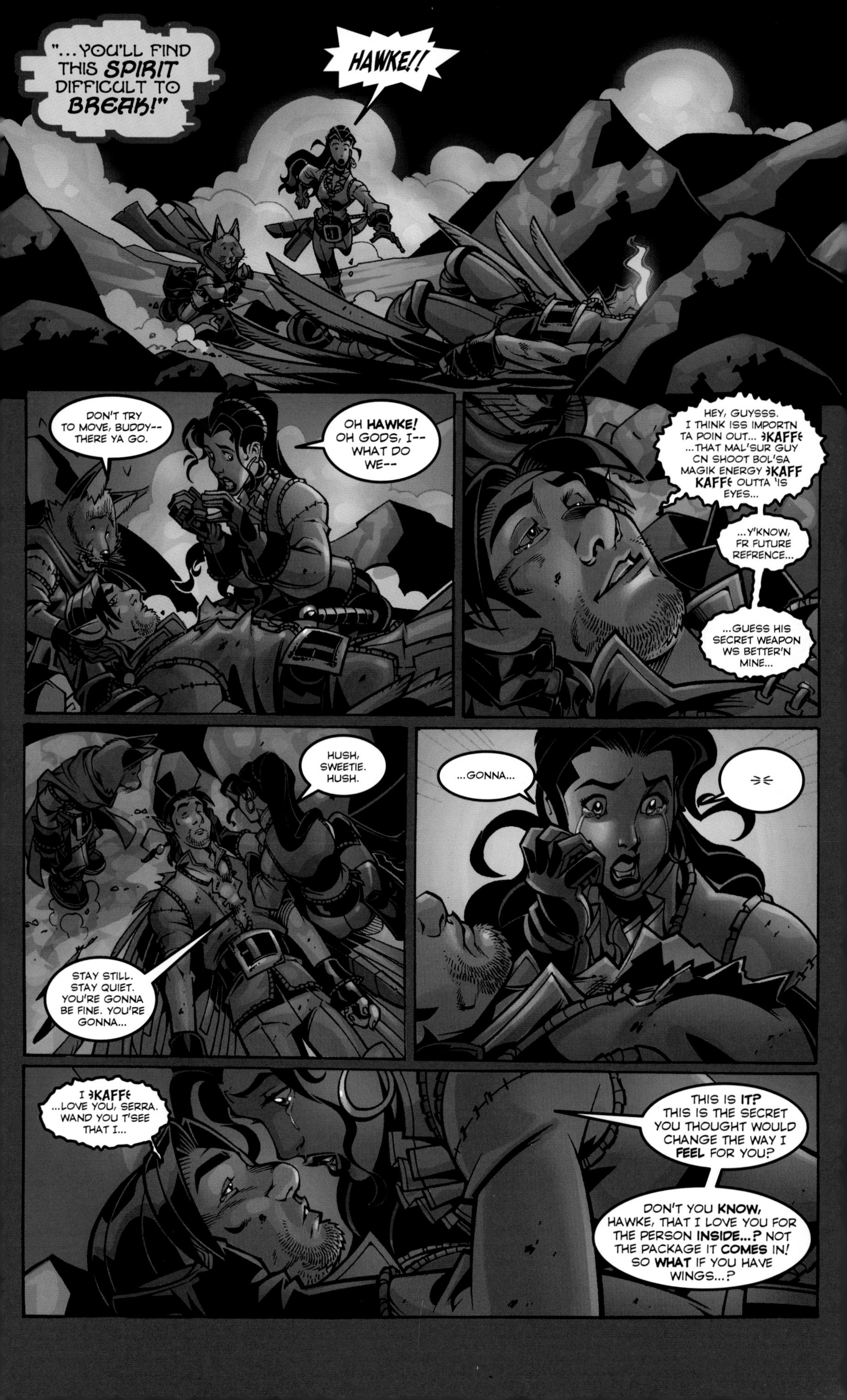
"...YOU'LL FIND THIS SPIRIT DIFFICULT TO BREAK!"
HAWKE!!
DON'T TRY TO MOVE, BUDDY-- THERE YA GO.
OH HAWKE! OH GODS, I-- WHAT DO WE--
HEY, GUYSSS. I THINK ISS IMPORTN TA POIN OUT... ƎKAFFƐ ...THAT MAL'SUR GUY CN SHOOT BOL'SA MAGIK ENERGY ƎKAFF KAFFƐ OUTTA 'IS EYES...
...Y'KNOW, FR FUTURE REFRENCE...
...GUESS HIS SECRET WEAPON WS BETTER'N MINE...
HUSH, SWEETIE. HUSH.
STAY STILL. STAY QUIET. YOU'RE GONNA BE FINE. YOU'RE GONNA...
...GONNA...
I ƎKAFFƐ ...LOVE YOU, SERRA. WAND YOU T'SEE THAT I...
THIS IS IT? THIS IS THE SECRET YOU THOUGHT WOULD CHANGE THE WAY I FEEL FOR YOU?
DON'T YOU KNOW, HAWKE, THAT I LOVE YOU FOR THE PERSON INSIDE...? NOT THE PACKAGE IT COMES IN! SO WHAT IF YOU HAVE WINGS...?

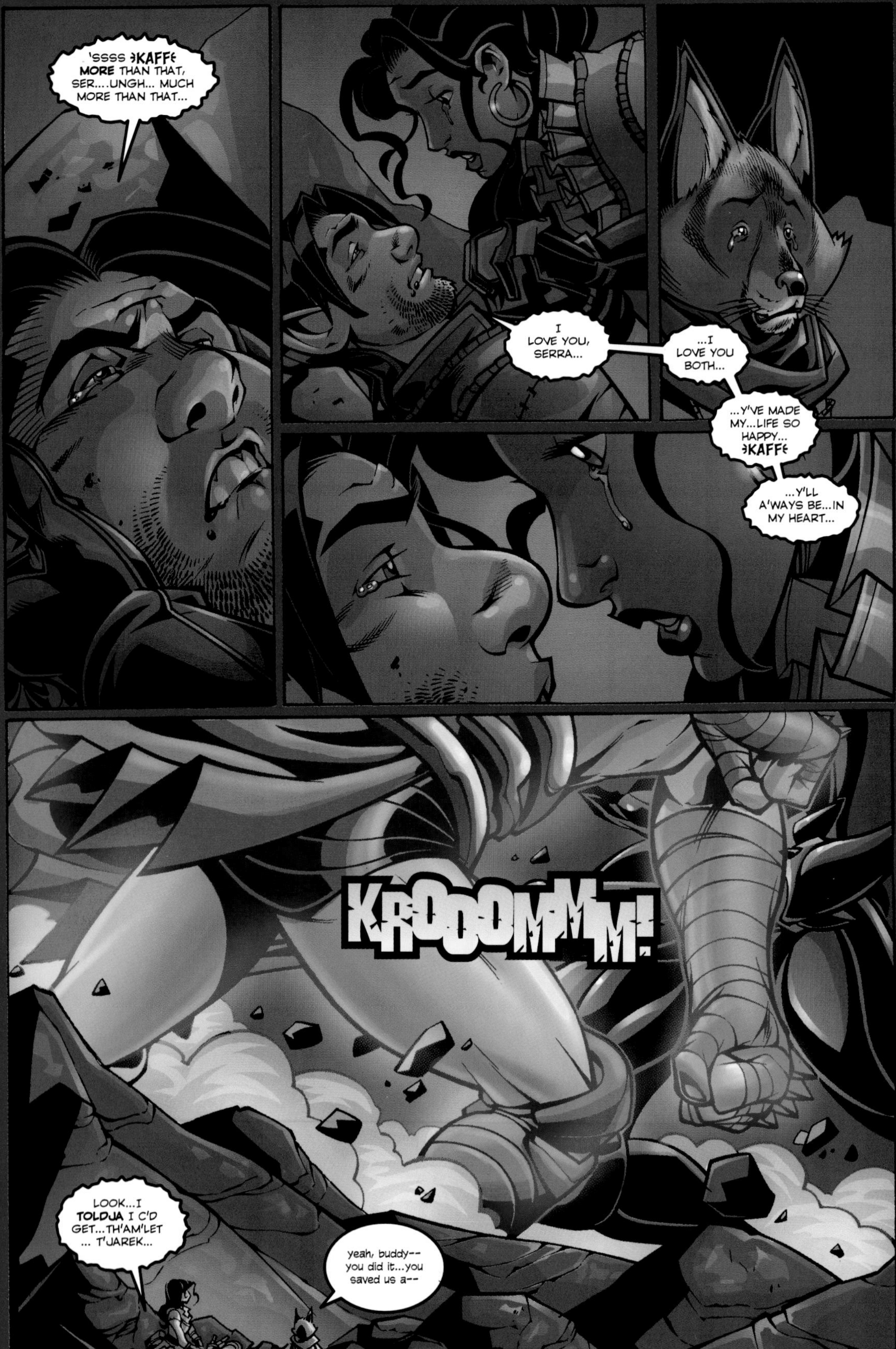
'SSSS *KAFF* MORE THAN THAT, SER.... UNGH... MUCH MORE THAN THAT...
I LOVE YOU, SERRA...
...I LOVE YOU BOTH...
...Y'VE MADE MY...LIFE SO HAPPY... *KAFF*
...Y'LL A'WAYS BE...IN MY HEART...
KROOOMMM!
LOOK...I TOLDJA I C'D GET...TH'AM'LET ... T'JAREK...
yeah, buddy-- you did it...you saved us a--

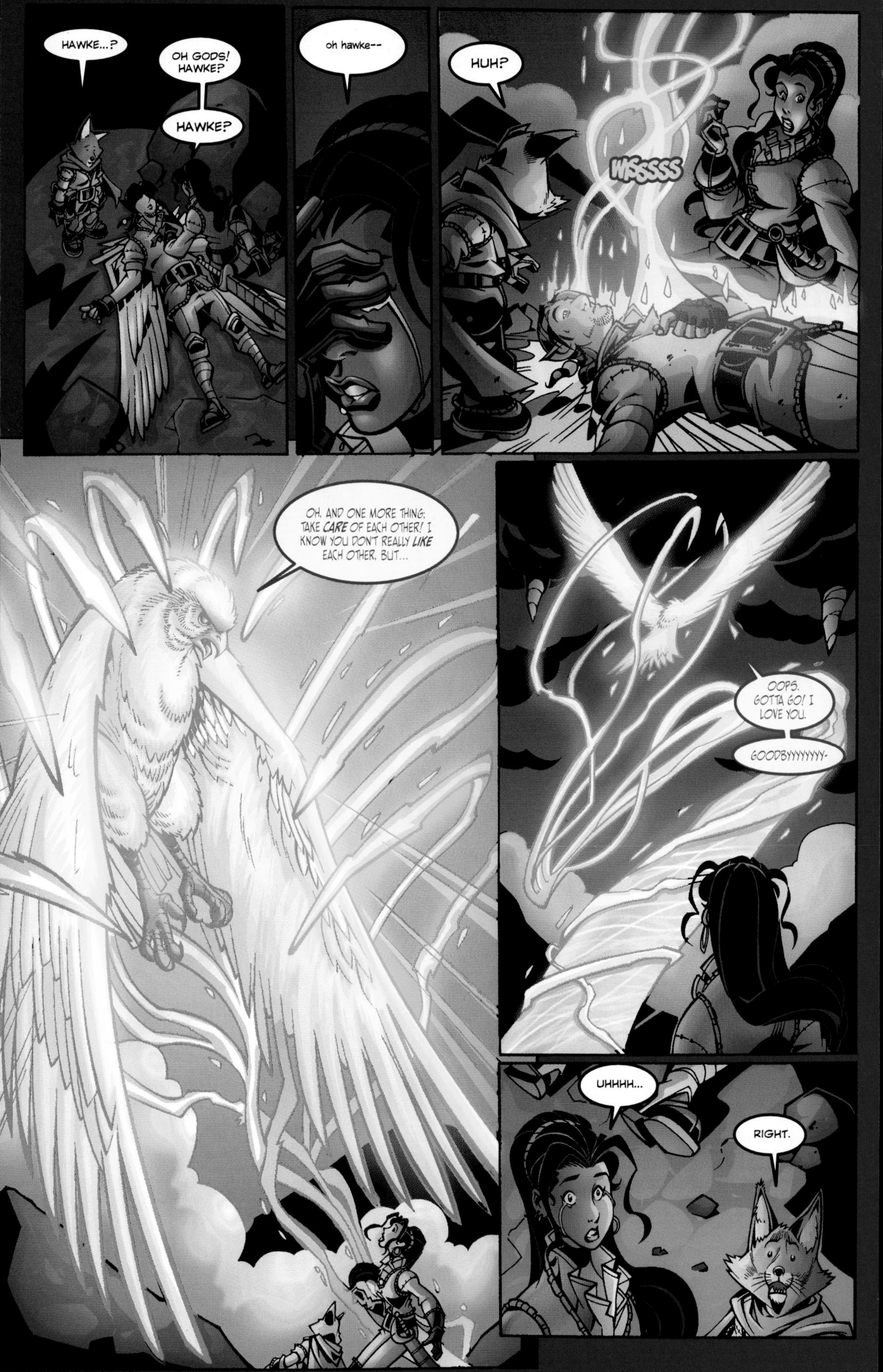
HAWKE...?
OH GODS! HAWKE?
HAWKE?
oh hawke--
HUH?
WISSSSS
OH, AND ONE MORE THING; TAKE CARE OF EACH OTHER! I KNOW YOU DON'T REALLY LIKE EACH OTHER, BUT...
OOPS. GOTTA GO! I LOVE YOU.
GOODBYYYYYYYY-
UHHHH...
RIGHT.

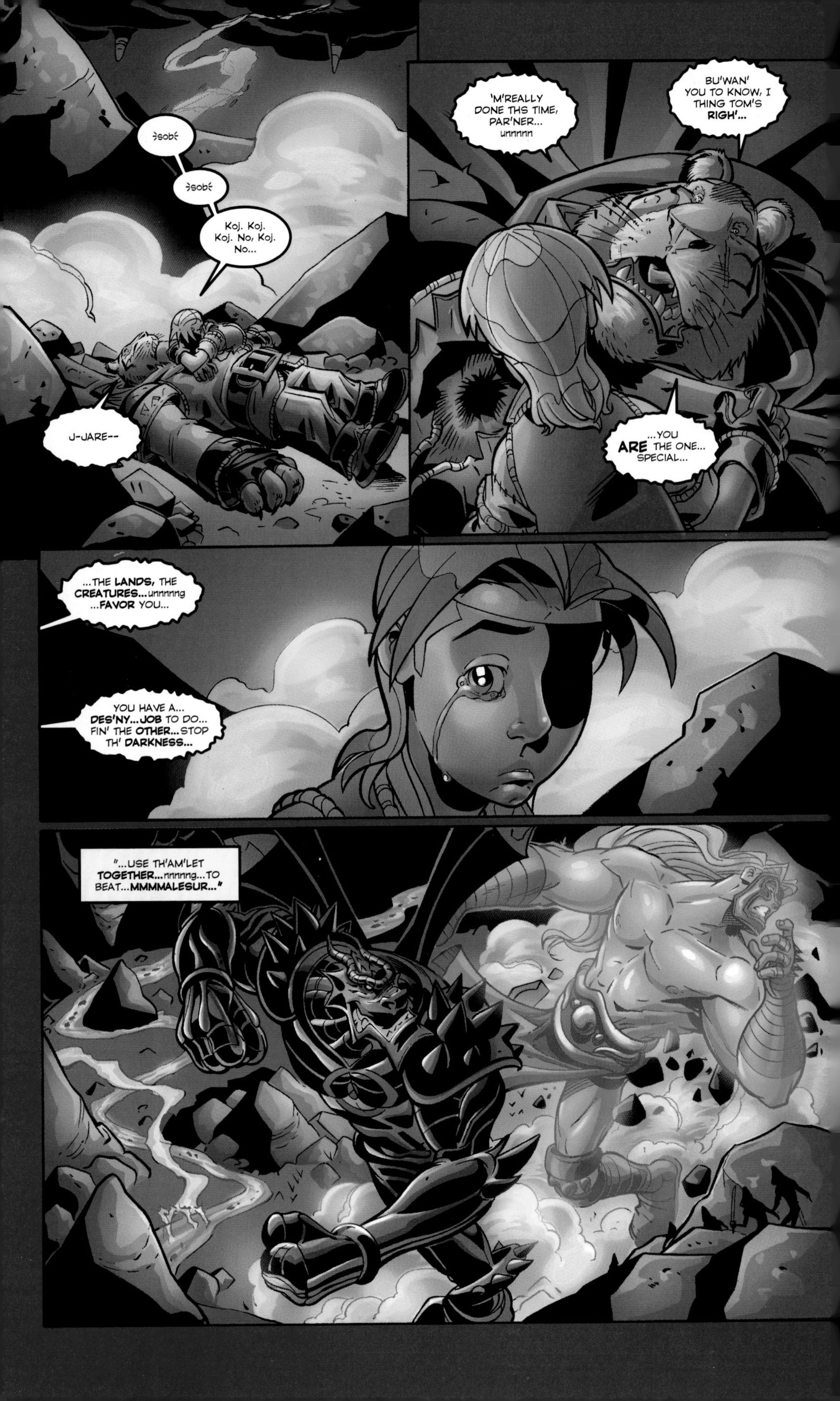

sob
sob
Koj. Koj. Koj. No, Koj. No...
J-JARE--
'M'REALLY DONE THS TIME, PAR'NER... unnnnn
BU'WAN' YOU TO KNOW, I THING TOM'S RIGH'...
...YOU ARE THE ONE... SPECIAL...
...THE LANDS, THE CREATURES...unnnnng ...FAVOR YOU...
YOU HAVE A... DES'NY...JOB TO DO... FIN' THE OTHER...STOP TH' DARKNESS...
"...USE TH'AM'LET TOGETHER...nnnnng...TO BEAT...MMMMALESUR..."

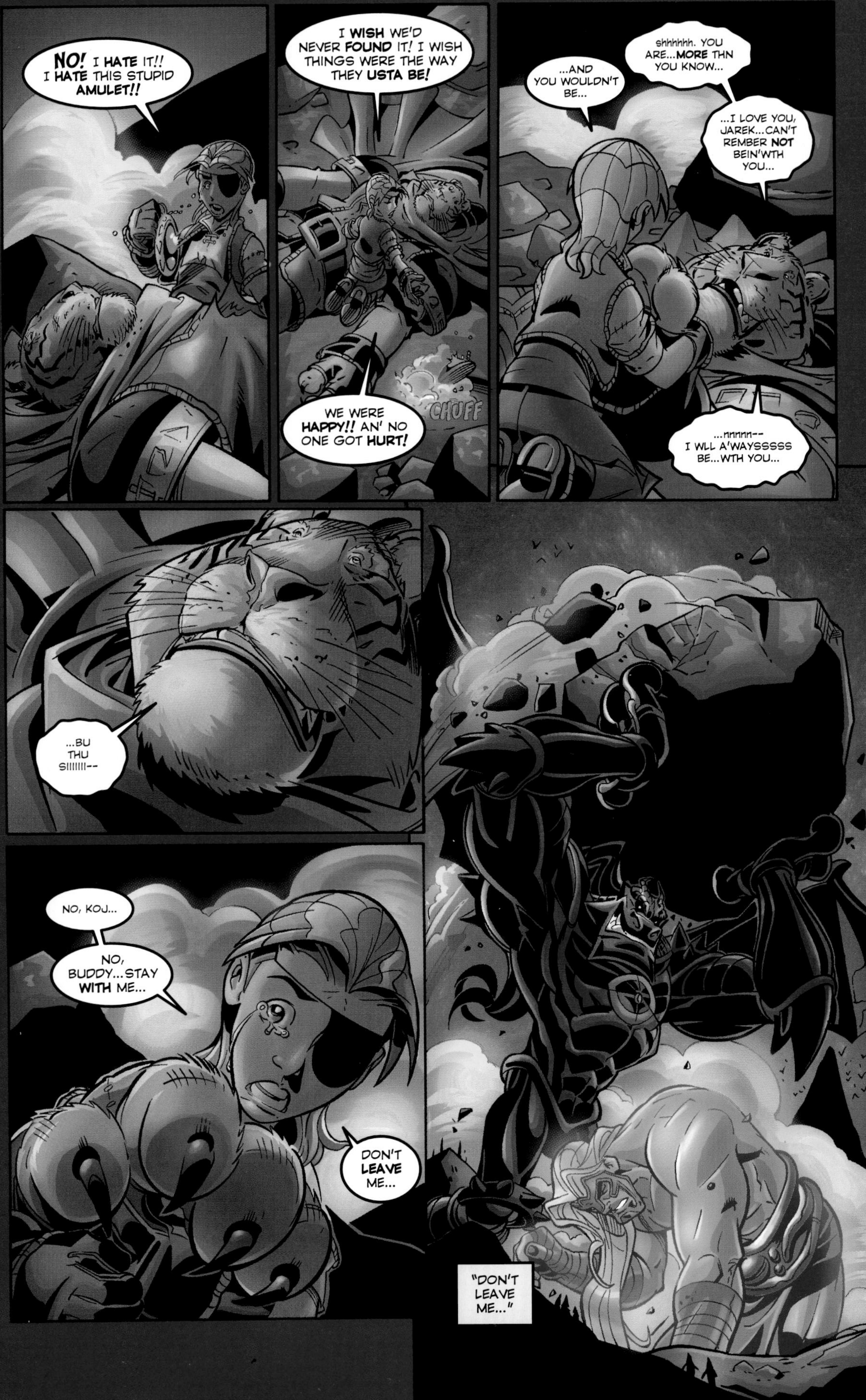
NO! I HATE IT!! I HATE THIS STUPID AMULET!!
I WISH WE'D NEVER FOUND IT! I WISH THINGS WERE THE WAY THEY USTA BE!
WE WERE HAPPY!! AN' NO ONE GOT HURT!
CHUFF
...AND YOU WOULDN'T BE...
shhhhhh. YOU ARE...MORE THN YOU KNOW...
...I LOVE YOU, JAREK...CAN'T REMBER NOT BEIN'WTH YOU...
...nnnnn-- I WLL A'WAYSSSS BE...WTH YOU...
...BU THU SIIIIII--
NO, KOJ...
NO, BUDDY...STAY WITH ME...
DON'T LEAVE ME...
"DON'T LEAVE ME..."

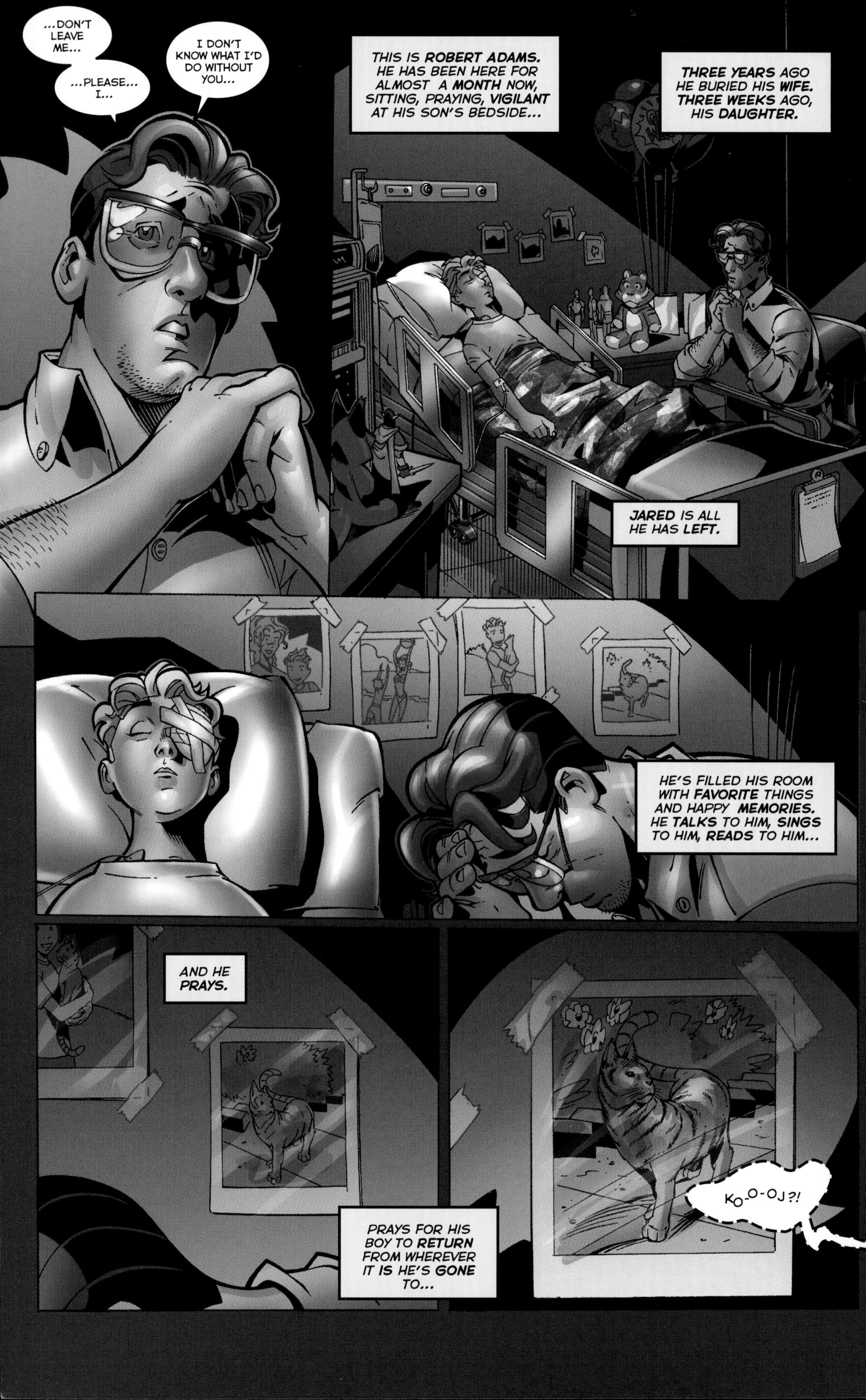
...DON'T LEAVE ME...
...PLEASE... I...
I DON'T KNOW WHAT I'D DO WITHOUT YOU...
THIS IS ROBERT ADAMS. HE HAS BEEN HERE FOR ALMOST A MONTH NOW, SITTING, PRAYING, VIGILANT AT HIS SON'S BEDSIDE...
THREE YEARS AGO HE BURIED HIS WIFE. THREE WEEKS AGO, HIS DAUGHTER.
JARED IS ALL HE HAS LEFT.
HE'S FILLED HIS ROOM WITH FAVORITE THINGS AND HAPPY MEMORIES. HE TALKS TO HIM, SINGS TO HIM, READS TO HIM...
AND HE PRAYS.
PRAYS FOR HIS BOY TO RETURN FROM WHEREVER IT IS HE'S GONE TO...
KO-O-OJ?!

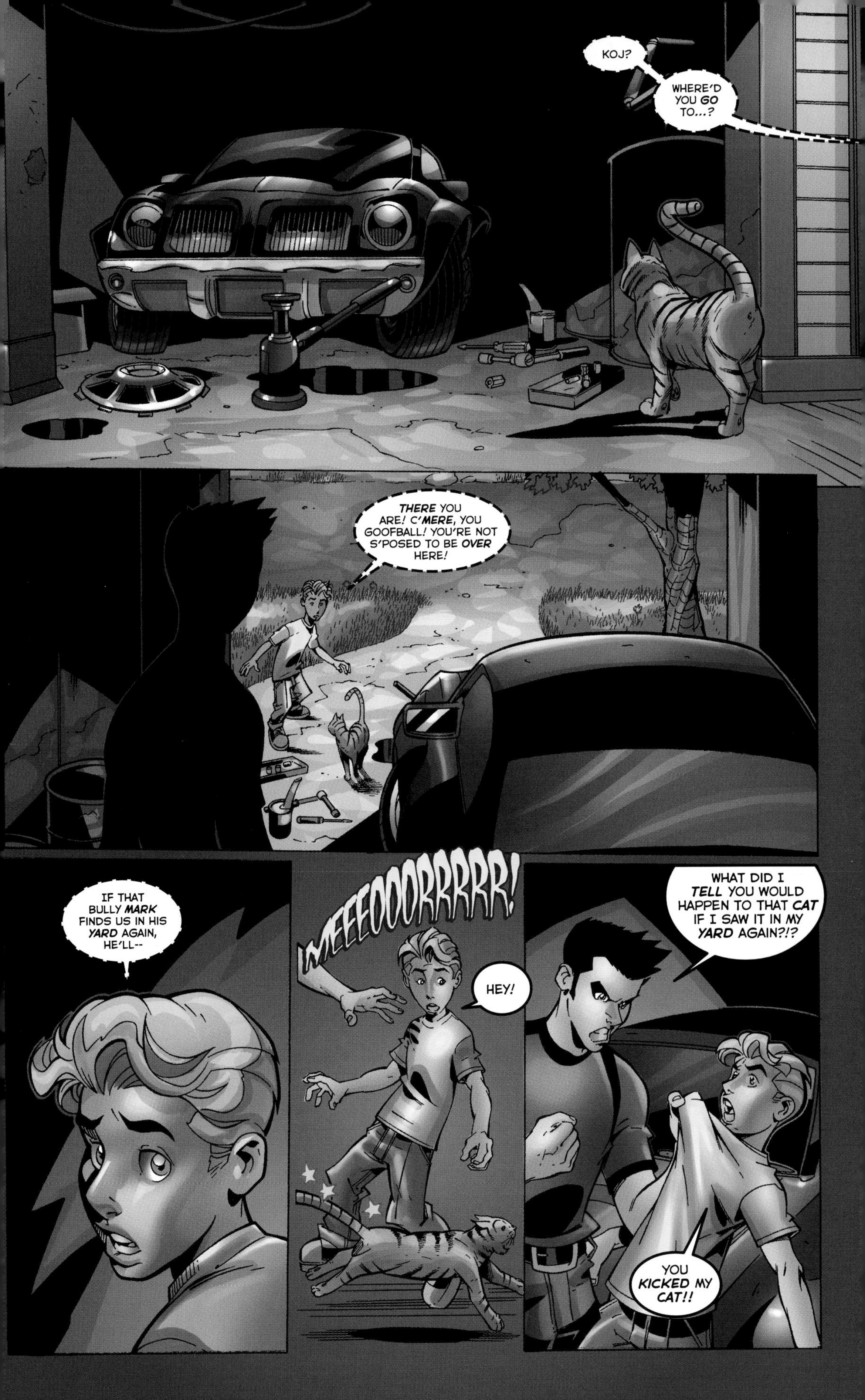
KOJ?
WHERE'D YOU GO TO...?
THERE YOU ARE! C'MERE, YOU GOOFBALL! YOU'RE NOT S'POSED TO BE OVER HERE!
IF THAT BULLY MARK FINDS US IN HIS YARD AGAIN, HE'LL--
MEEEOOORRRRR!
HEY!
WHAT DID I TELL YOU WOULD HAPPEN TO THAT CAT IF I SAW IT IN MY YARD AGAIN?!?
YOU KICKED MY CAT!!

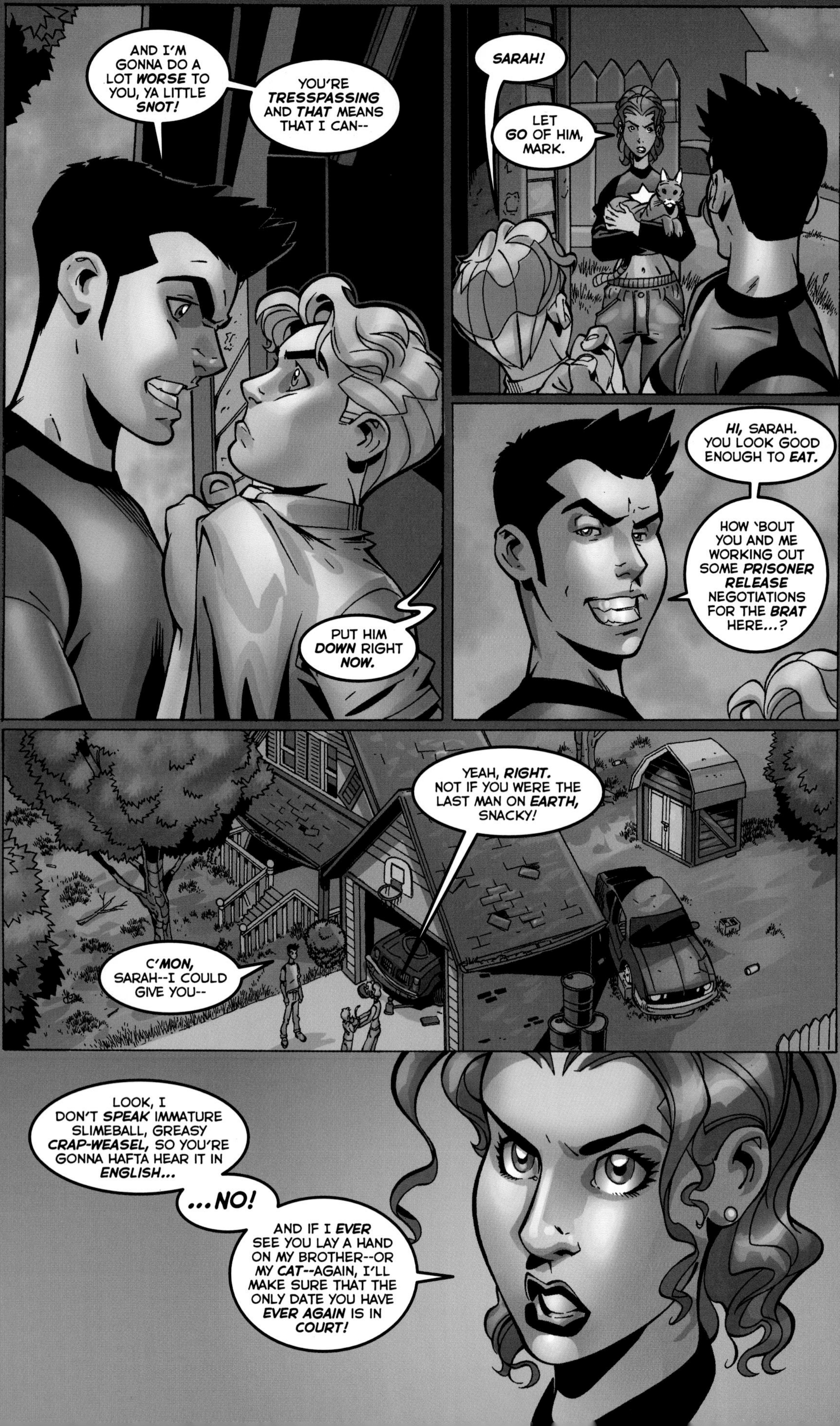

AND I'M GONNA DO A LOT WORSE TO YOU, YA LITTLE SNOT!
YOU'RE TRESSPASSING AND THAT MEANS THAT I CAN--
PUT HIM DOWN RIGHT NOW.
SARAH!
LET GO OF HIM, MARK.
HI, SARAH. YOU LOOK GOOD ENOUGH TO EAT.
HOW 'BOUT YOU AND ME WORKING OUT SOME PRISONER RELEASE NEGOTIATIONS FOR THE BRAT HERE...?
C'MON, SARAH--I COULD GIVE YOU--
YEAH, RIGHT. NOT IF YOU WERE THE LAST MAN ON EARTH, SNACKY!
LOOK, I DON'T SPEAK IMMATURE SLIMEBALL, GREASY CRAP-WEASEL, SO YOU'RE GONNA HAFTA HEAR IT IN ENGLISH...
...NO!
AND IF I EVER SEE YOU LAY A HAND ON MY BROTHER--OR MY CAT--AGAIN, I'LL MAKE SURE THAT THE ONLY DATE YOU HAVE EVER AGAIN IS IN COURT!

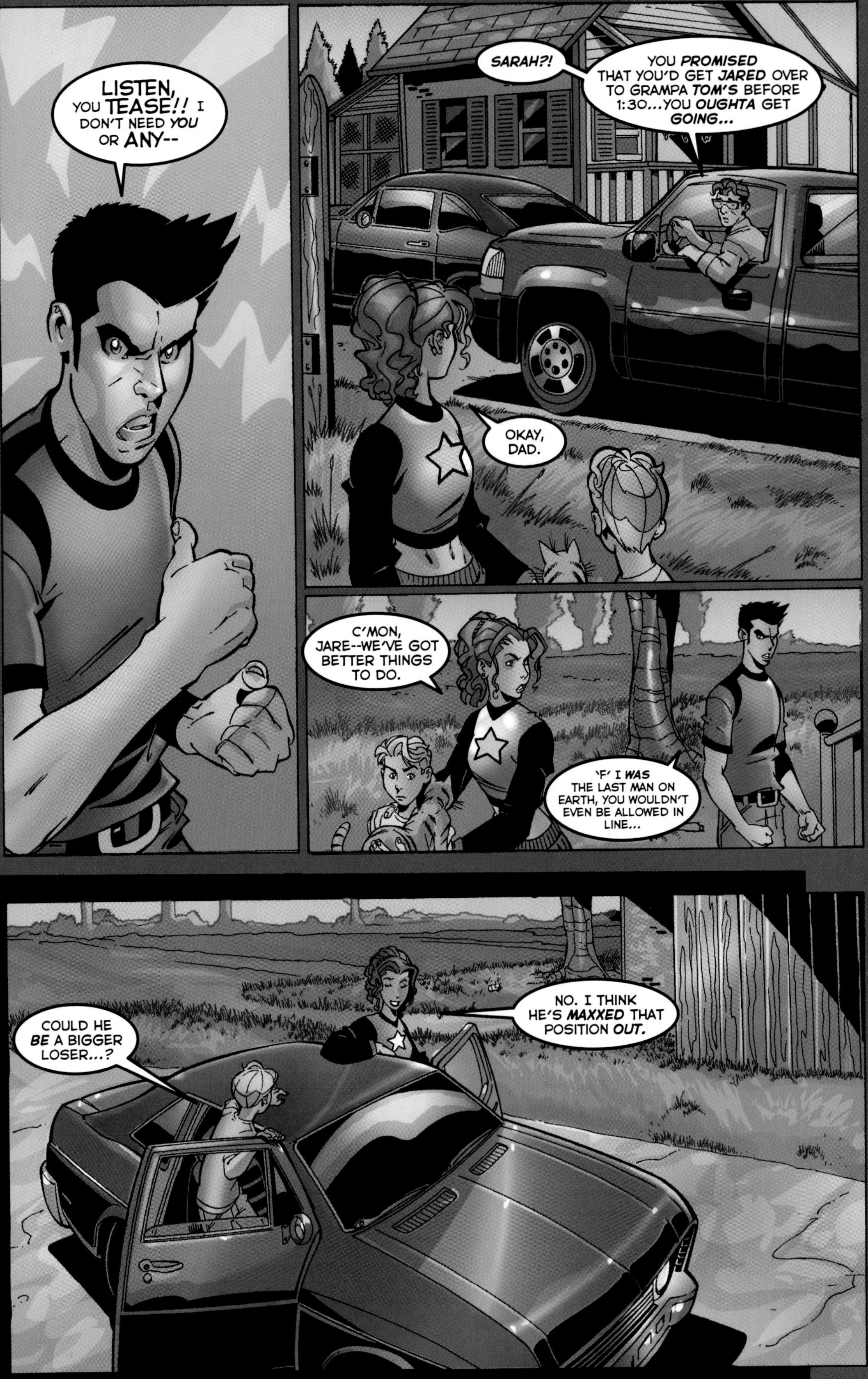
LISTEN, YOU TEASE!! I DON'T NEED YOU OR ANY--
SARAH?!
YOU PROMISED THAT YOU'D GET JARED OVER TO GRAMPA TOM'S BEFORE 1:30...YOU OUGHTA GET GOING...
OKAY, DAD.
C'MON, JARE--WE'VE GOT BETTER THINGS TO DO.
'F' I WAS THE LAST MAN ON EARTH, YOU WOULDN'T EVEN BE ALLOWED IN LINE...
COULD HE BE A BIGGER LOSER...?
NO. I THINK HE'S MAXXED THAT POSITION OUT.

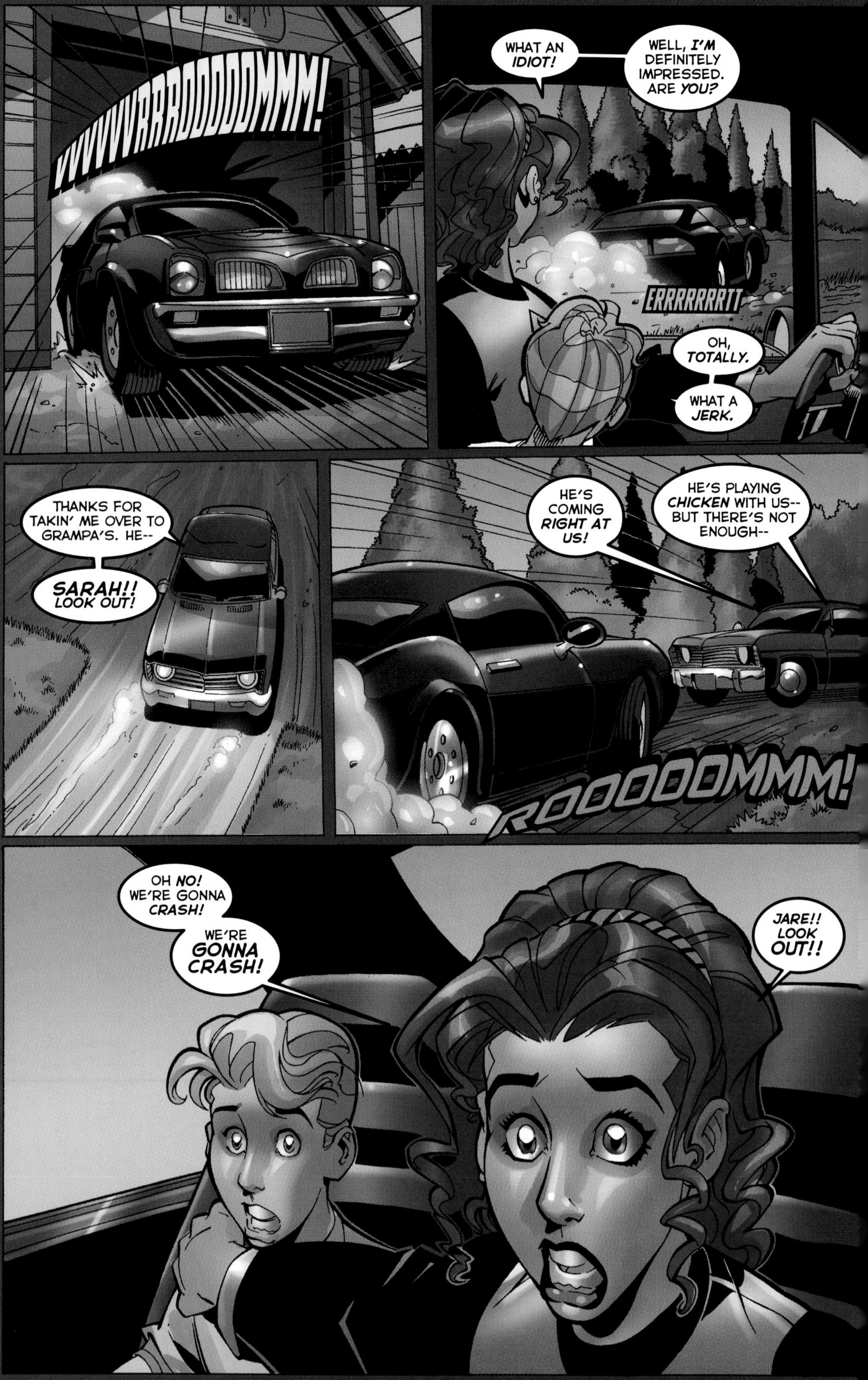
VVVVVVRRRROOOOOMMM!
WHAT AN IDIOT!
WELL, I'M DEFINITELY IMPRESSED. ARE YOU?
ERRRRRRRTT
OH, TOTALLY.
WHAT A JERK.
THANKS FOR TAKIN' ME OVER TO GRAMPA'S. HE--
SARAH!! LOOK OUT!
HE'S COMING RIGHT AT US!
HE'S PLAYING CHICKEN WITH US-- BUT THERE'S NOT ENOUGH--
ROOOOOMMM!
OH NO! WE'RE GONNA CRASH!
WE'RE GONNA CRASH!
JARE!! LOOK OUT!!

TO BE CONCLUDED.

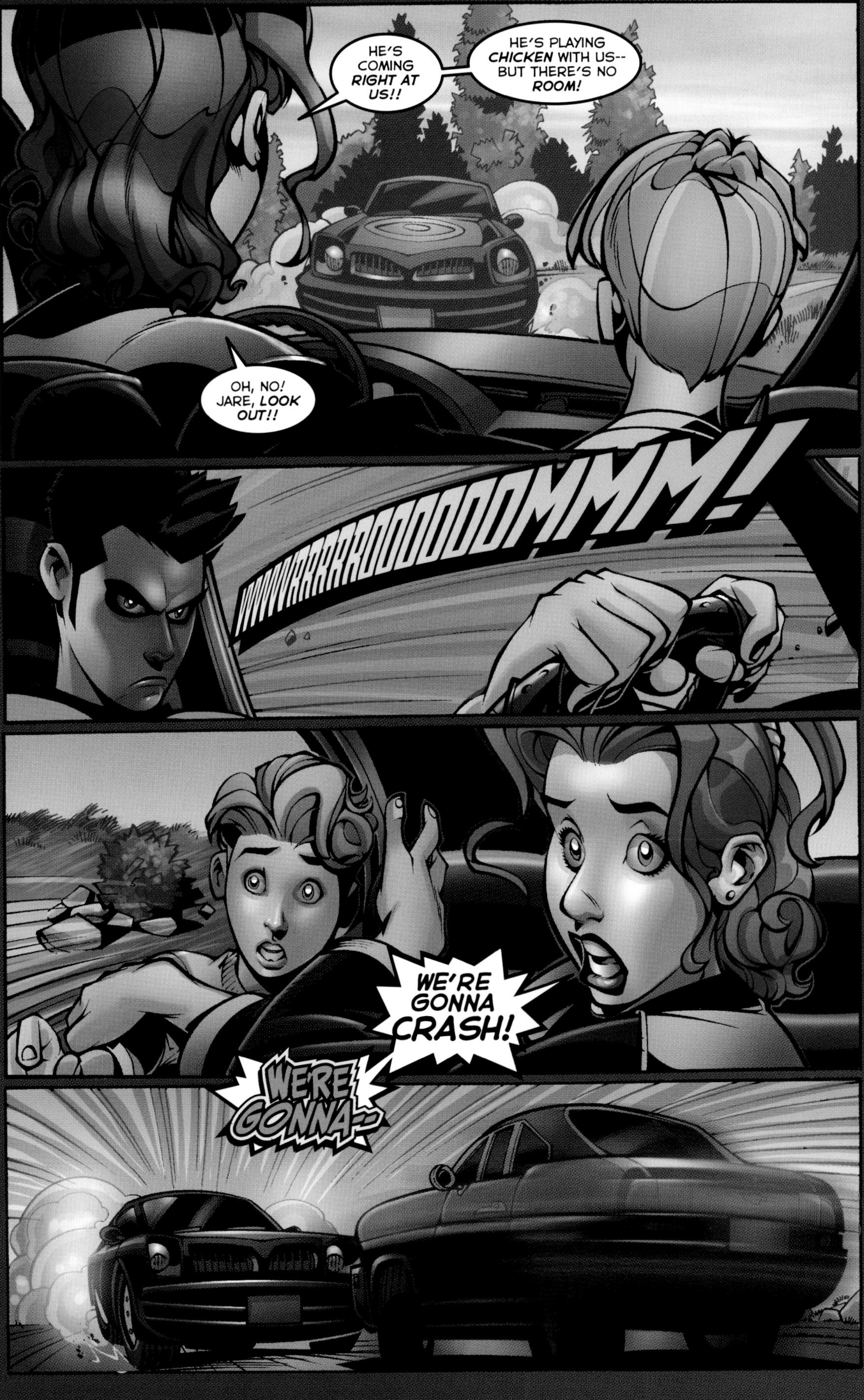
HE'S COMING RIGHT AT US!!
HE'S PLAYING CHICKEN WITH US-- BUT THERE'S NO ROOM!
OH, NO! JARE, LOOK OUT!!
WWWVRRRROOOOOOOMMMM!
WE'RE GONNA CRASH!
WE'RE GONNA--

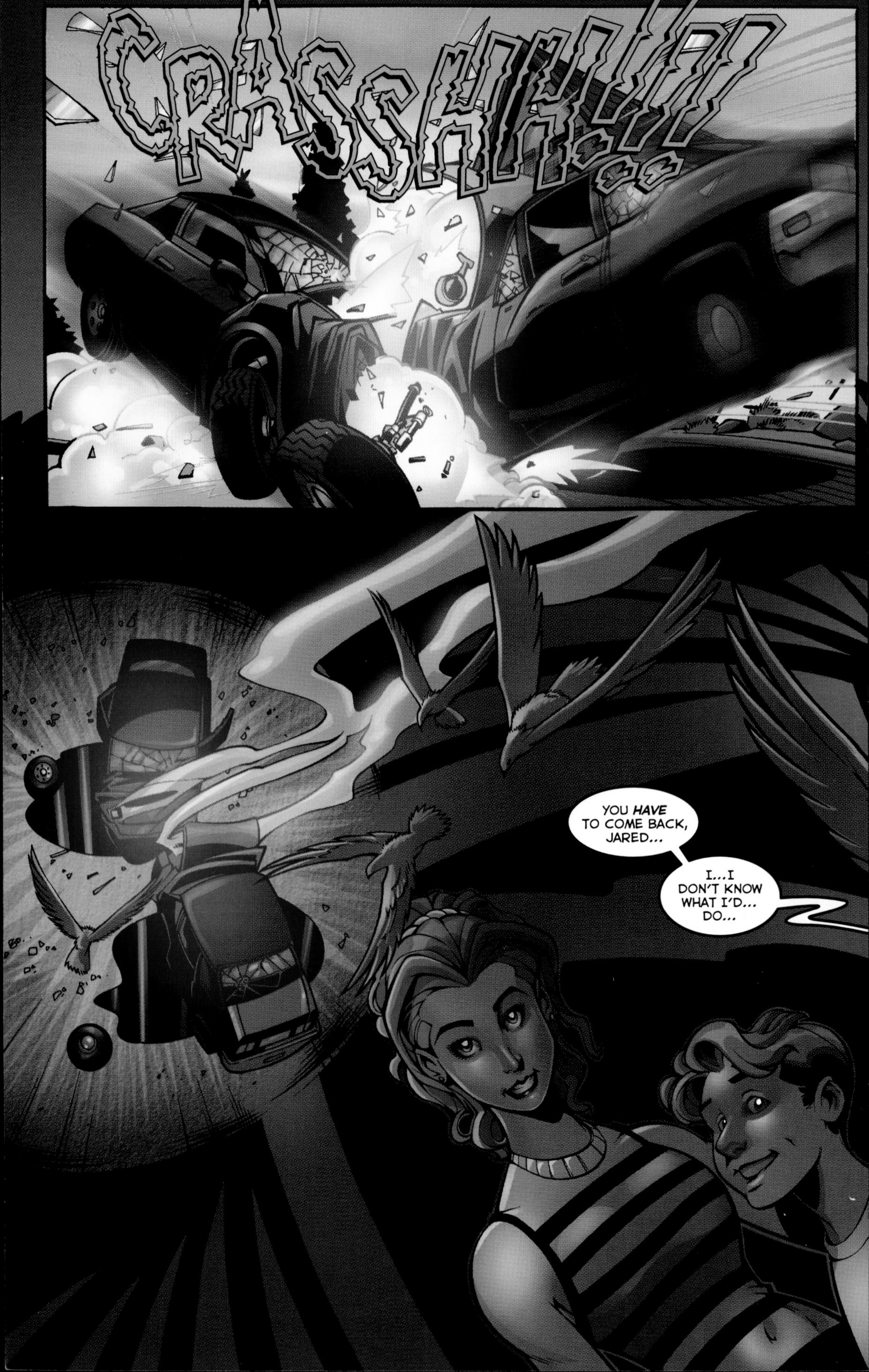
YOU HAVE TO COME BACK, JARED...
I...I DON'T KNOW WHAT I'D... DO...

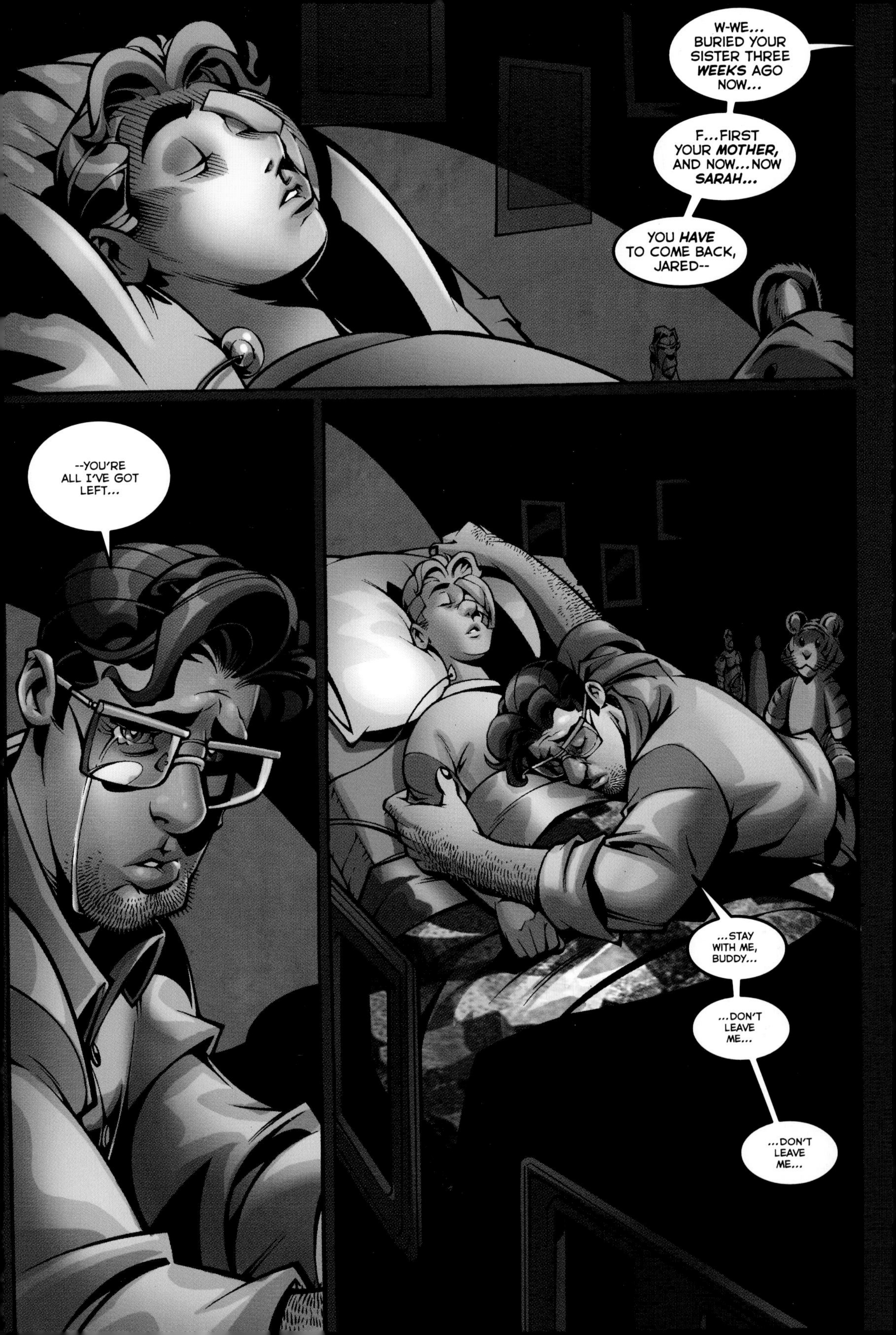
W-WE... BURIED YOUR SISTER THREE WEEKS AGO NOW...
F...FIRST YOUR MOTHER, AND NOW...NOW SARAH...
YOU HAVE TO COME BACK, JARED--
--YOU'RE ALL I'VE GOT LEFT...
...STAY WITH ME, BUDDY...
...DON'T LEAVE ME...
...DON'T LEAVE ME...

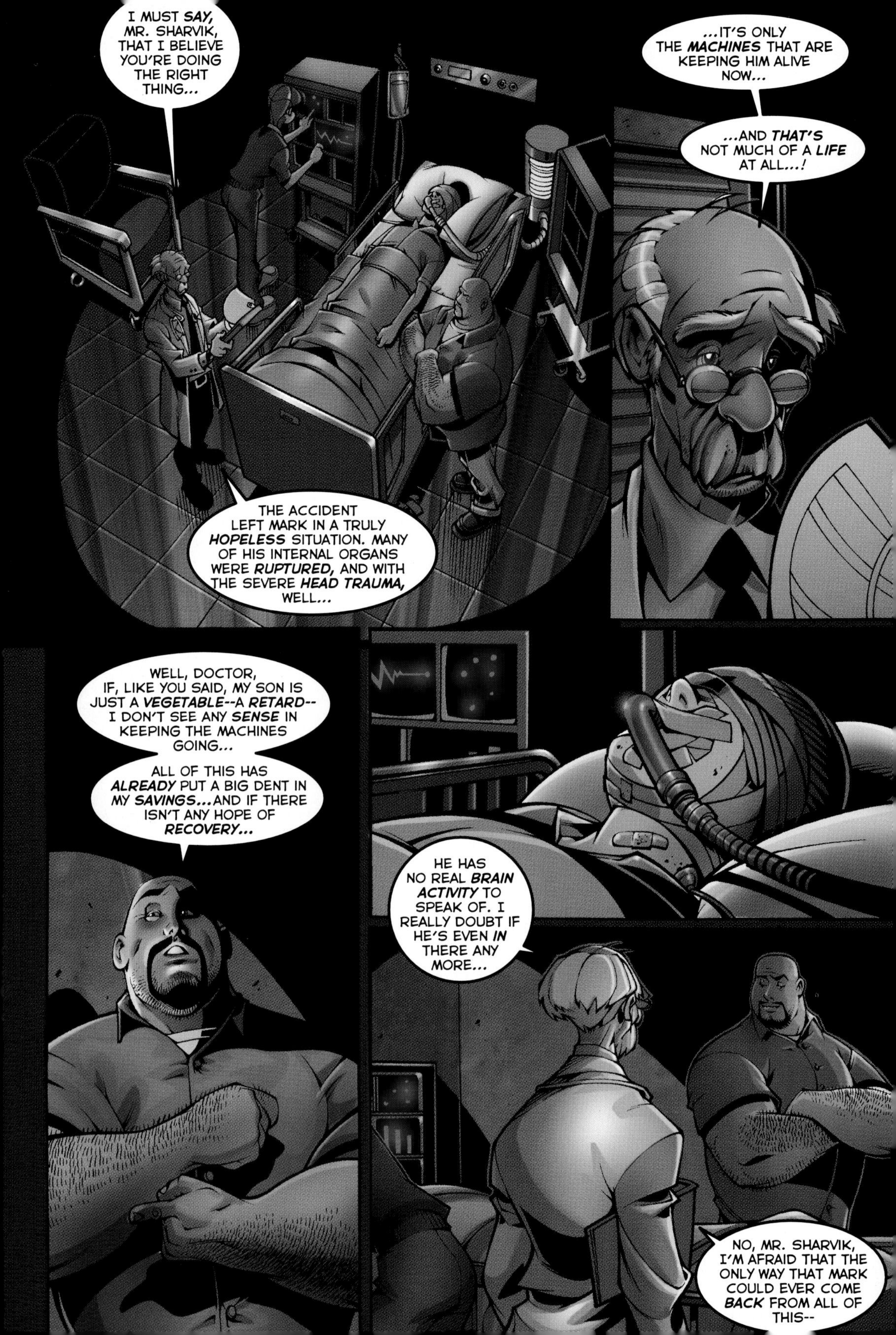
I MUST SAY, MR. SHARVIK, THAT I BELIEVE YOU'RE DOING THE RIGHT THING...
THE ACCIDENT LEFT MARK IN A TRULY HOPELESS SITUATION. MANY OF HIS INTERNAL ORGANS WERE RUPTURED, AND WITH THE SEVERE HEAD TRAUMA, WELL...
...IT'S ONLY THE MACHINES THAT ARE KEEPING HIM ALIVE NOW...
...AND THAT'S NOT MUCH OF A LIFE AT ALL...!
WELL, DOCTOR, IF, LIKE YOU SAID, MY SON IS JUST A VEGETABLE--A RETARD-- I DON'T SEE ANY SENSE IN KEEPING THE MACHINES GOING...
ALL OF THIS HAS ALREADY PUT A BIG DENT IN MY SAVINGS...AND IF THERE ISN'T ANY HOPE OF RECOVERY...
HE HAS NO REAL BRAIN ACTIVITY TO SPEAK OF. I REALLY DOUBT IF HE'S EVEN IN THERE ANY MORE...
NO, MR. SHARVIK, I'M AFRAID THAT THE ONLY WAY THAT MARK COULD EVER COME BACK FROM ALL OF THIS--

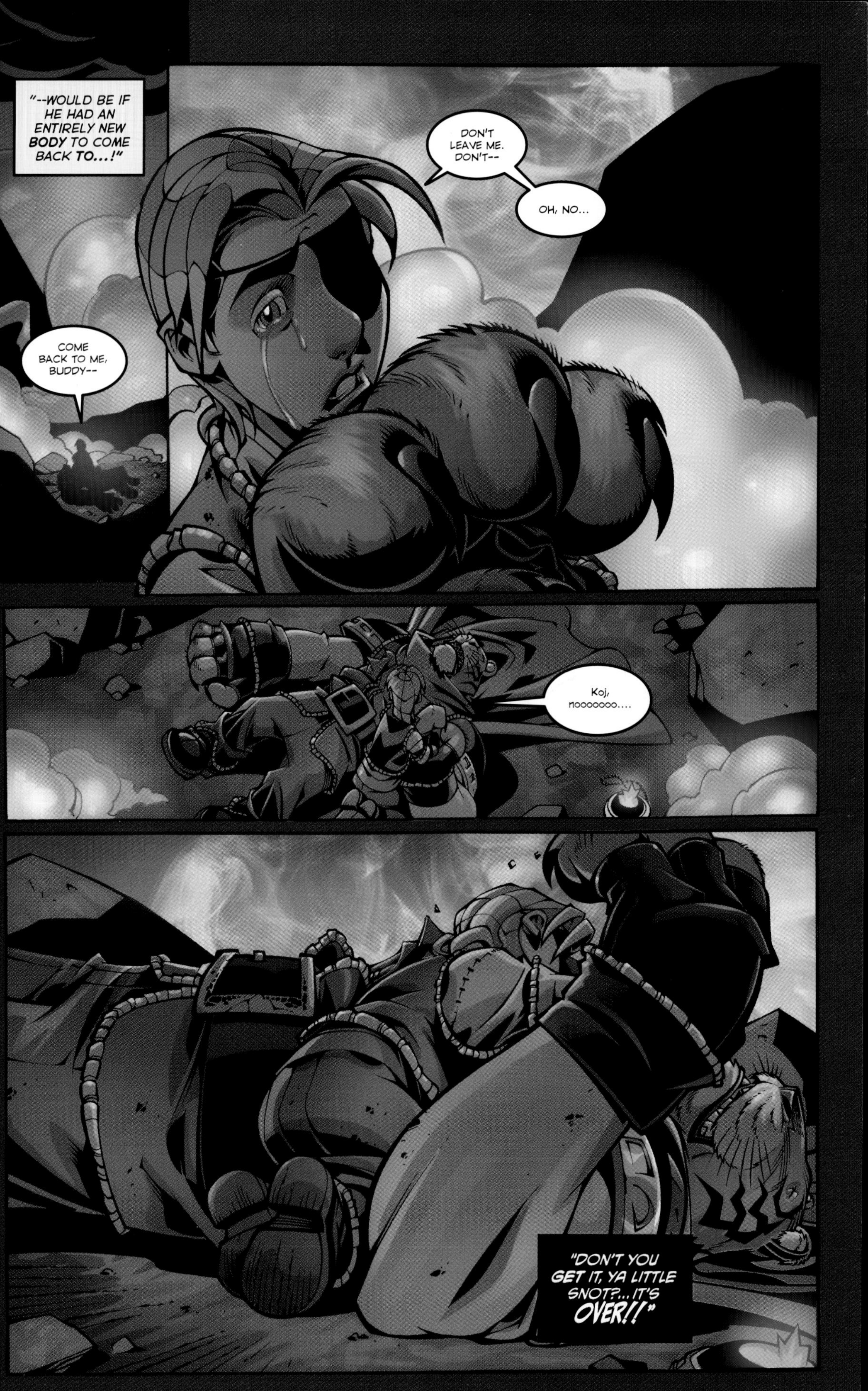
"--WOULD BE IF HE HAD AN ENTIRELY NEW BODY TO COME BACK TO...!"
DON'T LEAVE ME. DON'T--
OH, NO...
COME BACK TO ME, BUDDY--
Koj, noooooooo....
"DON'T YOU GET IT, YA LITTLE SNOT?... IT'S OVER!!"

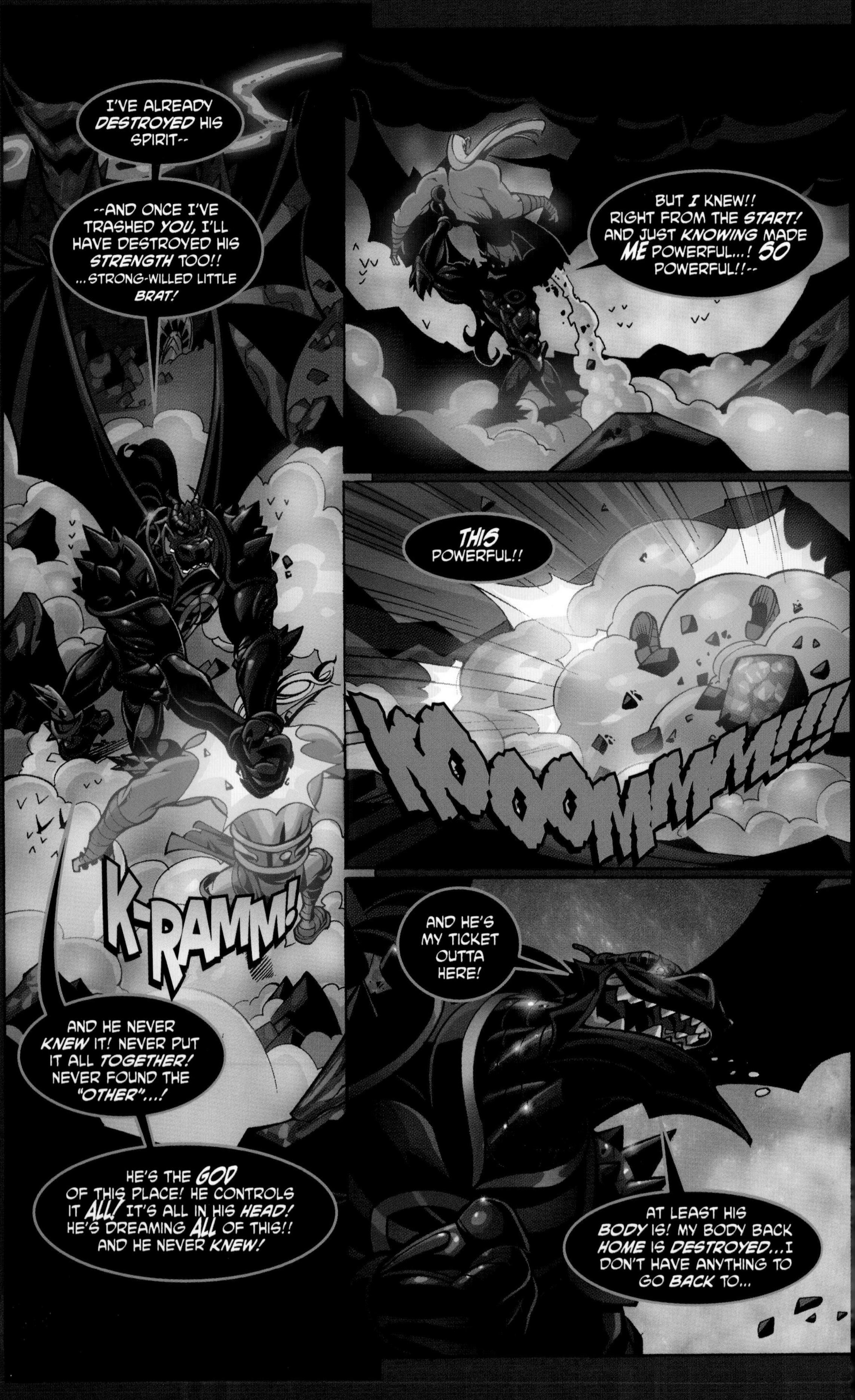
I'VE ALREADY DESTROYED HIS SPIRIT--
--AND ONCE I'VE TRASHED YOU, I'LL HAVE DESTROYED HIS STRENGTH TOO!! ...STRONG-WILLED LITTLE BRAT!
K-RAMM!
AND HE NEVER KNEW IT! NEVER PUT IT ALL TOGETHER! NEVER FOUND THE "OTHER"...!
HE'S THE GOD OF THIS PLACE! HE CONTROLS IT ALL! IT'S ALL IN HIS HEAD! HE'S DREAMING ALL OF THIS!! AND HE NEVER KNEW!
BUT I KNEW!! RIGHT FROM THE START! AND JUST KNOWING MADE ME POWERFUL...! SO POWERFUL!!--
THIS POWERFUL!!
KROOOMMM!!!
AND HE'S MY TICKET OUTTA HERE!
AT LEAST HIS BODY IS! MY BODY BACK HOME IS DESTROYED...I DON'T HAVE ANYTHING TO GO BACK TO...

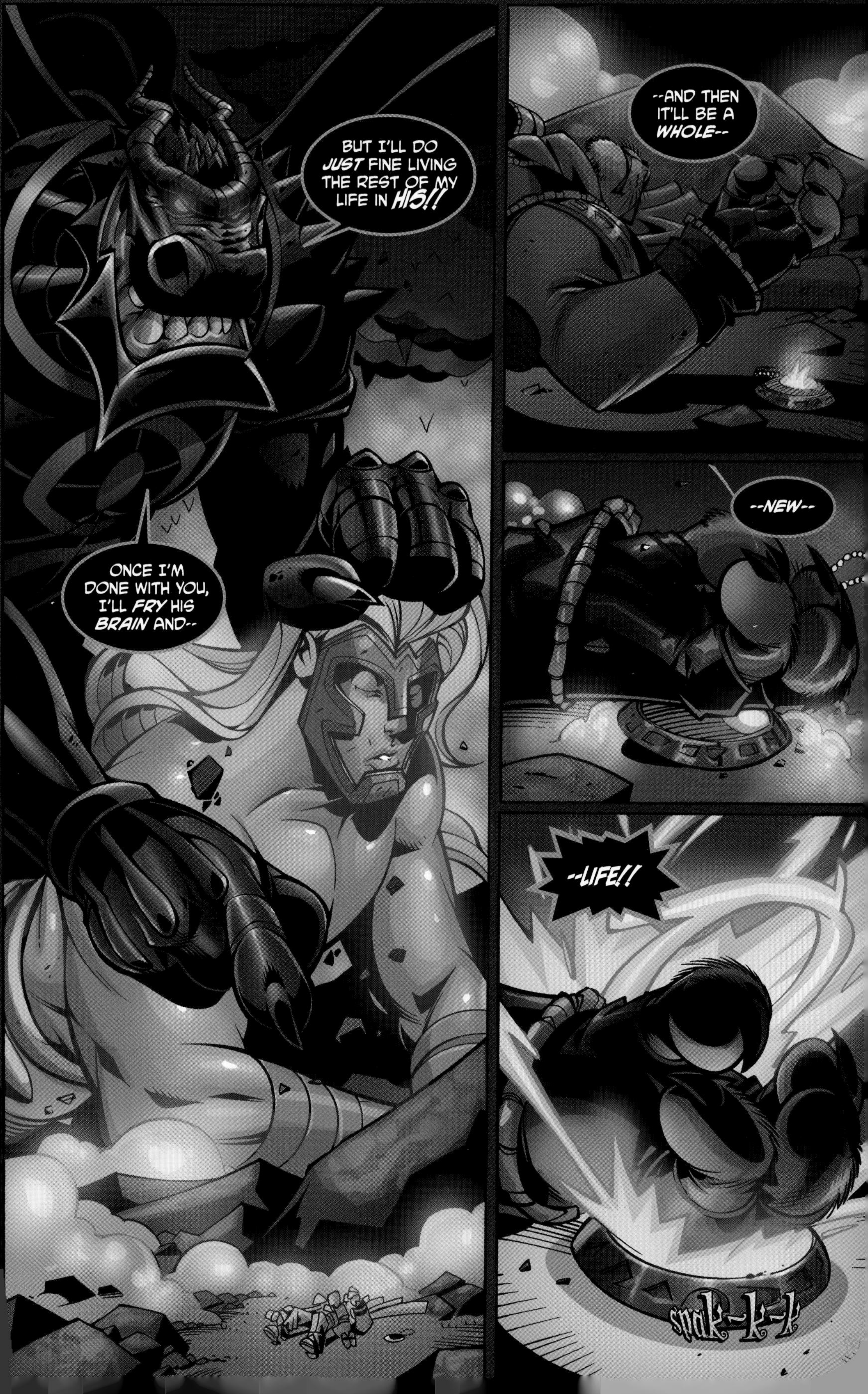
BUT I'LL DO JUST FINE LIVING THE REST OF MY LIFE IN HIS!!
ONCE I'M DONE WITH YOU, I'LL FRY HIS BRAIN AND--
--AND THEN IT'LL BE A WHOLE--
--NEW--
--LIFE!!
spak-k-k

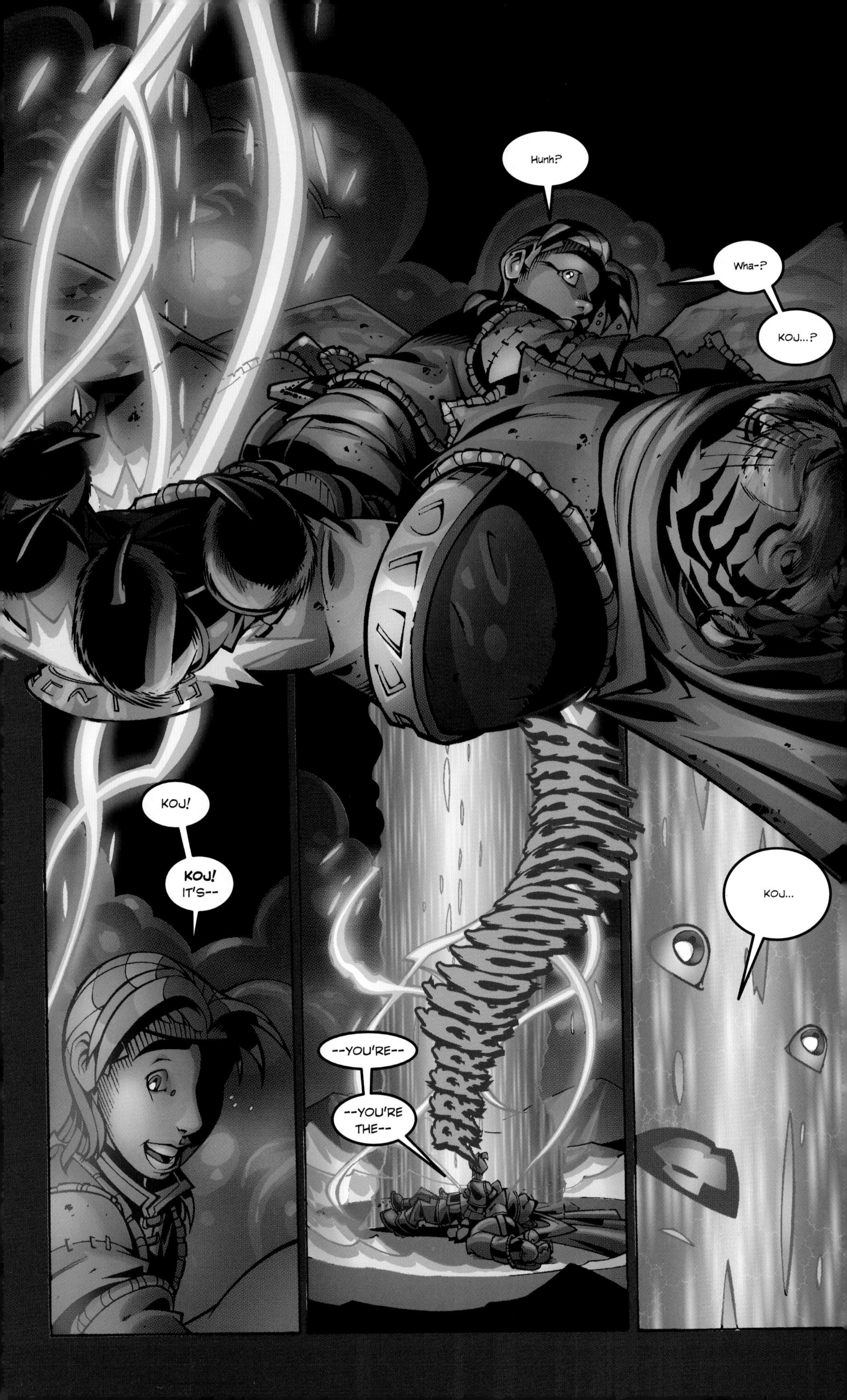
Hunh?
Wha-?
KOJ...?
KOJ!
KOJ! IT'S--
--YOU'RE--
--YOU'RE THE--
KOJ...

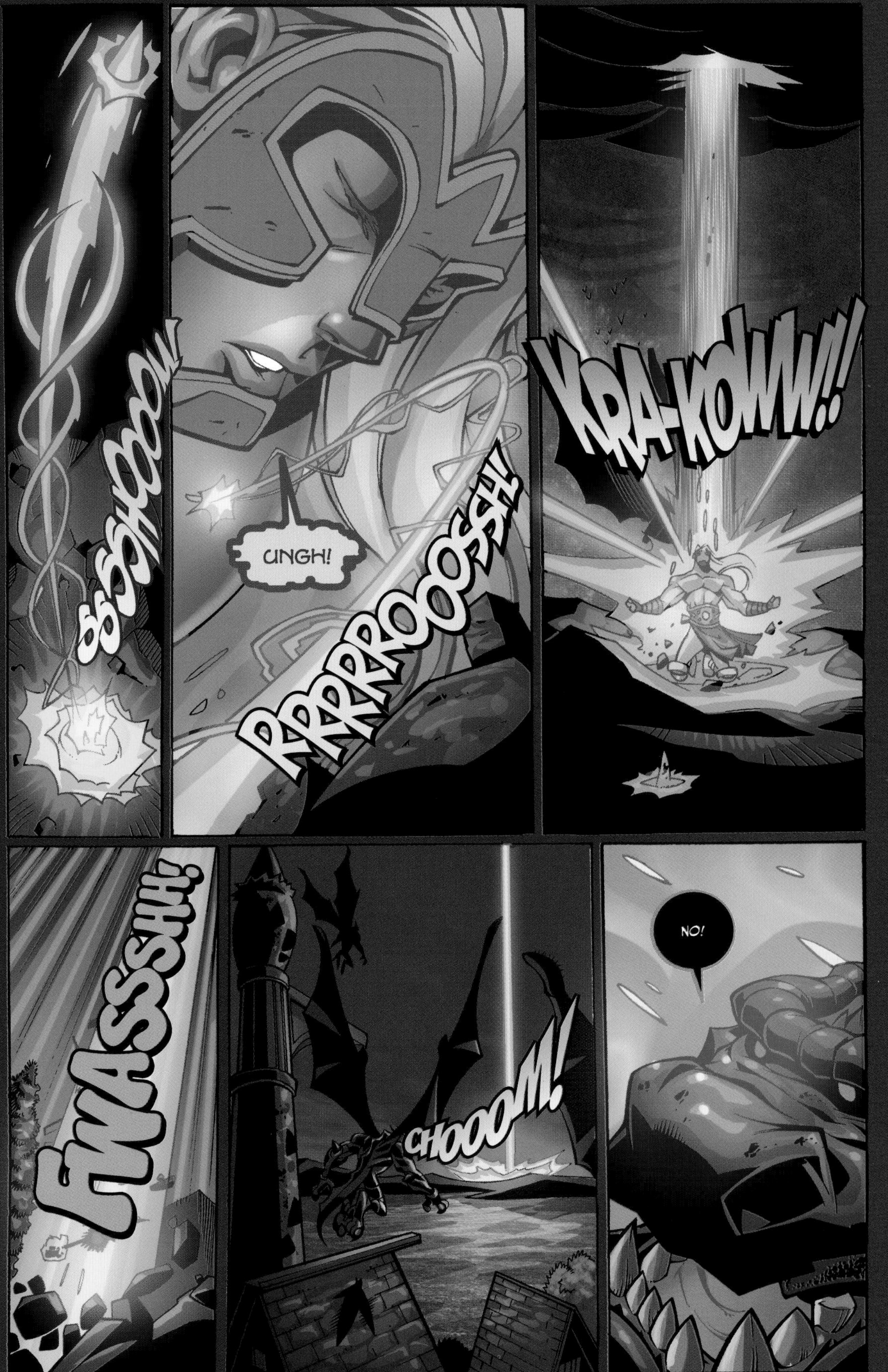
SSSHOOOM!
UNGH!
RRRRROOOSSH!
KRA-KOWW!!
FWASSSHH!
CHOOOM!
NO!

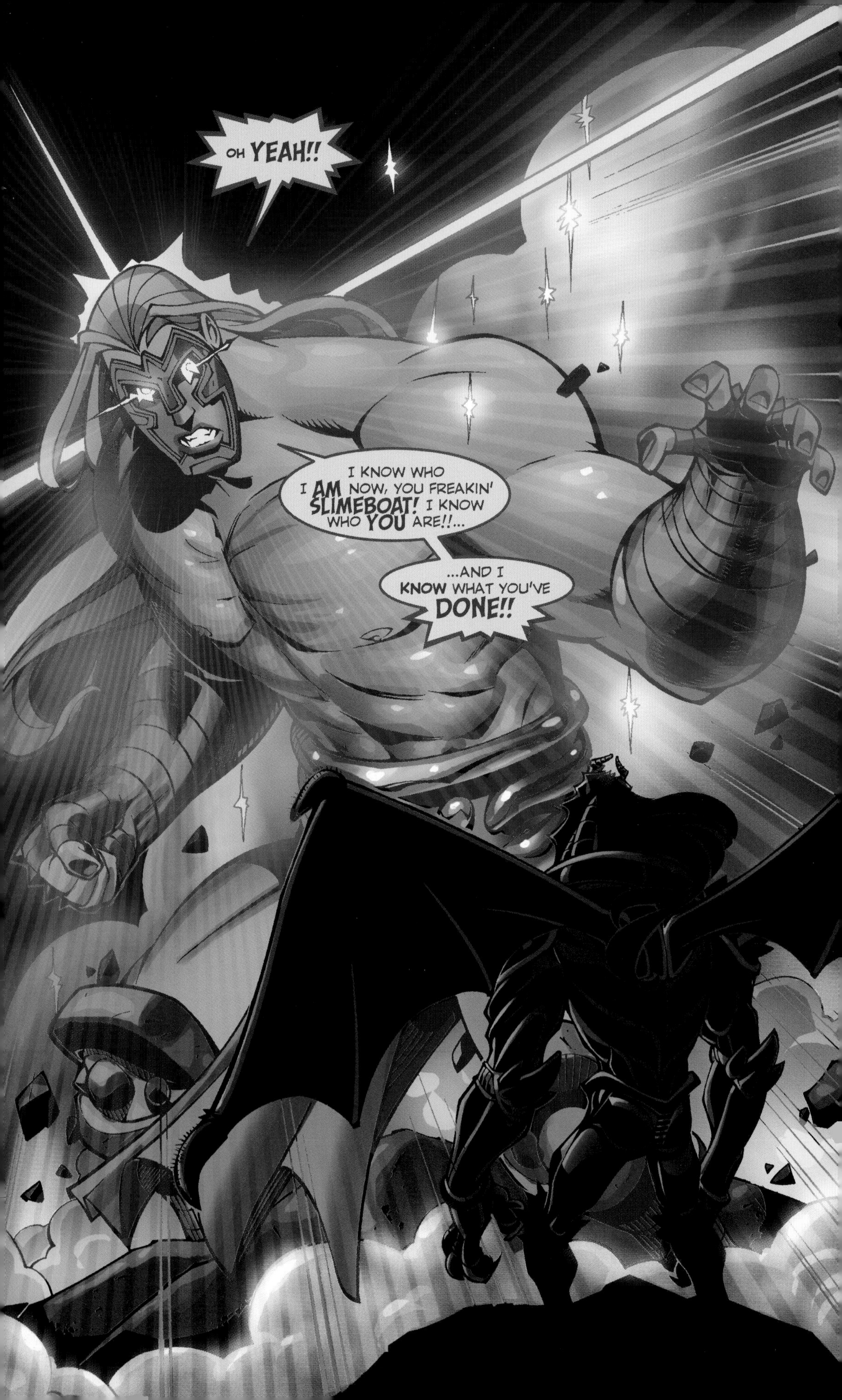
OH YEAH!!
I KNOW WHO I AM NOW, YOU FREAKIN' SLIMEBOAT! I KNOW WHO YOU ARE!!...
...AND I KNOW WHAT YOU'VE DONE!!

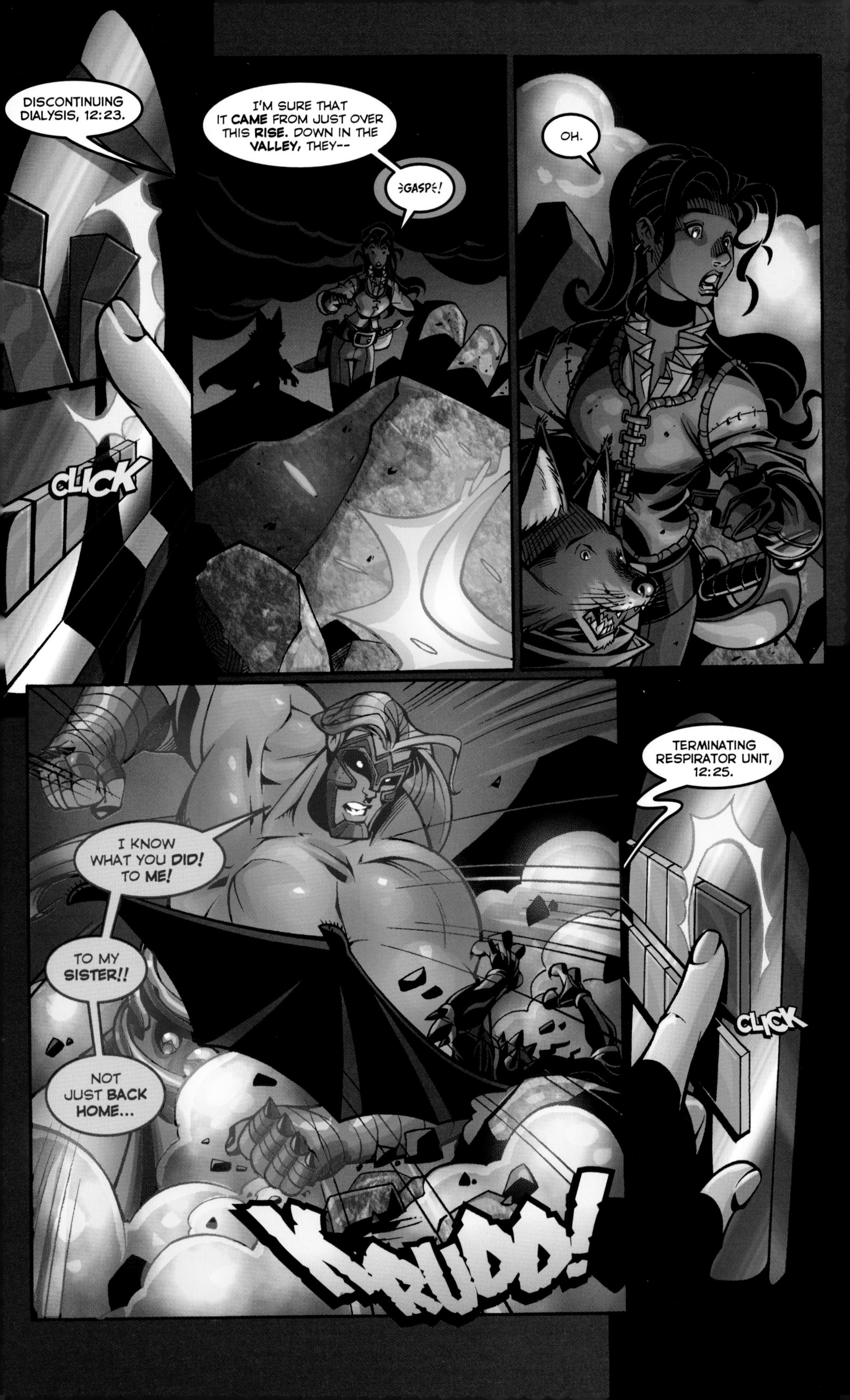
DISCONTINUING DIALYSIS, 12:23.
CLICK
I'M SURE THAT IT CAME FROM JUST OVER THIS RISE. DOWN IN THE VALLEY, THEY--
GASP!
OH.
TERMINATING RESPIRATOR UNIT, 12:25.
I KNOW WHAT YOU DID! TO ME!
TO MY SISTER!!
NOT JUST BACK HOME...
CLICK
KRUDD!

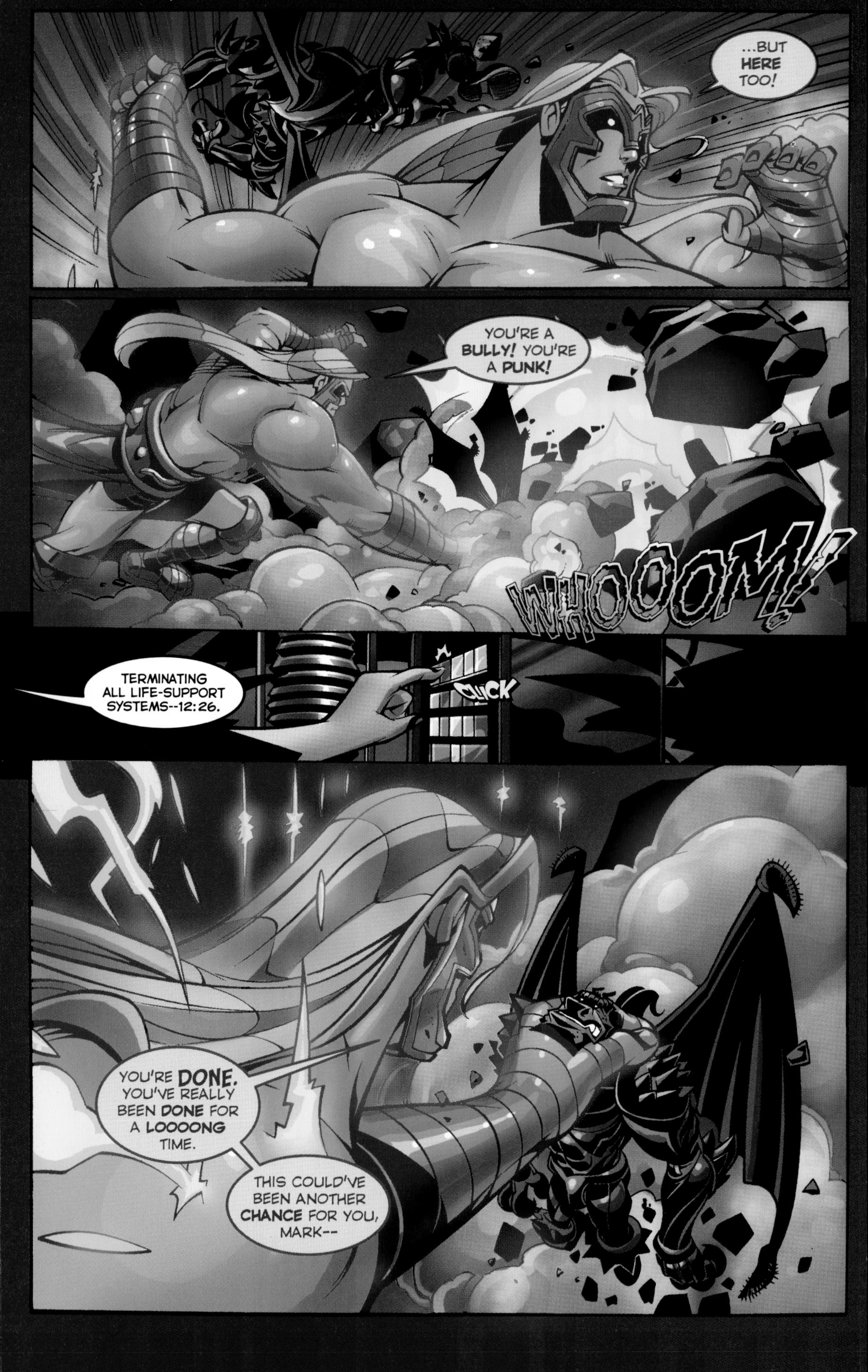
...BUT HERE TOO!
YOU'RE A BULLY! YOU'RE A PUNK!
WHOOOOM!
TERMINATING ALL LIFE-SUPPORT SYSTEMS--12:26.
CLICK
YOU'RE DONE. YOU'VE REALLY BEEN DONE FOR A LOOOONG TIME.
THIS COULD'VE BEEN ANOTHER CHANCE FOR YOU, MARK--

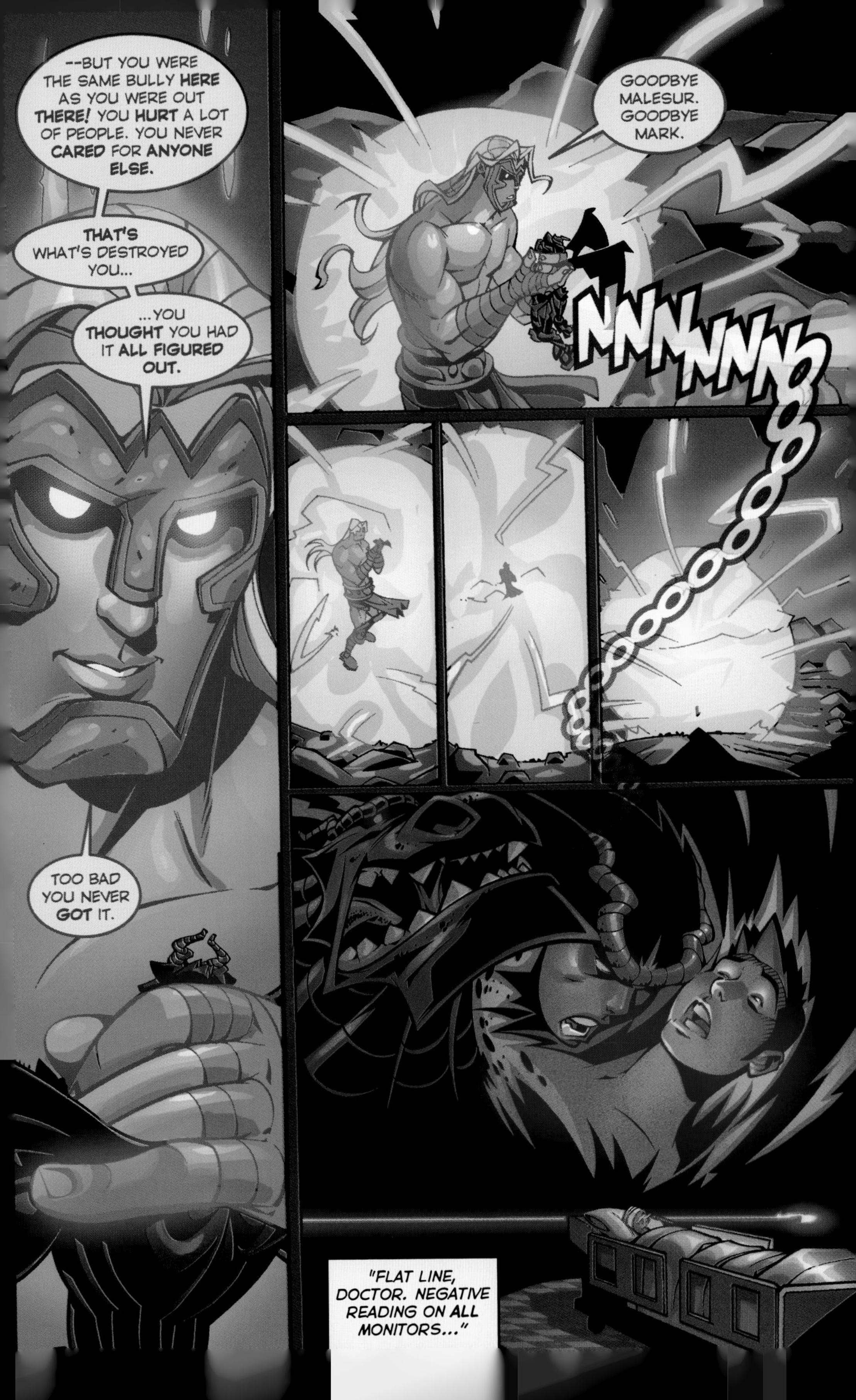
--BUT YOU WERE THE SAME BULLY HERE AS YOU WERE OUT THERE! YOU HURT A LOT OF PEOPLE. YOU NEVER CARED FOR ANYONE ELSE.
THAT'S WHAT'S DESTROYED YOU...
...YOU THOUGHT YOU HAD IT ALL FIGURED OUT.
TOO BAD YOU NEVER GOT IT.
GOODBYE MALESUR. GOODBYE MARK.
NNNNNNN
"FLAT LINE, DOCTOR. NEGATIVE READING ON ALL MONITORS..."

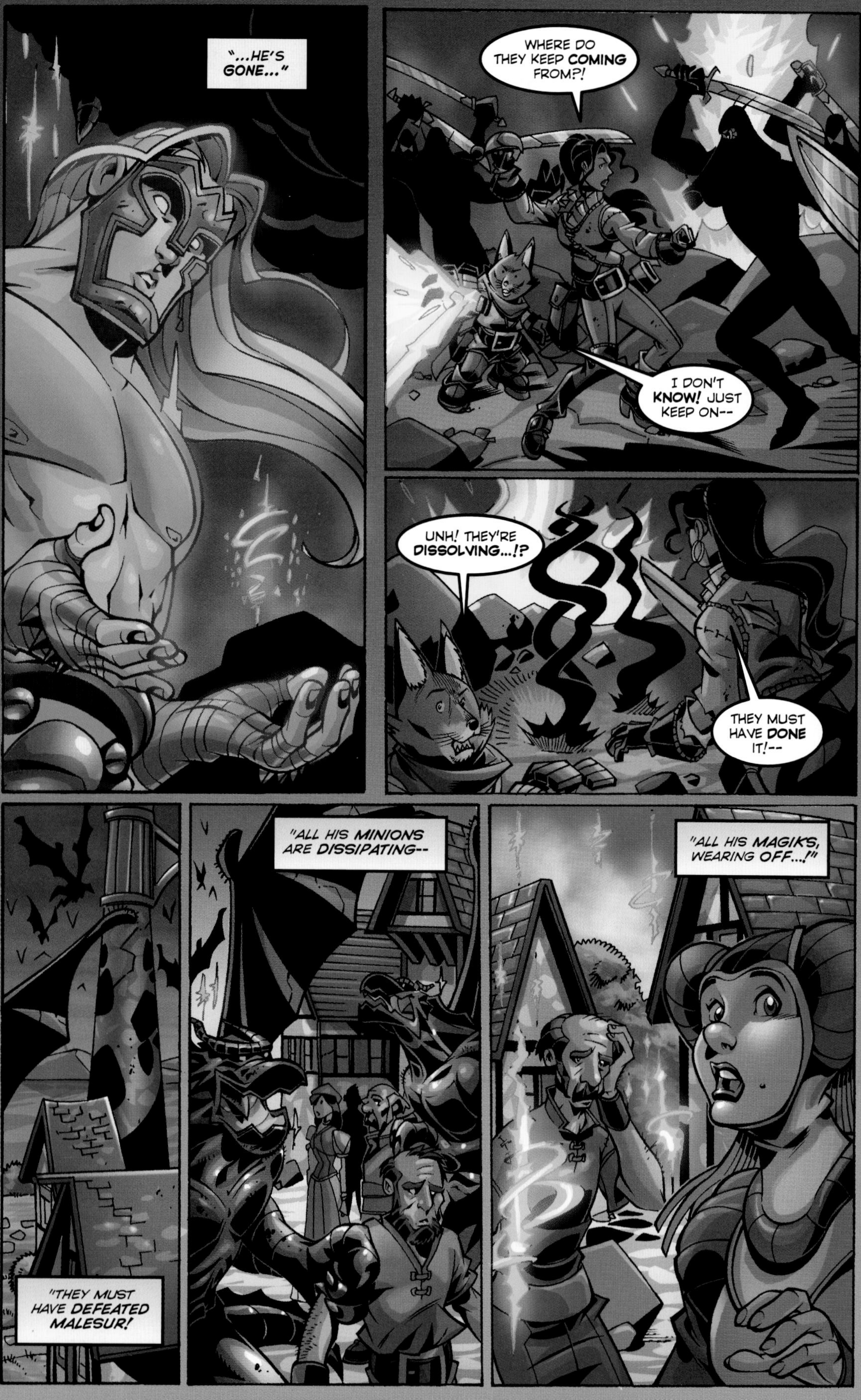
"...HE'S GONE..."
WHERE DO THEY KEEP COMING FROM?!
I DON'T KNOW! JUST KEEP ON--
UNH! THEY'RE DISSOLVING...!?
THEY MUST HAVE DONE IT!--
"THEY MUST HAVE DEFEATED MALESUR!
"ALL HIS MINIONS ARE DISSIPATING--
"ALL HIS MAGIKS, WEARING OFF...!"

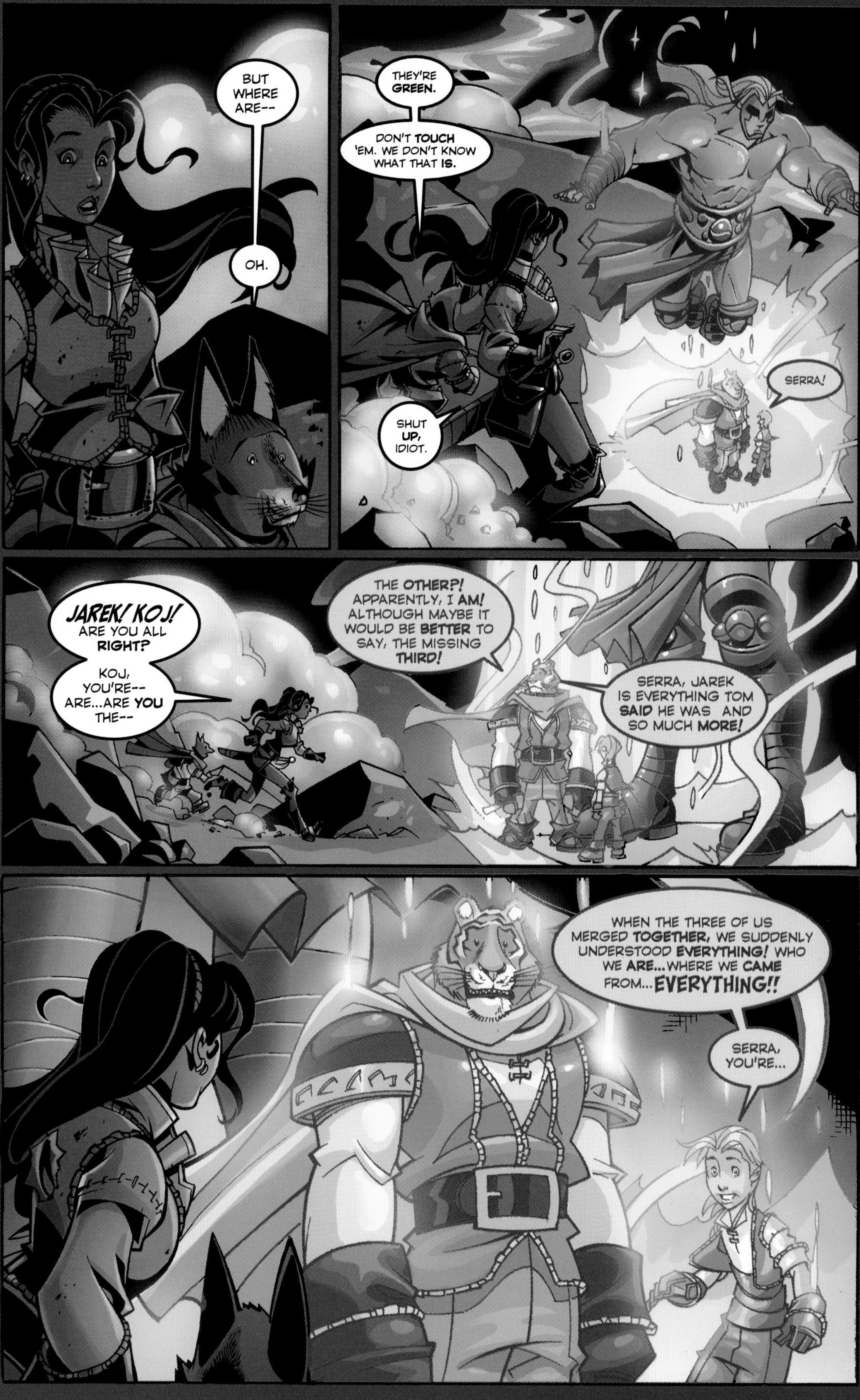
BUT WHERE ARE--
OH.
THEY'RE **GREEN.**
DON'T **TOUCH** 'EM. WE DON'T KNOW WHAT THAT **IS.**
SERRA!
SHUT **UP,** IDIOT.
JAREK! KOJ! ARE YOU ALL **RIGHT?**
KOJ, YOU'RE-- ARE...ARE **YOU** THE--
THE **OTHER?!** APPARENTLY, I **AM!** ALTHOUGH MAYBE IT WOULD BE **BETTER** TO SAY, THE MISSING **THIRD!**
SERRA, JAREK IS EVERYTHING TOM **SAID** HE WAS AND SO MUCH **MORE!**
WHEN THE THREE OF US MERGED **TOGETHER,** WE SUDDENLY UNDERSTOOD **EVERYTHING!** WHO WE **ARE...**WHERE WE **CAME** FROM...**EVERYTHING!!**
SERRA, YOU'RE...

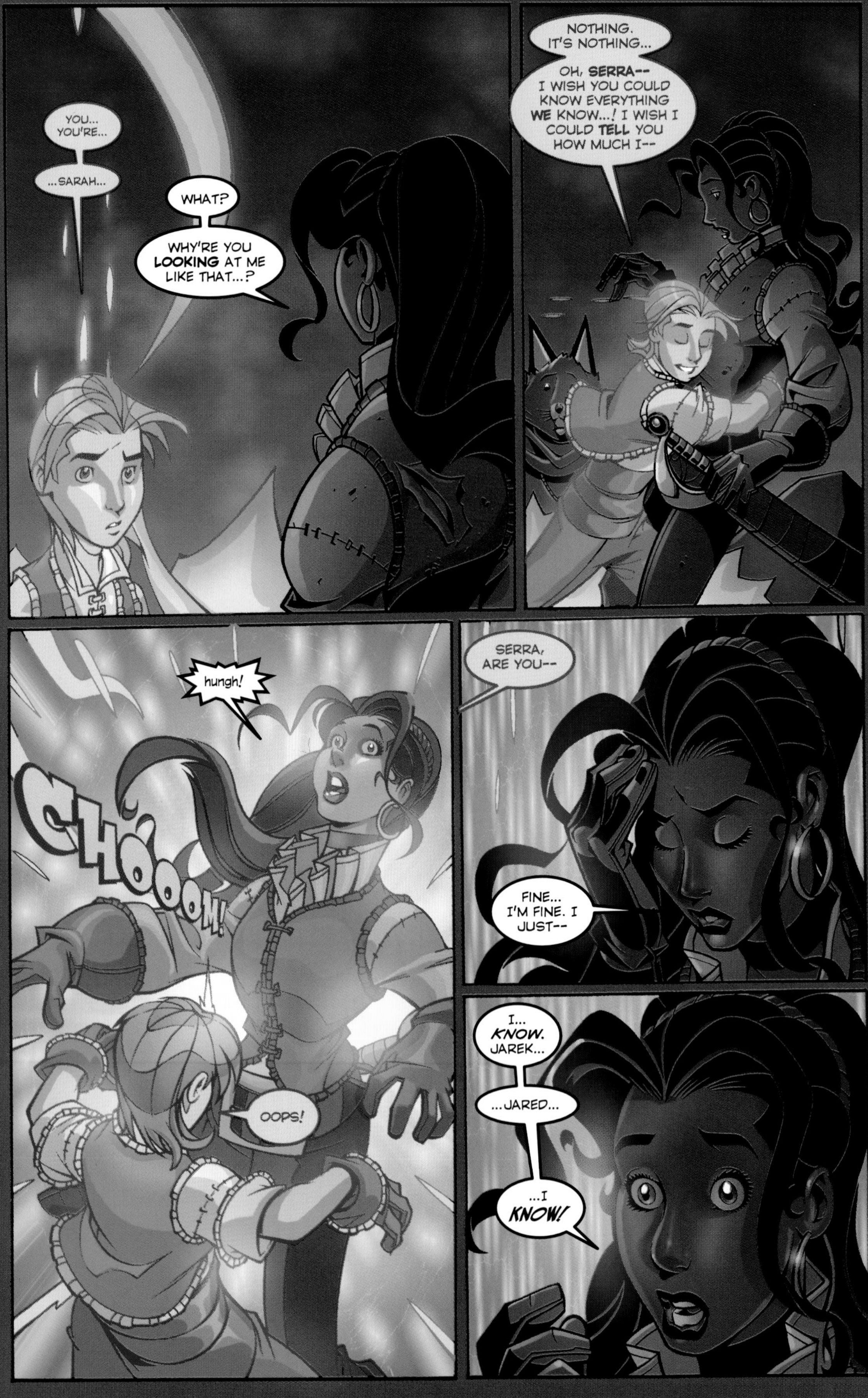
YOU... YOU'RE...
...SARAH...
WHAT?
WHY'RE YOU **LOOKING** AT ME LIKE THAT...?
NOTHING. IT'S NOTHING...
OH, **SERRA--** I WISH YOU COULD KNOW EVERYTHING **WE** KNOW...! I WISH I COULD **TELL** YOU HOW MUCH I--
hungh!
CHOOOOM!
OOPS!
SERRA, ARE YOU--
FINE... I'M FINE. I JUST--
I... ***KNOW.*** JAREK...
...JARED...
...I ***KNOW!***

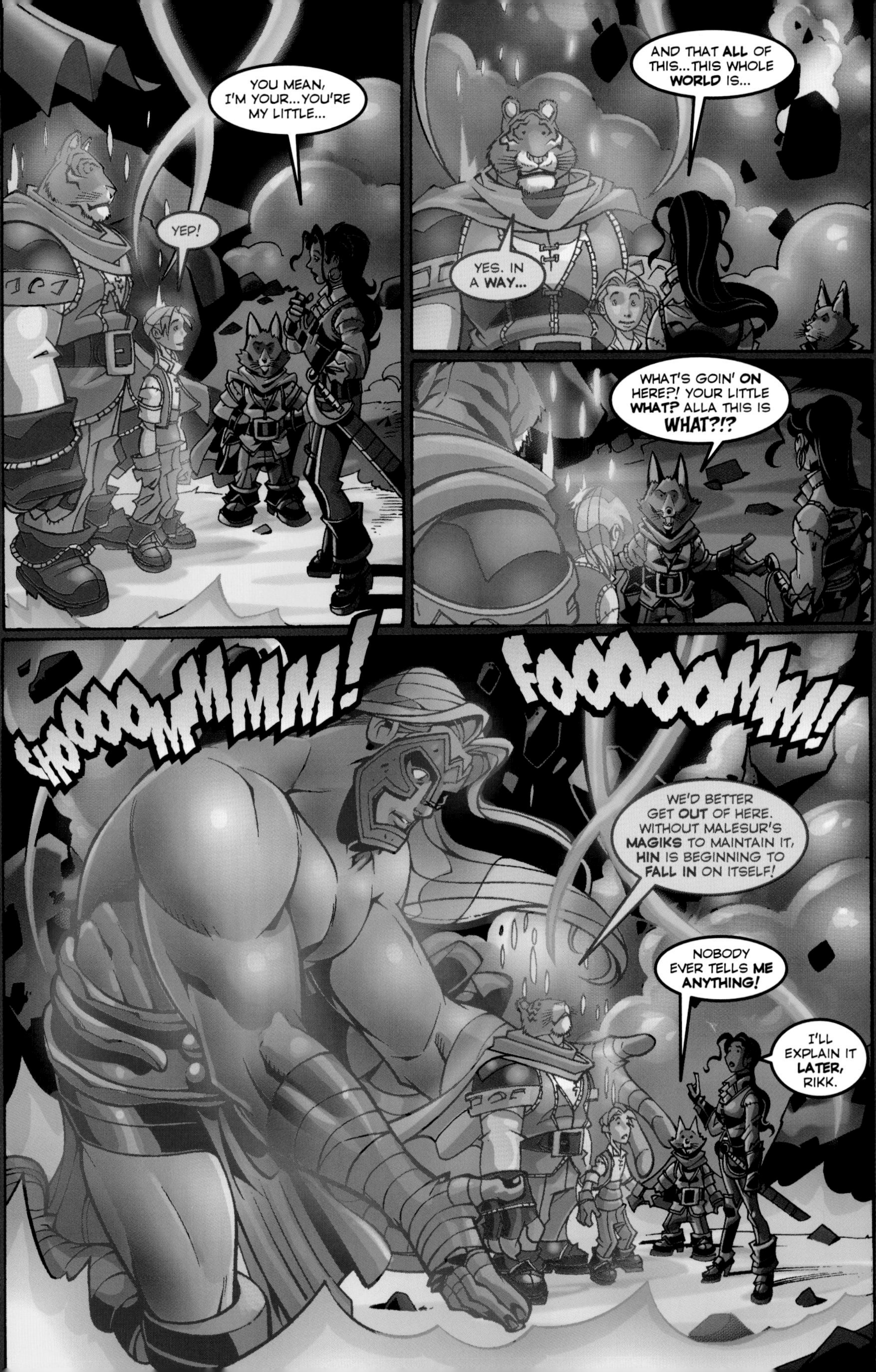

YOU MEAN, I'M YOUR...YOU'RE MY LITTLE...
YEP!
AND THAT ALL OF THIS...THIS WHOLE WORLD IS...
YES. IN A WAY...
WHAT'S GOIN' ON HERE?! YOUR LITTLE WHAT? ALLA THIS IS WHAT?!?
SHOOOOMMMM!
FOOOOOMM!!
WE'D BETTER GET OUT OF HERE. WITHOUT MALESUR'S MAGIKS TO MAINTAIN IT, HIN IS BEGINNING TO FALL IN ON ITSELF!
NOBODY EVER TELLS ME ANYTHING!
I'LL EXPLAIN IT LATER, RIKK.

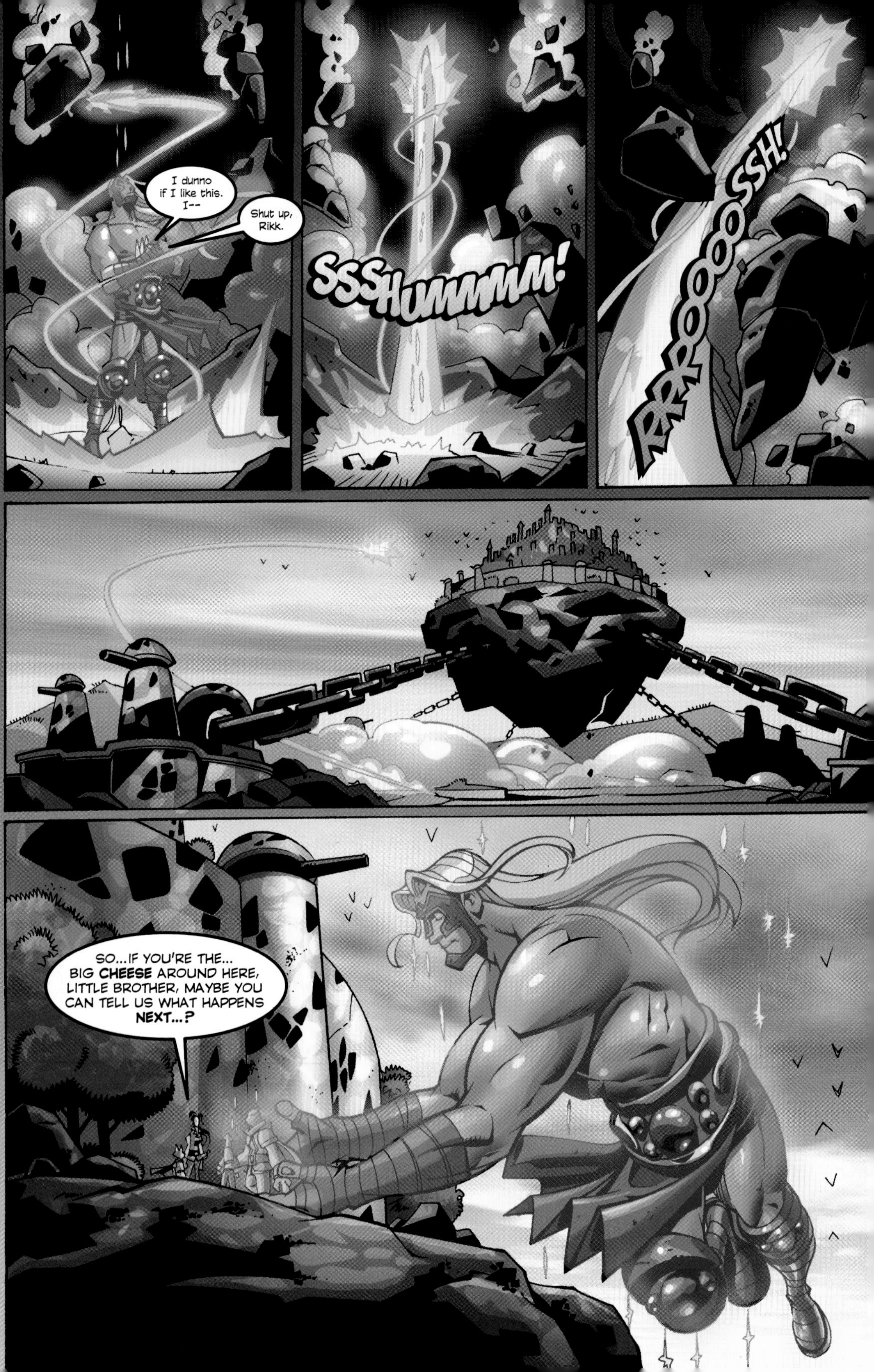
I dunno if I like this. I--
Shut up, Rikk.
SSSHUMMMM!
RRROOOOSSH!
SO...IF YOU'RE THE... BIG CHEESE AROUND HERE, LITTLE BROTHER, MAYBE YOU CAN TELL US WHAT HAPPENS NEXT...?

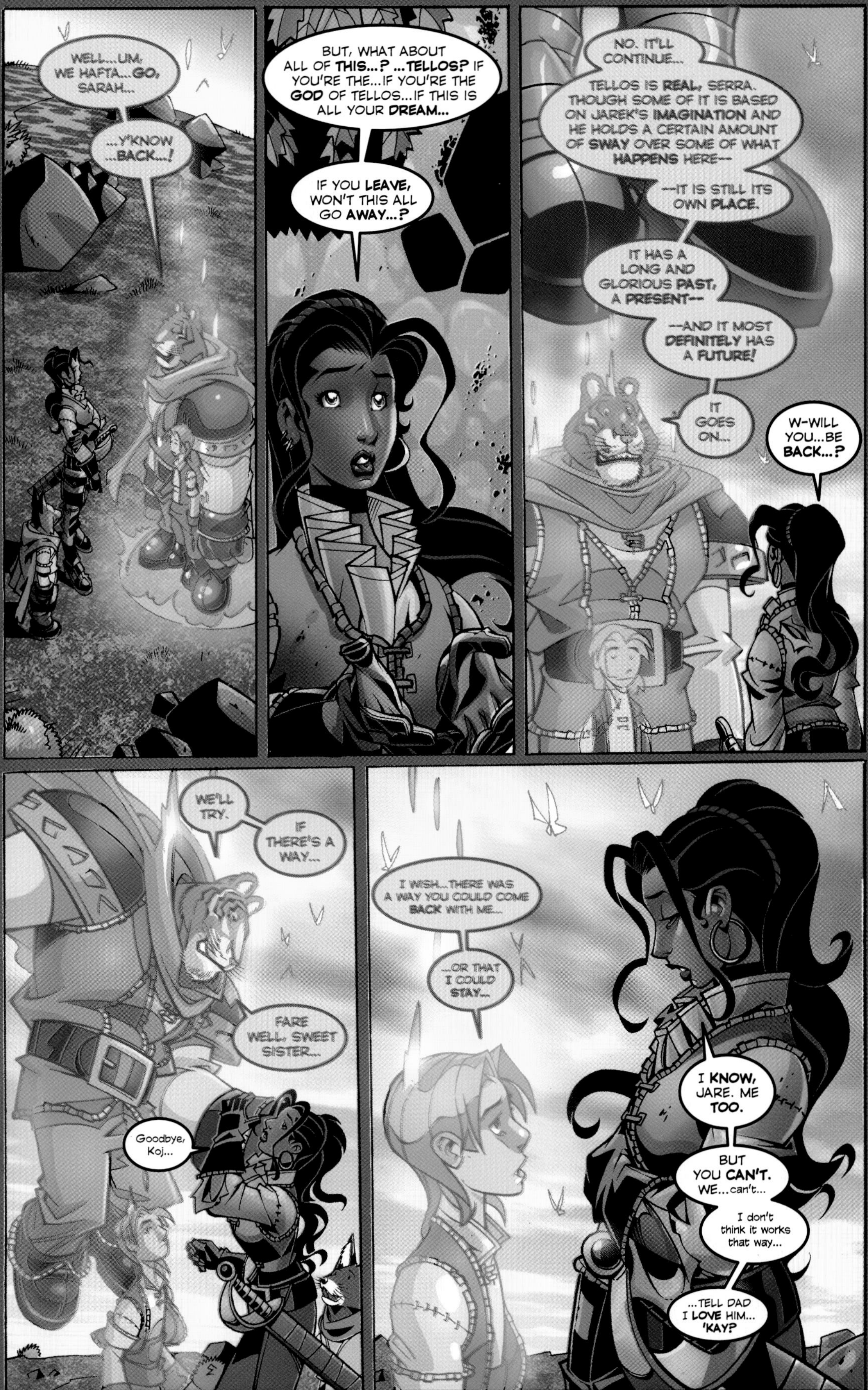

WELL...UM. WE HAFTA...GO, SARAH...
...Y'KNOW ...BACK...!
BUT, WHAT ABOUT ALL OF THIS...? ...TELLOS? IF YOU'RE THE...IF YOU'RE THE GOD OF TELLOS...IF THIS IS ALL YOUR DREAM...
IF YOU LEAVE, WON'T THIS ALL GO AWAY...?
NO. IT'LL CONTINUE...
TELLOS IS REAL, SERRA. THOUGH SOME OF IT IS BASED ON JAREK'S IMAGINATION AND HE HOLDS A CERTAIN AMOUNT OF SWAY OVER SOME OF WHAT HAPPENS HERE--
--IT IS STILL ITS OWN PLACE.
IT HAS A LONG AND GLORIOUS PAST, A PRESENT--
--AND IT MOST DEFINITELY HAS A FUTURE!
IT GOES ON...
W-WILL YOU...BE BACK...?
WE'LL TRY.
IF THERE'S A WAY...
FARE WELL, SWEET SISTER...
Goodbye, Koj...
I WISH...THERE WAS A WAY YOU COULD COME BACK WITH ME...
...OR THAT I COULD STAY...
I KNOW, JARE. ME TOO.
BUT YOU CAN'T. WE...can't...
I don't think it works that way...
...TELL DAD I LOVE HIM... 'KAY?

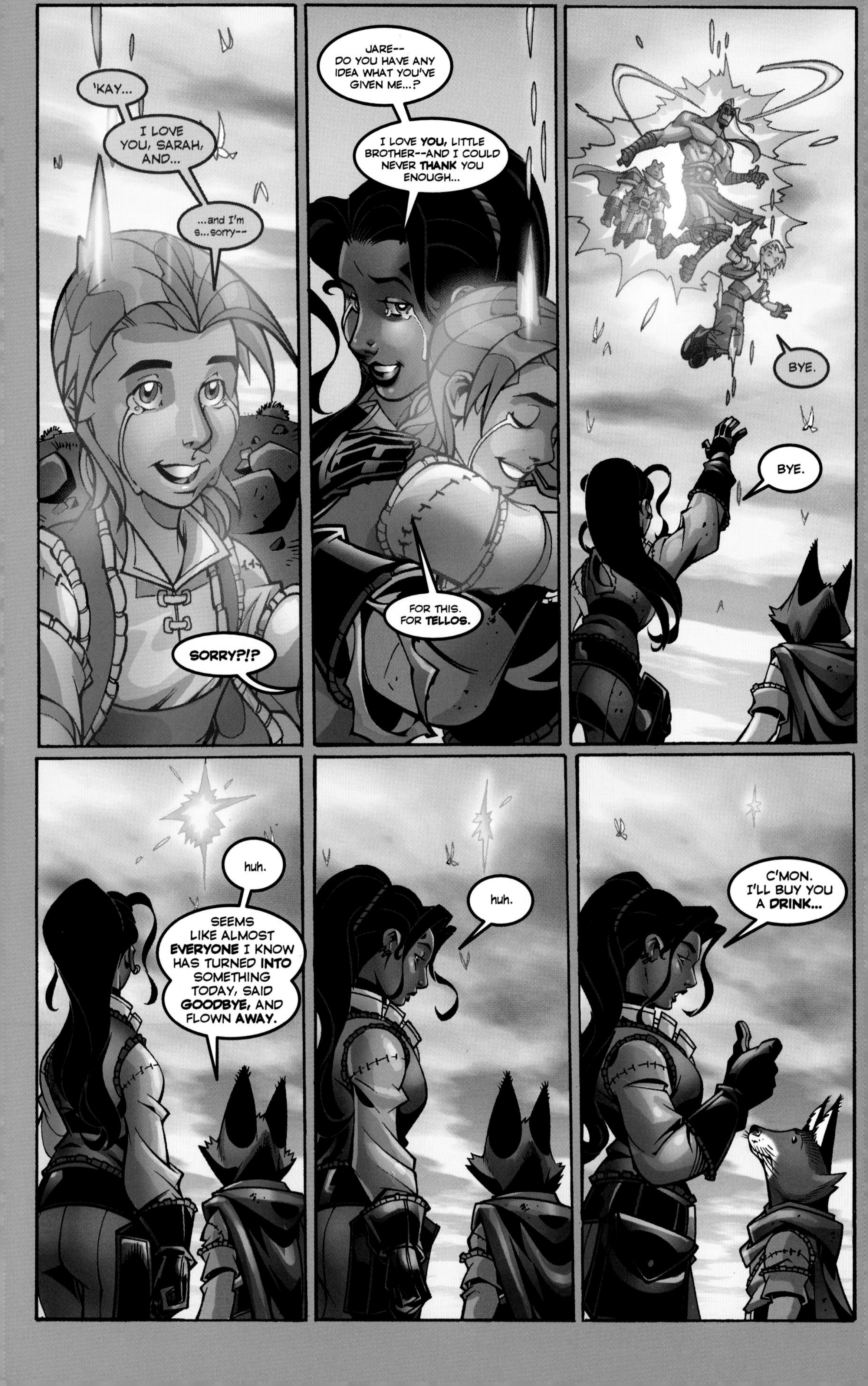
'KAY...
I LOVE YOU, SARAH, AND...
...and I'm s...sorry--
SORRY?!?
JARE-- DO YOU HAVE ANY IDEA WHAT YOU'VE GIVEN ME...?
I LOVE YOU, LITTLE BROTHER--AND I COULD NEVER THANK YOU ENOUGH...
FOR THIS. FOR TELLOS.
BYE.
BYE.
huh.
SEEMS LIKE ALMOST EVERYONE I KNOW HAS TURNED INTO SOMETHING TODAY, SAID GOODBYE, AND FLOWN AWAY.
huh.
C'MON. I'LL BUY YOU A DRINK...

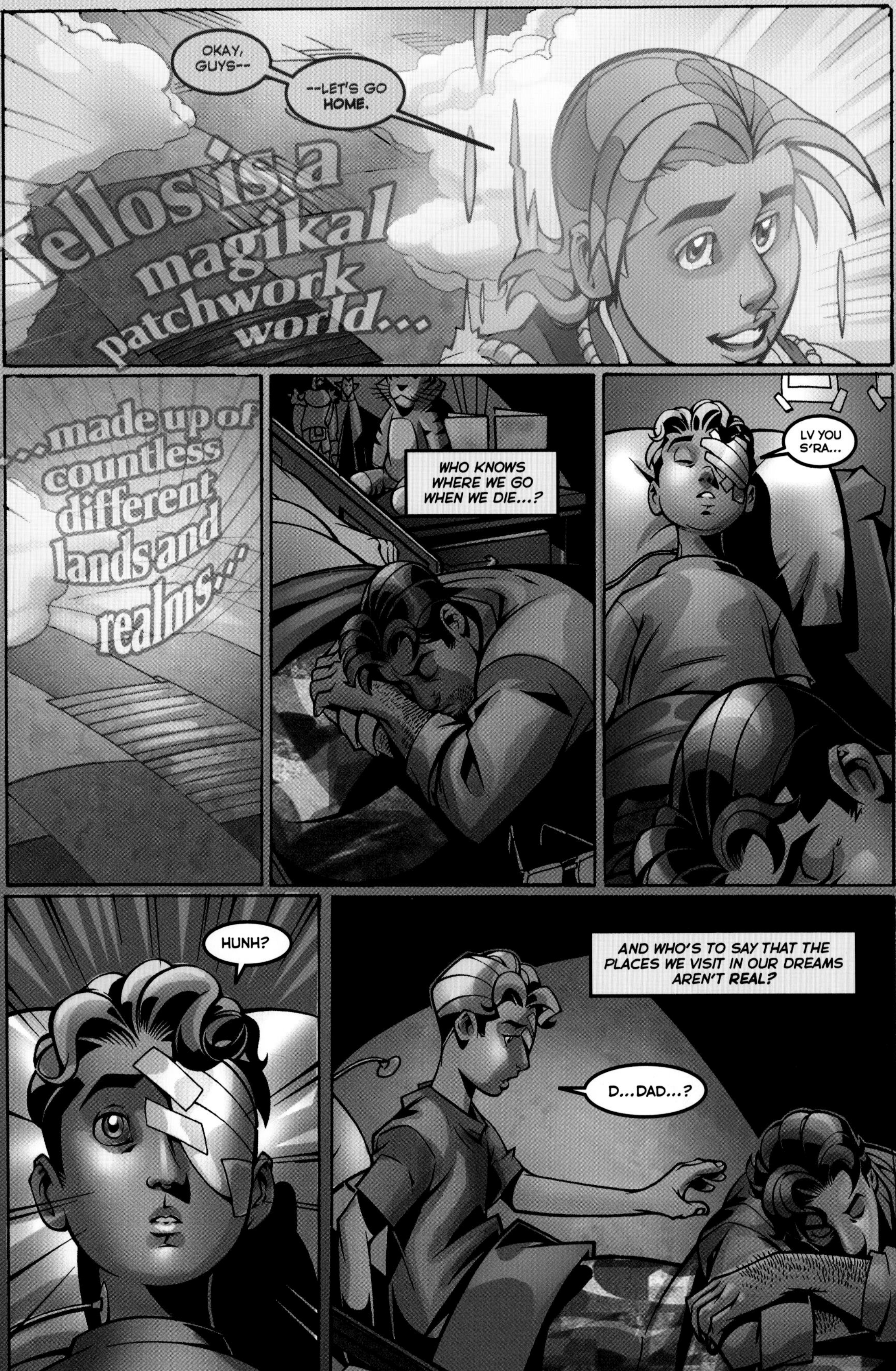

OKAY, GUYS--
--LET'S GO HOME.
Tellos is a magikal patchwork world...
...made up of countless different lands and realms...
WHO KNOWS WHERE WE GO WHEN WE DIE...?
LV YOU S'RA...
HUNH?
AND WHO'S TO SAY THAT THE PLACES WE VISIT IN OUR DREAMS AREN'T REAL?
D...DAD...?

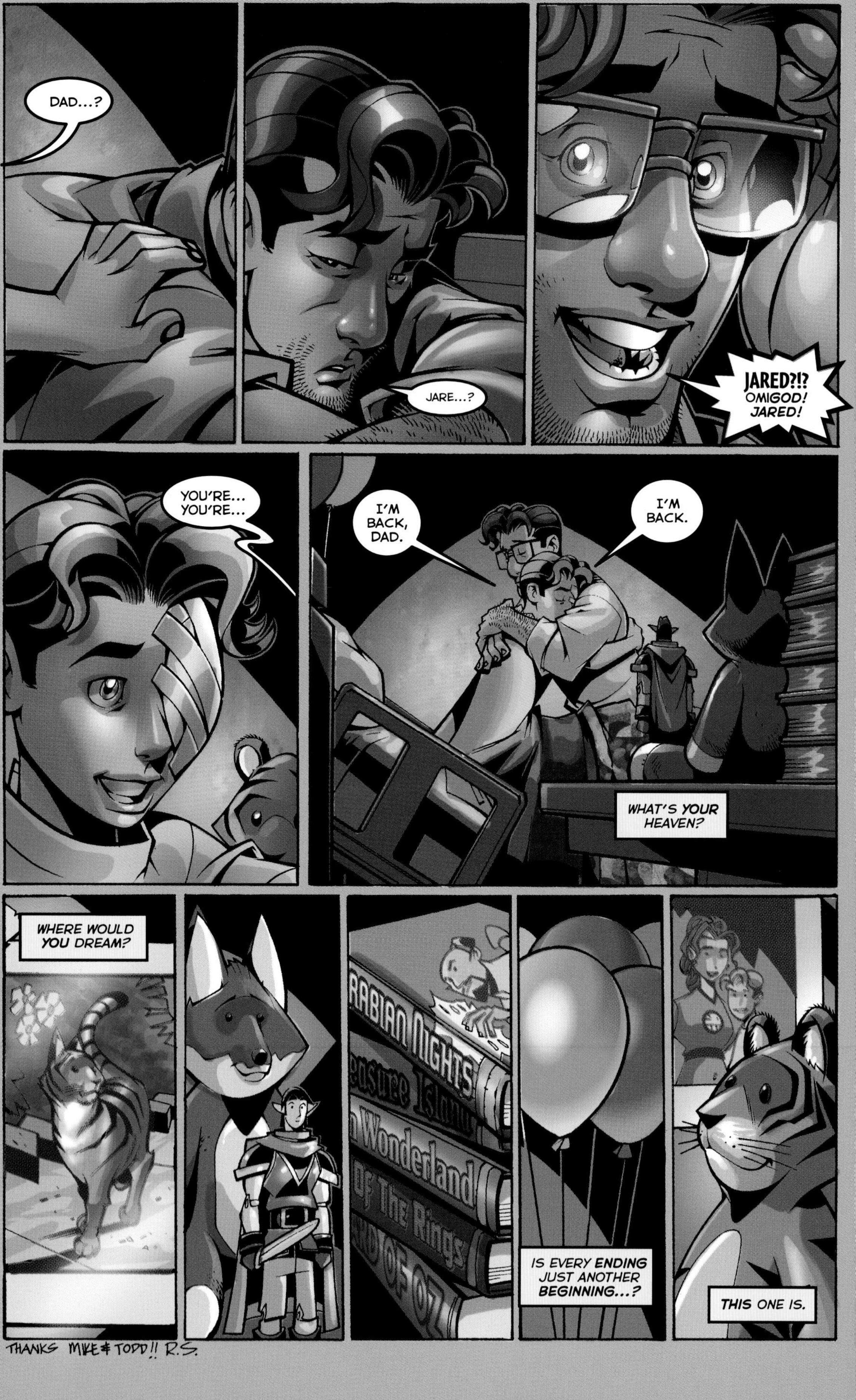
DAD...?
JARE...?
JARED?!? OMIGOD! JARED!
YOU'RE... YOU'RE...
I'M BACK, DAD.
I'M BACK.
WHAT'S YOUR HEAVEN?
WHERE WOULD YOU DREAM?
ARABIAN NIGHTS
Treasure Island
in Wonderland
OF THE RINGS
IS EVERY ENDING JUST ANOTHER BEGINNING...?
THIS ONE IS.

THANKS MIKE & TODD!! R.S.

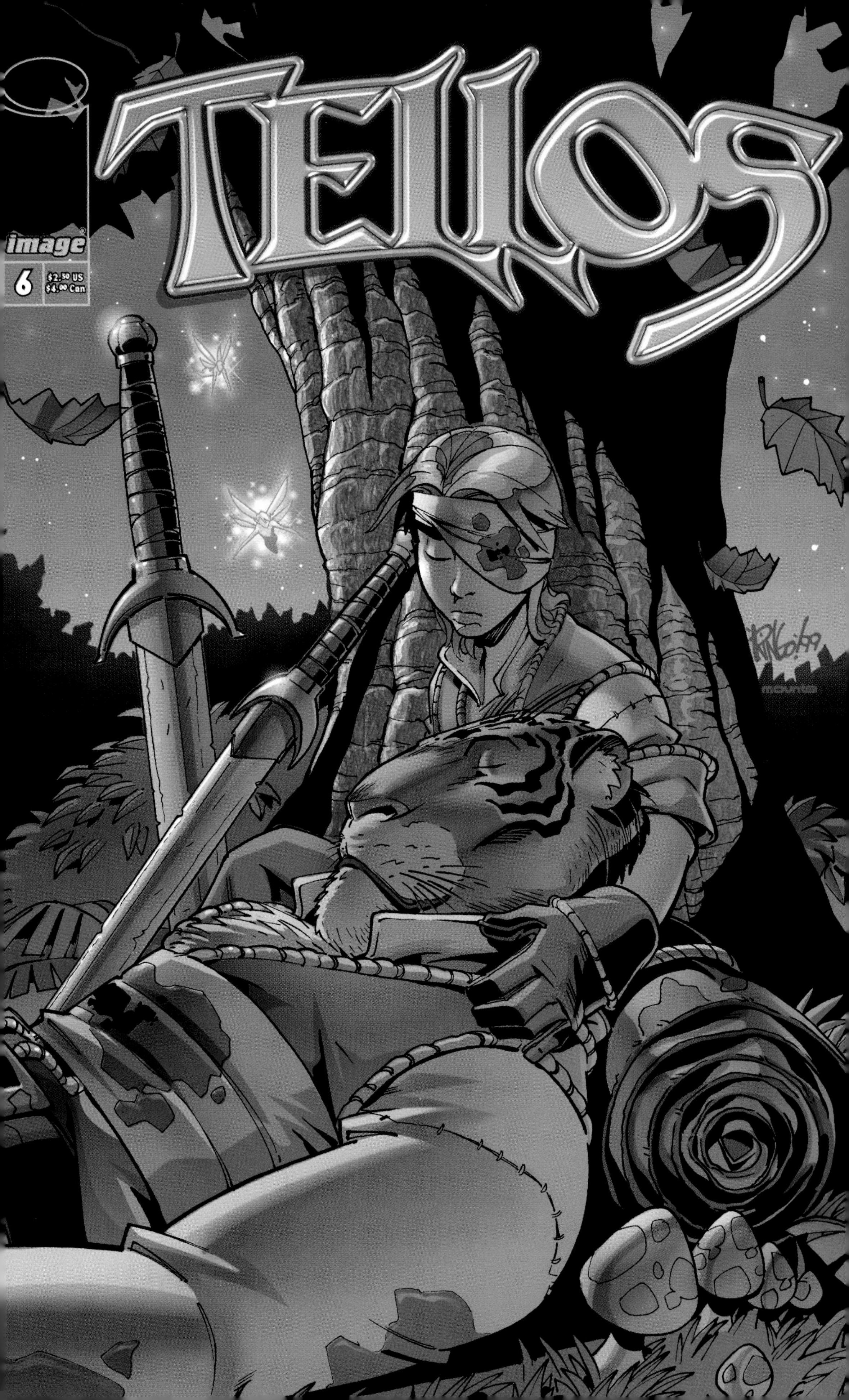
image
6
$2.50 US
$4.00 Can
TELLOS

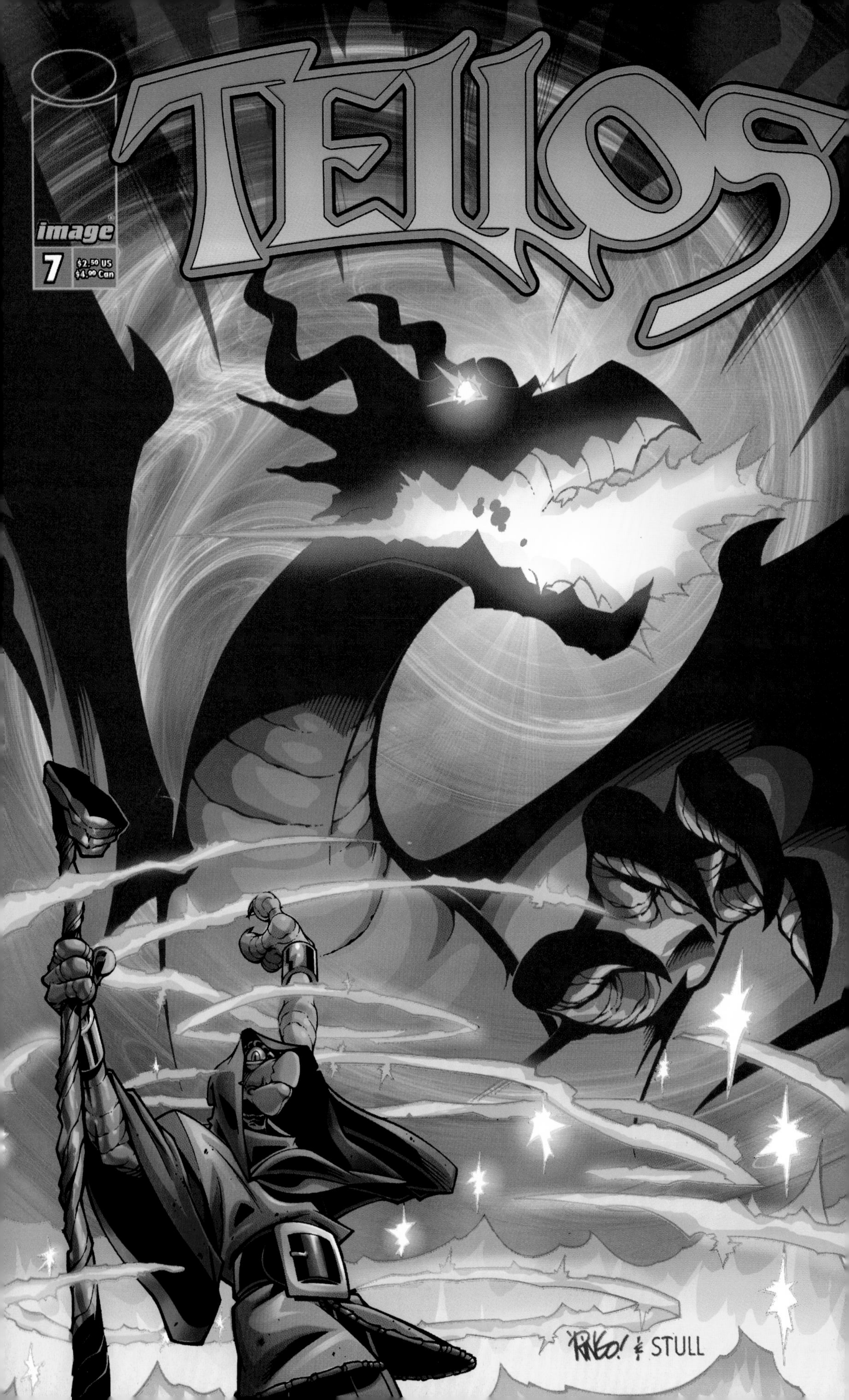
TELLOS
image
7
$2.50 US
$4.00 Can
'RINGO! & STULL

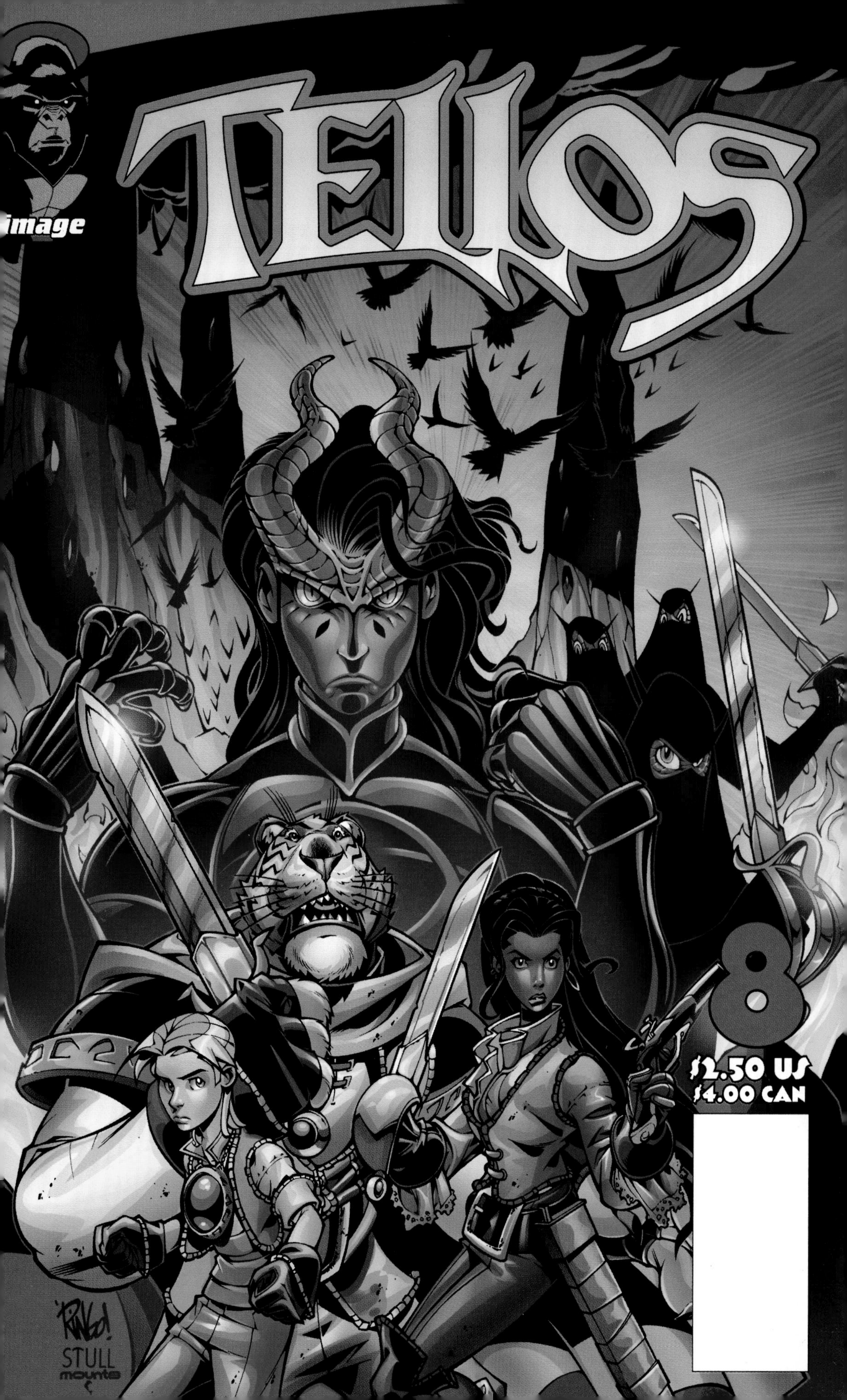

image
TELLOS
8
$2.50 US
$4.00 CAN
RINGO!
STULL
mounts

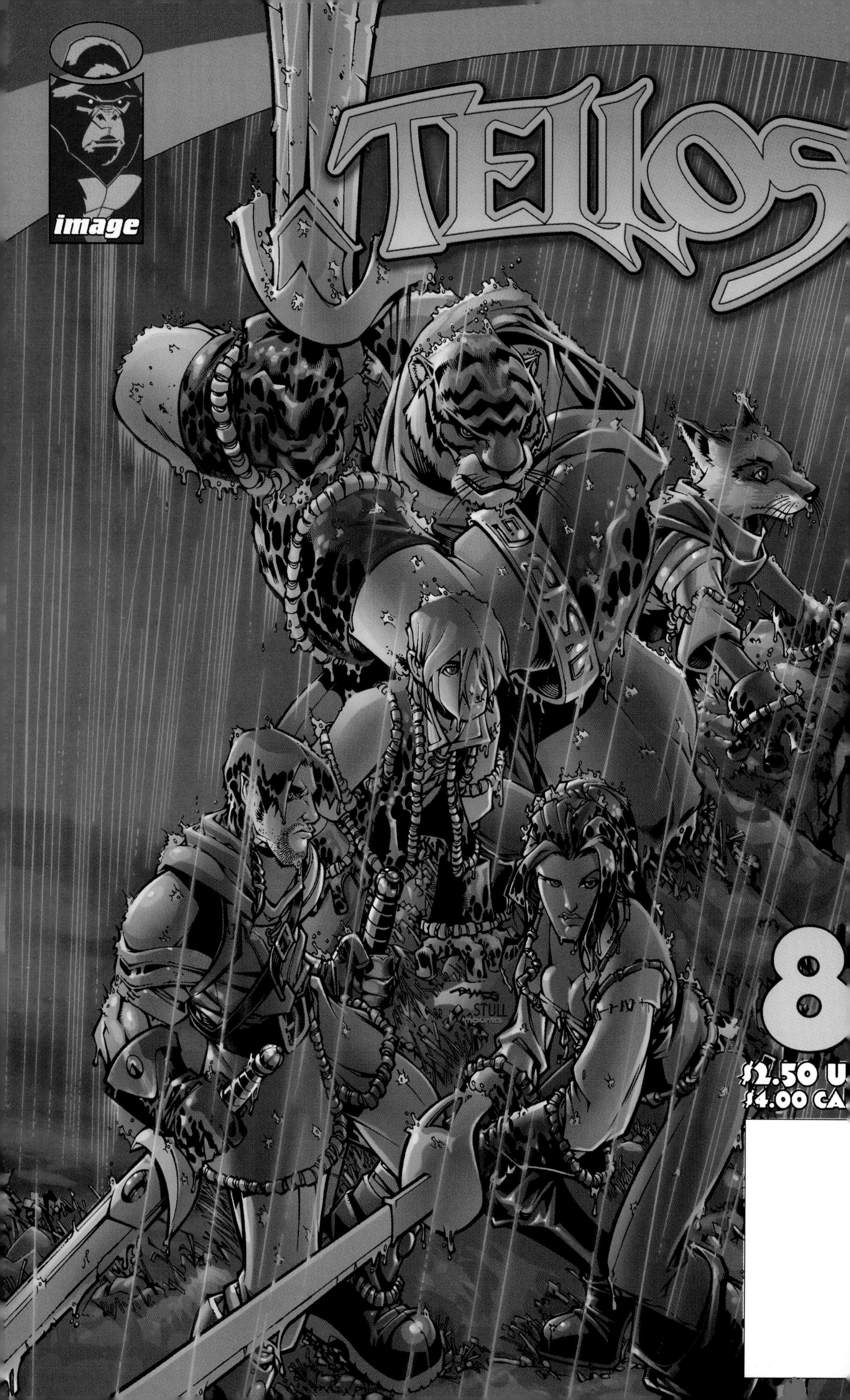
image
TELLOS
8
$2.50 U
$4.00 CA
STULL

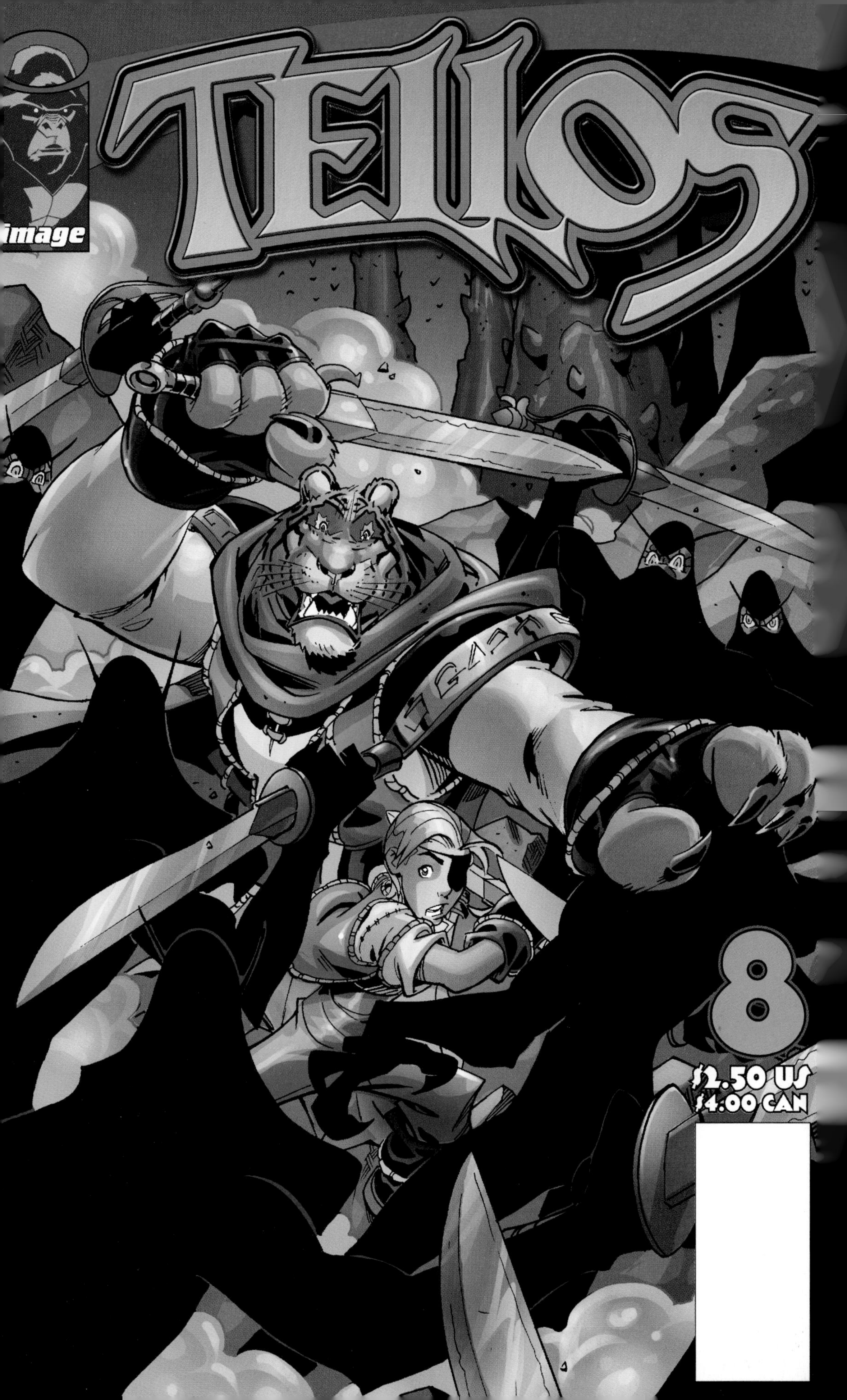
image
TELLOS
8
$2.50 US
$4.00 CAN

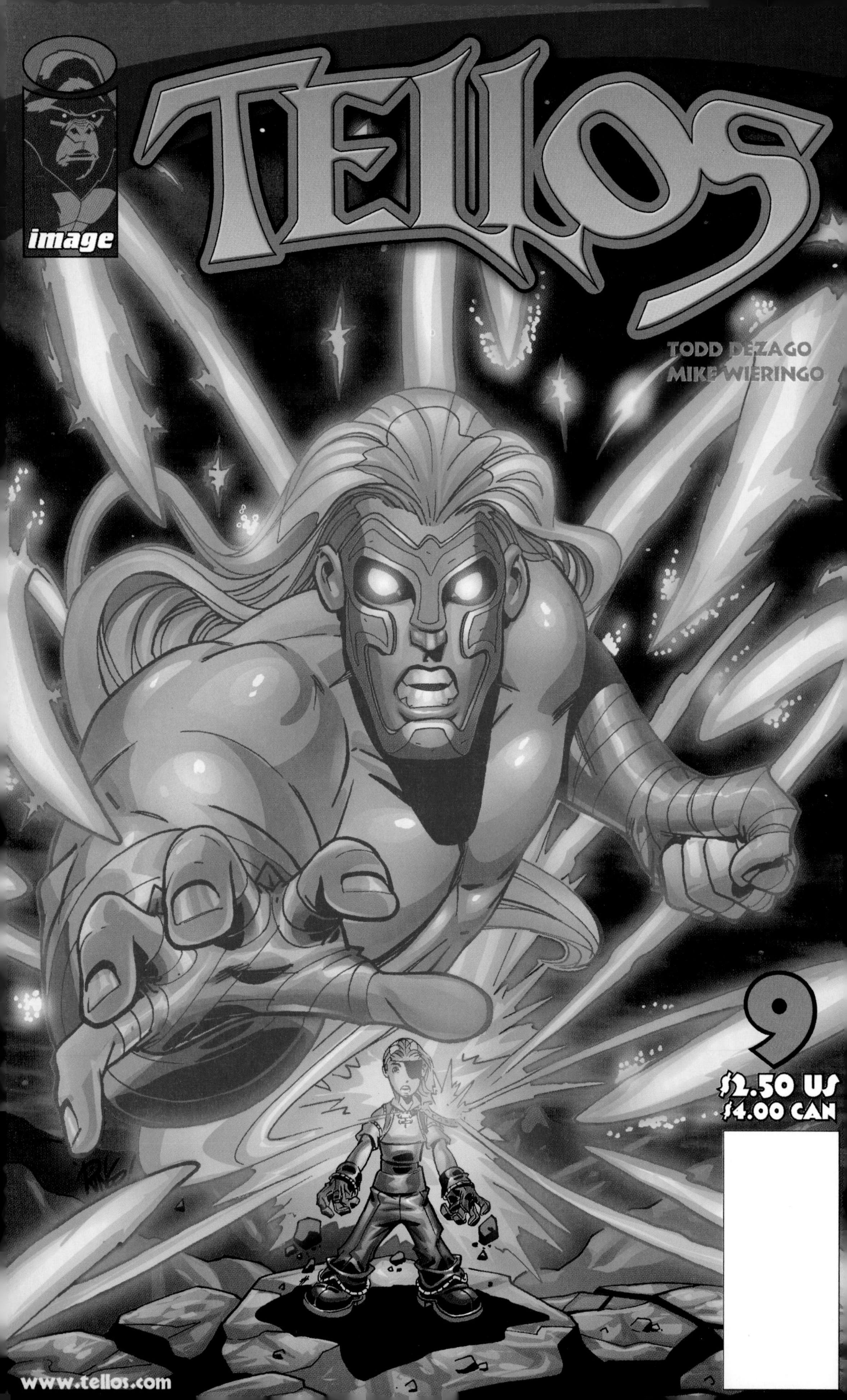
image
TELLOS
TODD DEZAGO
MIKE WIERINGO
9
$2.50 US
$4.00 CAN
www.tellos.com

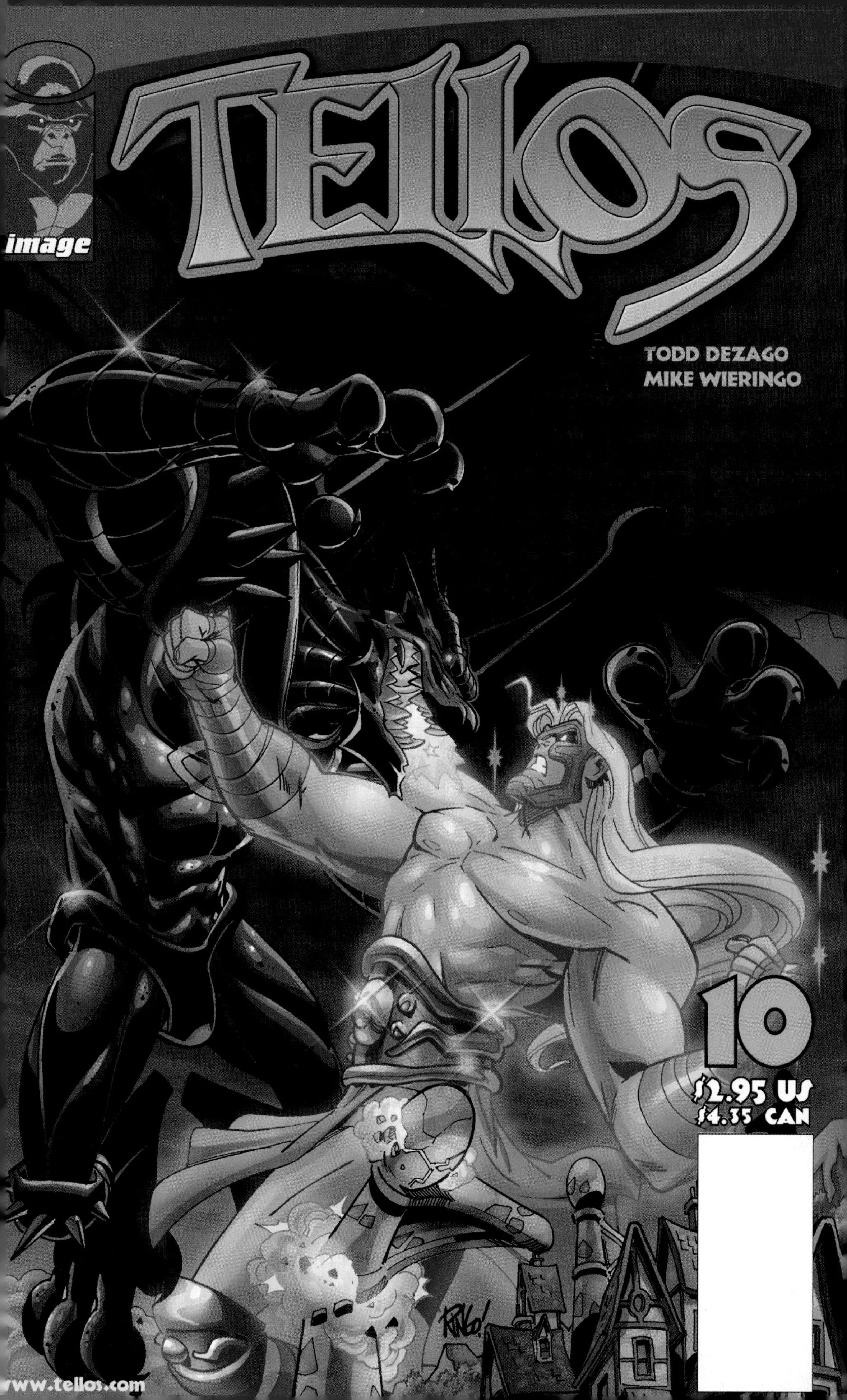
image
TELLOS
TODD DEZAGO
MIKE WIERINGO
10
$2.95 US
$4.35 CAN
RINGO!
www.tellos.com

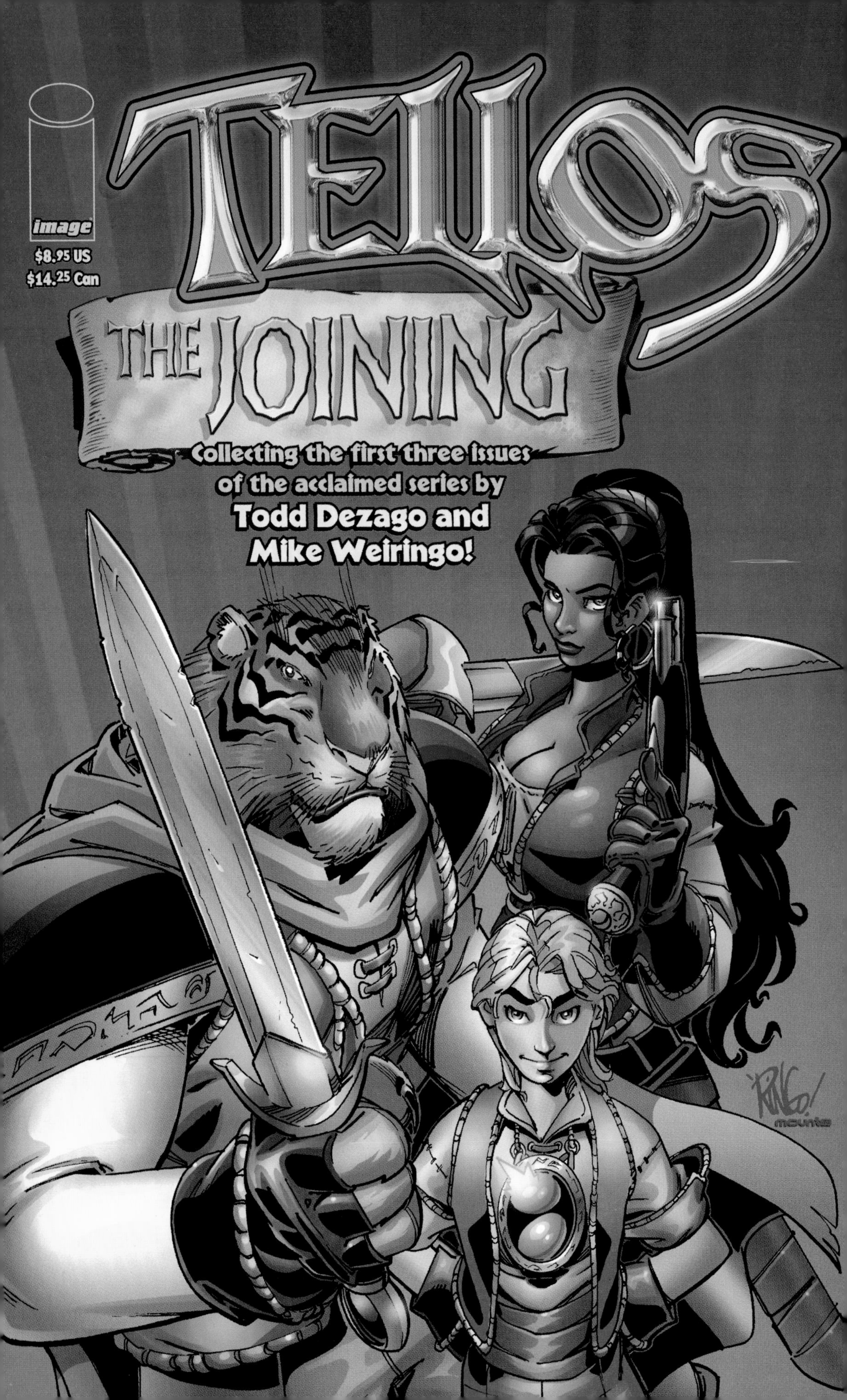
image
$8.95 US
$14.25 Can
TELLOS
THE JOINING
Collecting the first three issues
of the acclaimed series by
Todd Dezago and
Mike Weiringo!
Ringo!
mounts

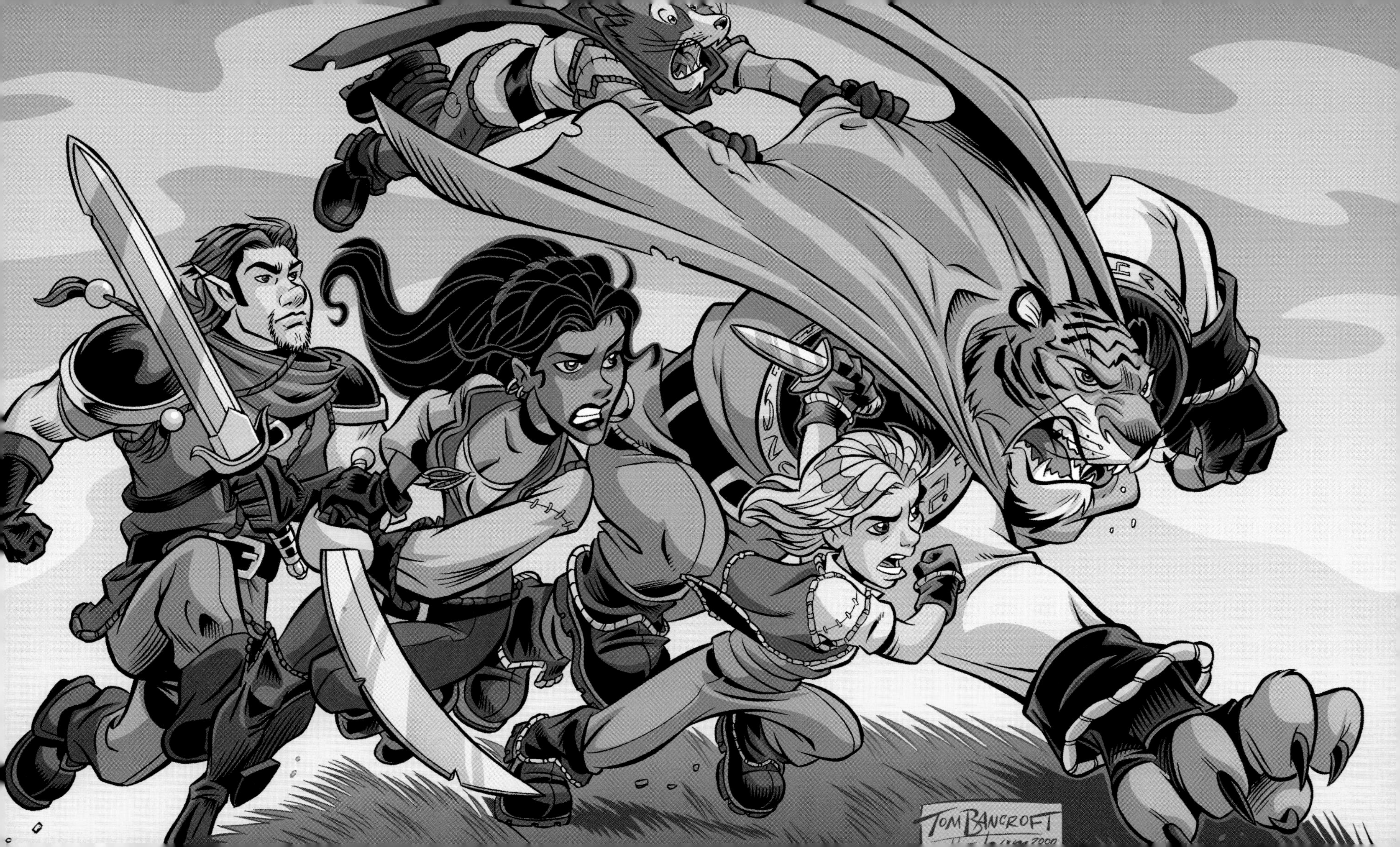
TOM BANCROFT

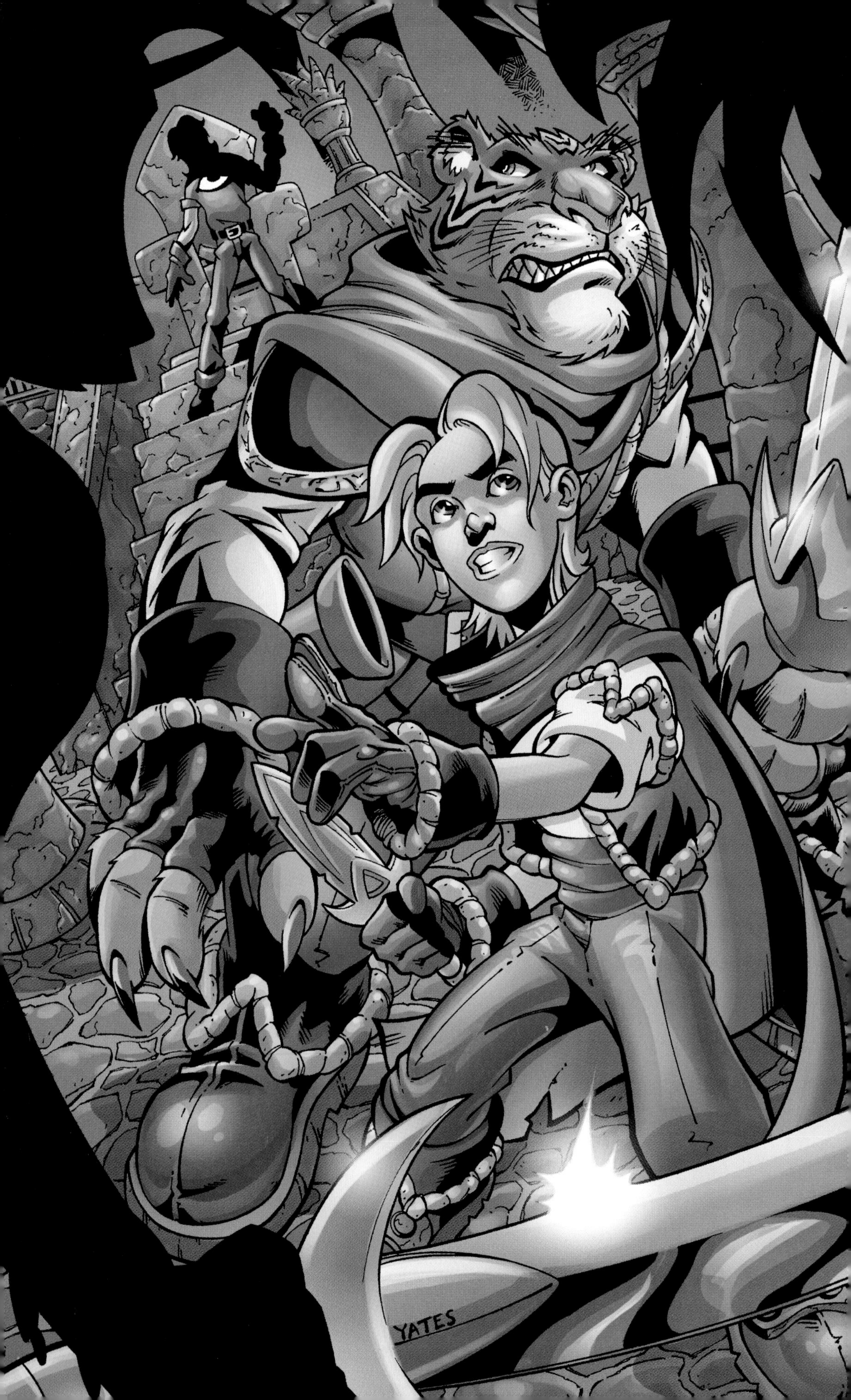
YATES

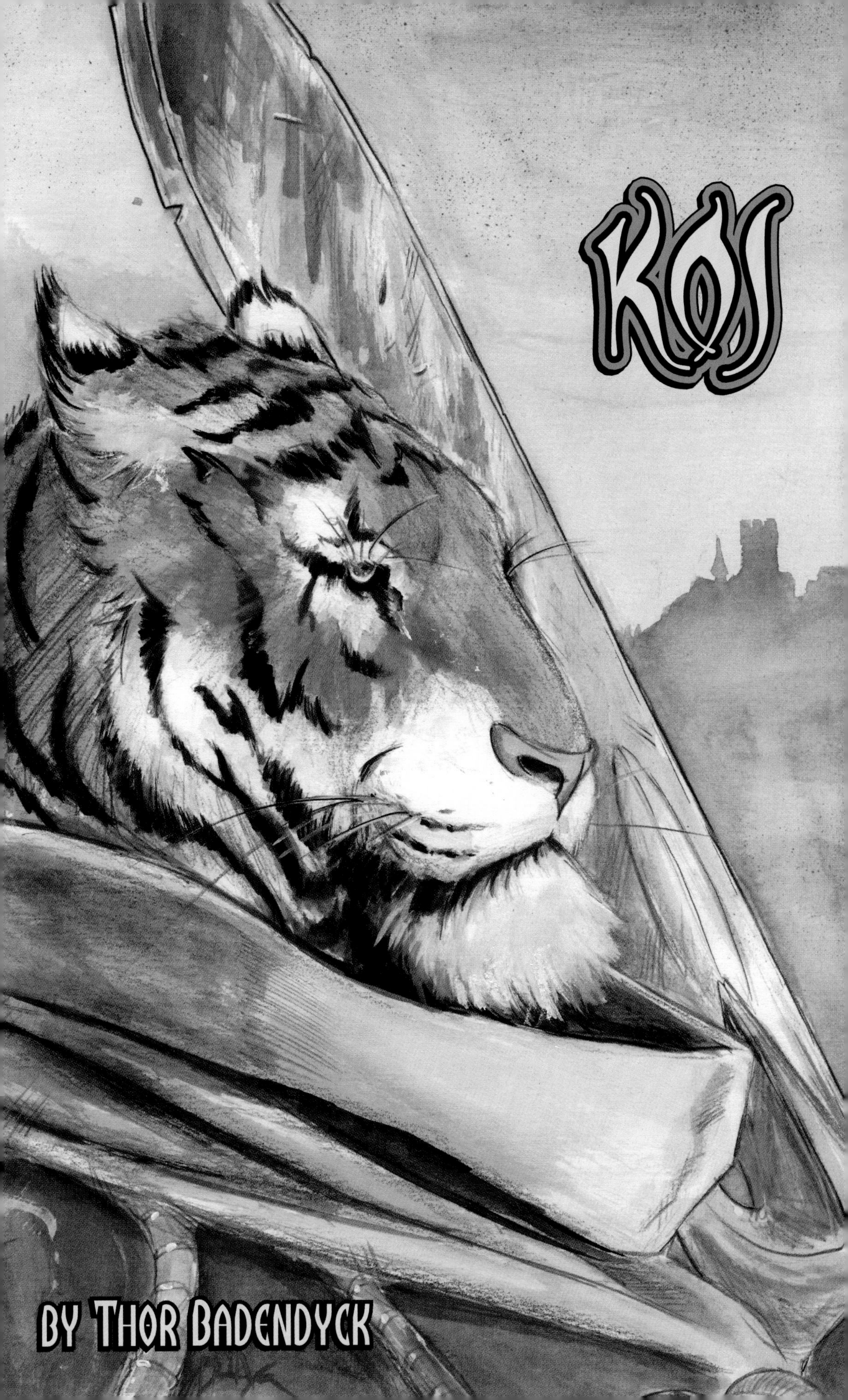
By Thor Badendyck

The SCATTERJACK Story...

Last year, Mike and I found ourselves in League with some of the best storytellers in comics today, as we launched the well-intended but short-lived GORILLA COMICS. While the sad story of Gorilla's brief existence (and desperate struggle to remain viable) will surely go down in Comics History, I can sum up the problem in one word: money. We thought we had it. And at the last minute, our financial backers backed out. A lesson learned. A painful lesson.

Anyway, enough about that; good things came from this experience too. Aside from the friendships we cultivated with our Gorilla Brothers, Mike and I also cranked out the following 5-page Tellos story, which appeared in Karl Kesel and Tom Grummett's awesome (if I may say so myself) SECTION ZERO #1, in an attempt to show unity throughout the Gorilla Books. With my eye already on the possibility of an anthology book growing out of Tellos, I wanted to introduce our occasional narrator, SCATTERJACK, in a tiny little jaunt that would introduce New Readers to the World of Tellos.

Many people ask us where our ideas come from, and especially in regards to our characters and their names (and especially because Mike and I actually do put a lot of thought into that...). Scatterjack is based on and named for my late Grandfather, my Mom's Step-Father, Jack Scattergood, who was quite a rambling storyteller himself and always good for a mealtime yarn that would get us all laughing and squirting milk out our noses. This is for him.

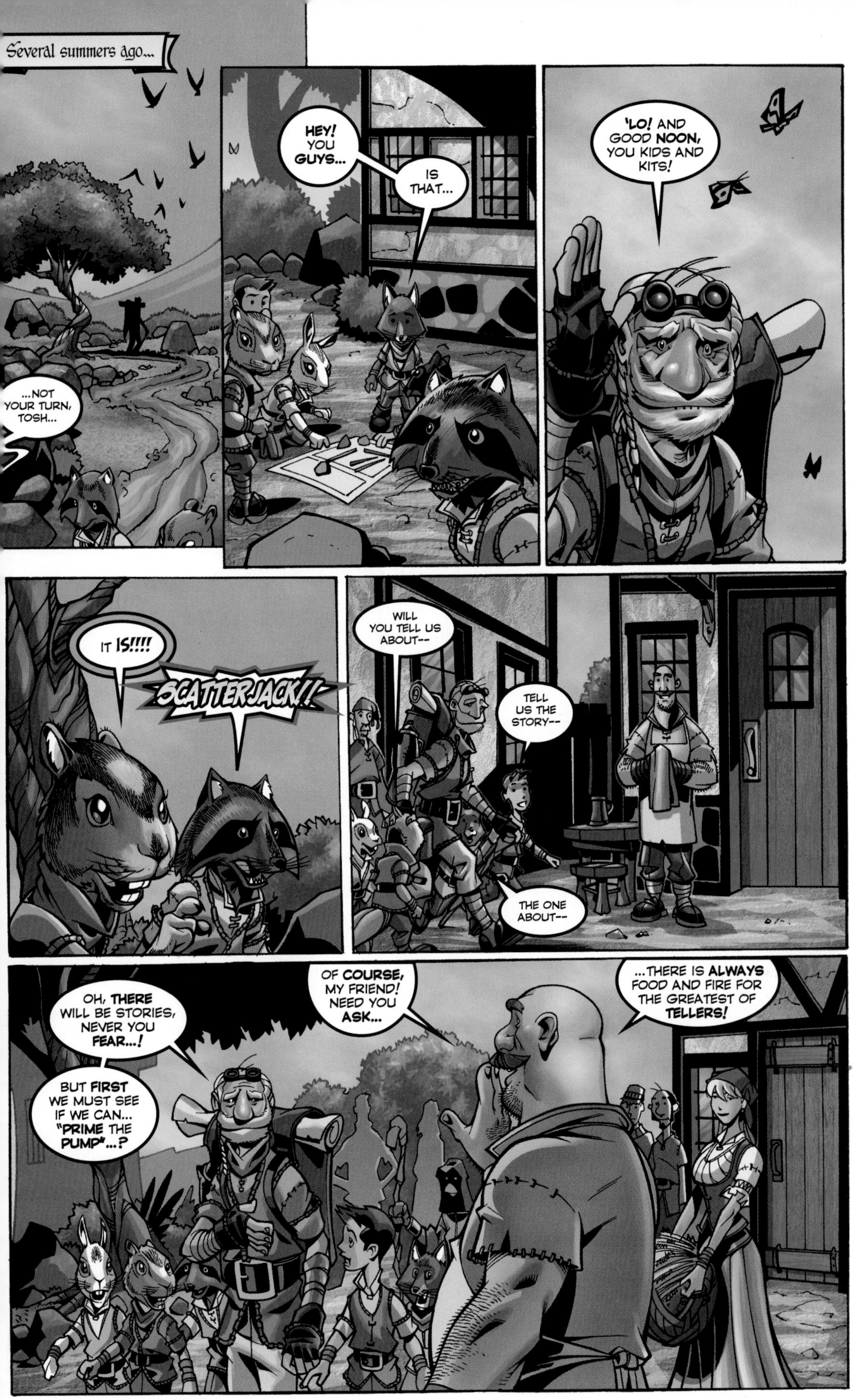
Several summers ago...
...NOT YOUR TURN, TOSH...
HEY! YOU GUYS...
IS THAT...
'LO! AND GOOD NOON, YOU KIDS AND KITS!
IT IS!!!!
SCATTERJACK!!
WILL YOU TELL US ABOUT--
TELL US THE STORY--
THE ONE ABOUT--
OH, THERE WILL BE STORIES, NEVER YOU FEAR...!
BUT FIRST WE MUST SEE IF WE CAN... "PRIME THE PUMP"...?
OF COURSE, MY FRIEND! NEED YOU ASK...
...THERE IS ALWAYS FOOD AND FIRE FOR THE GREATEST OF TELLERS!

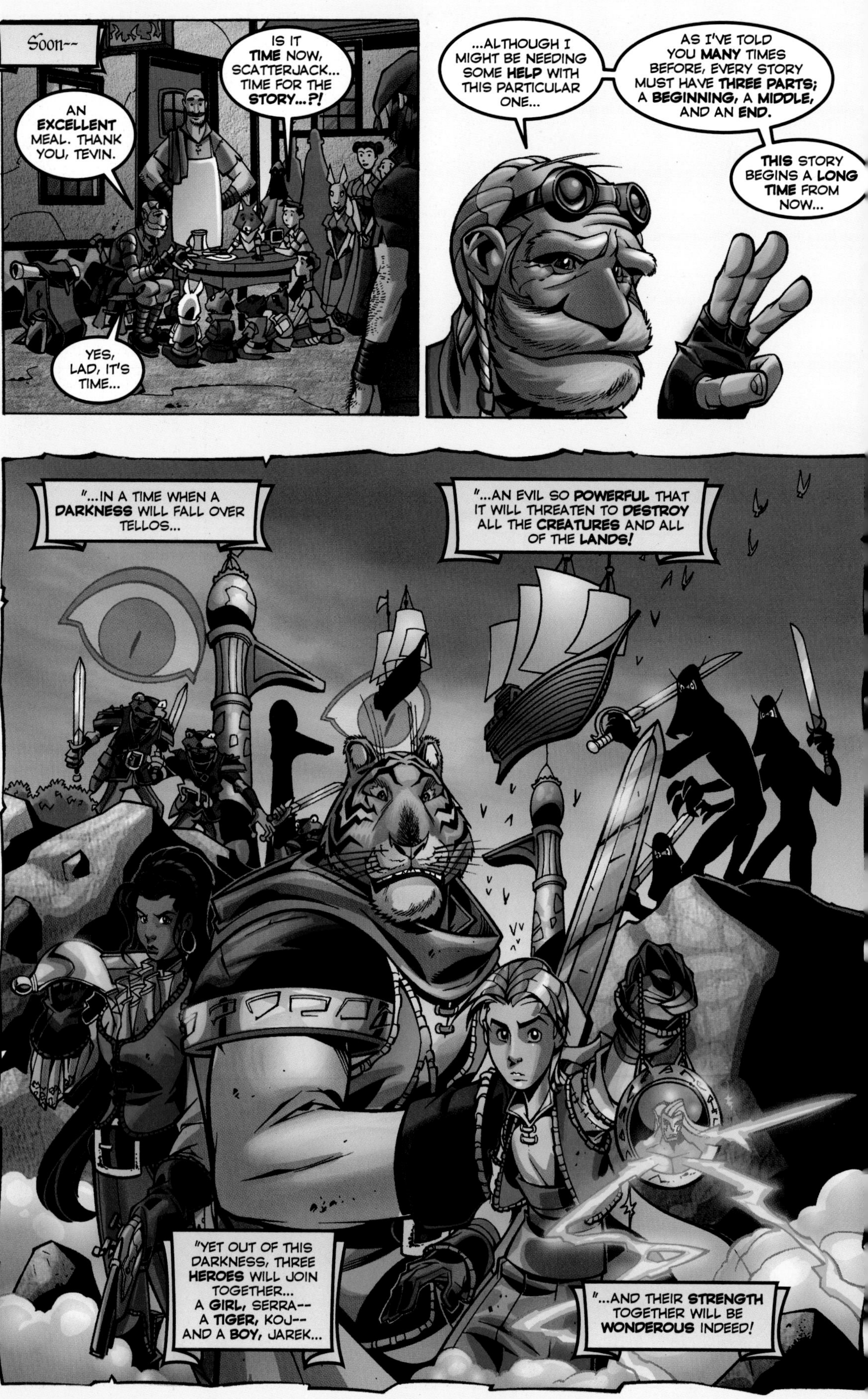
Soon--
AN EXCELLENT MEAL. THANK YOU, TEVIN.
IS IT TIME NOW, SCATTERJACK... TIME FOR THE STORY...?!
YES, LAD, IT'S TIME...
...ALTHOUGH I MIGHT BE NEEDING SOME HELP WITH THIS PARTICULAR ONE...
AS I'VE TOLD YOU MANY TIMES BEFORE, EVERY STORY MUST HAVE THREE PARTS; A BEGINNING, A MIDDLE, AND AN END.
THIS STORY BEGINS A LONG TIME FROM NOW...
"...IN A TIME WHEN A DARKNESS WILL FALL OVER TELLOS...
"...AN EVIL SO POWERFUL THAT IT WILL THREATEN TO DESTROY ALL THE CREATURES AND ALL OF THE LANDS!
"YET OUT OF THIS DARKNESS, THREE HEROES WILL JOIN TOGETHER... A GIRL, SERRA-- A TIGER, KOJ-- AND A BOY, JAREK...
"...AND THEIR STRENGTH TOGETHER WILL BE WONDEROUS INDEED!

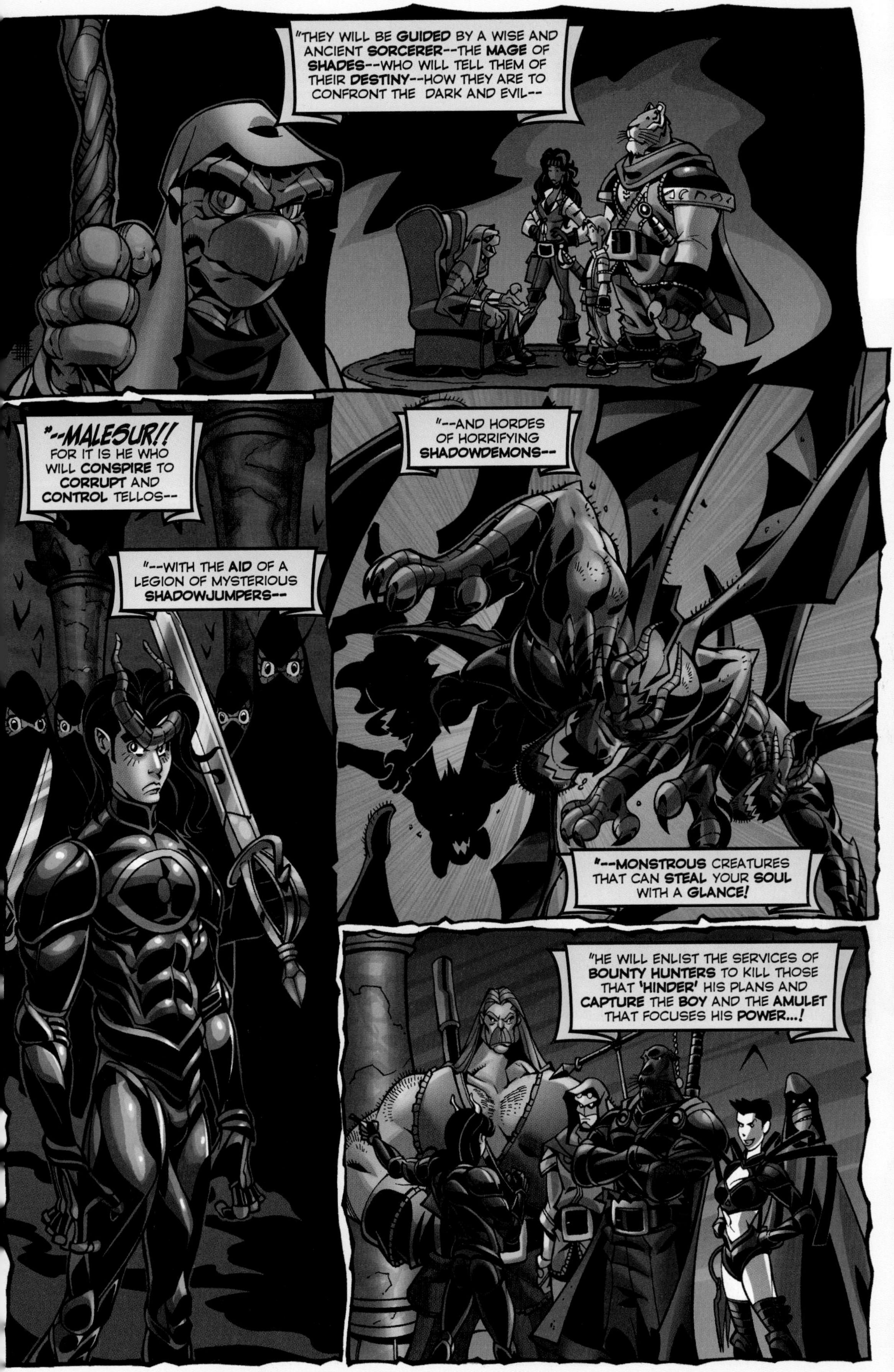
"THEY WILL BE GUIDED BY A WISE AND ANCIENT SORCERER--THE MAGE OF SHADES--WHO WILL TELL THEM OF THEIR DESTINY--HOW THEY ARE TO CONFRONT THE DARK AND EVIL--
"--MALESUR!! FOR IT IS HE WHO WILL CONSPIRE TO CORRUPT AND CONTROL TELLOS--
"--WITH THE AID OF A LEGION OF MYSTERIOUS SHADOWJUMPERS--
"--AND HORDES OF HORRIFYING SHADOWDEMONS--
"--MONSTROUS CREATURES THAT CAN STEAL YOUR SOUL WITH A GLANCE!
"HE WILL ENLIST THE SERVICES OF BOUNTY HUNTERS TO KILL THOSE THAT 'HINDER' HIS PLANS AND CAPTURE THE BOY AND THE AMULET THAT FOCUSES HIS POWER...!

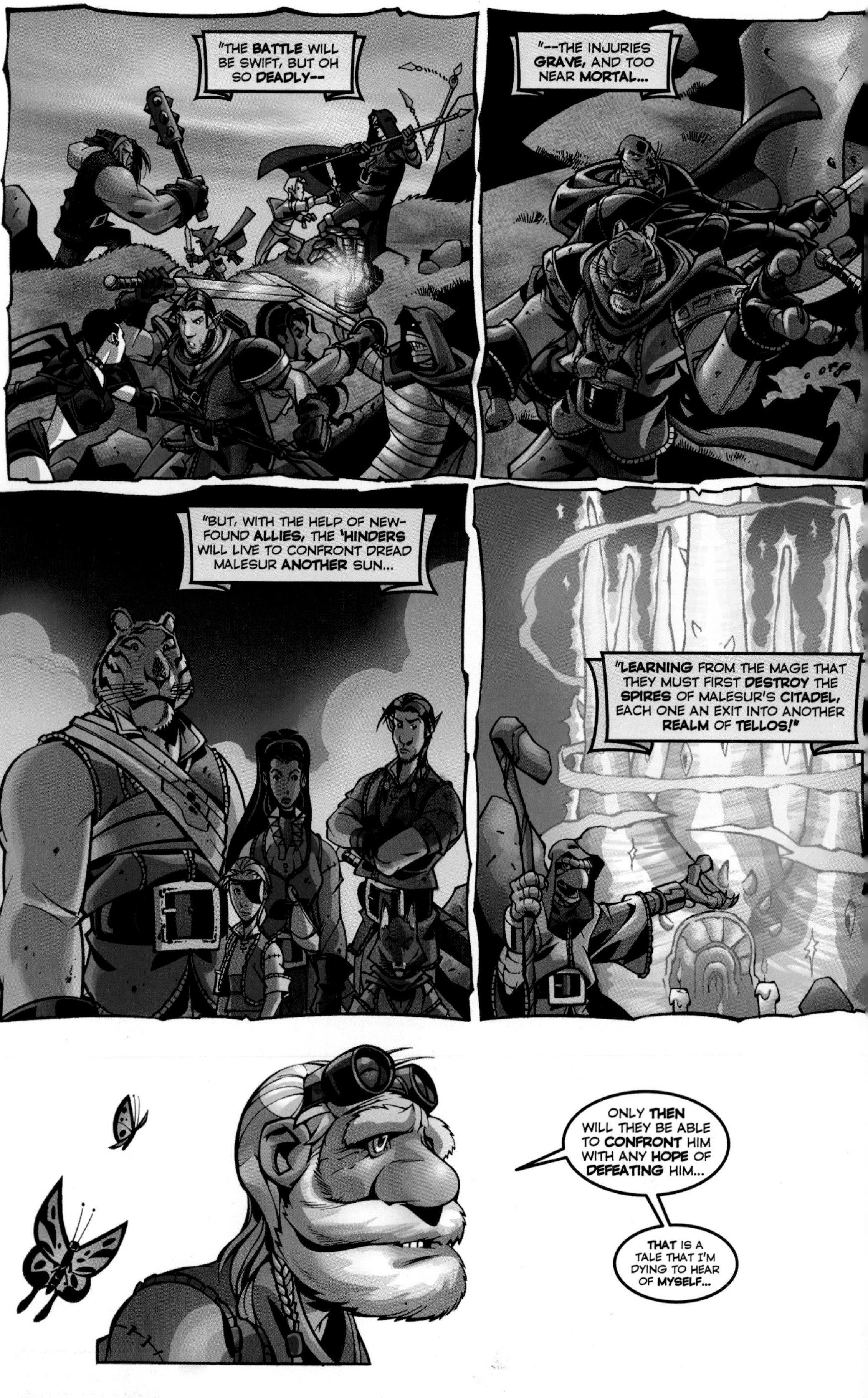
"THE BATTLE WILL BE SWIFT, BUT OH SO DEADLY--
"--THE INJURIES GRAVE, AND TOO NEAR MORTAL...
"BUT, WITH THE HELP OF NEW-FOUND ALLIES, THE 'HINDERS WILL LIVE TO CONFRONT DREAD MALESUR ANOTHER SUN...
"LEARNING FROM THE MAGE THAT THEY MUST FIRST DESTROY THE SPIRES OF MALESUR'S CITADEL, EACH ONE AN EXIT INTO ANOTHER REALM OF TELLOS!"
ONLY THEN WILL THEY BE ABLE TO CONFRONT HIM WITH ANY HOPE OF DEFEATING HIM...
THAT IS A TALE THAT I'M DYING TO HEAR OF MYSELF...

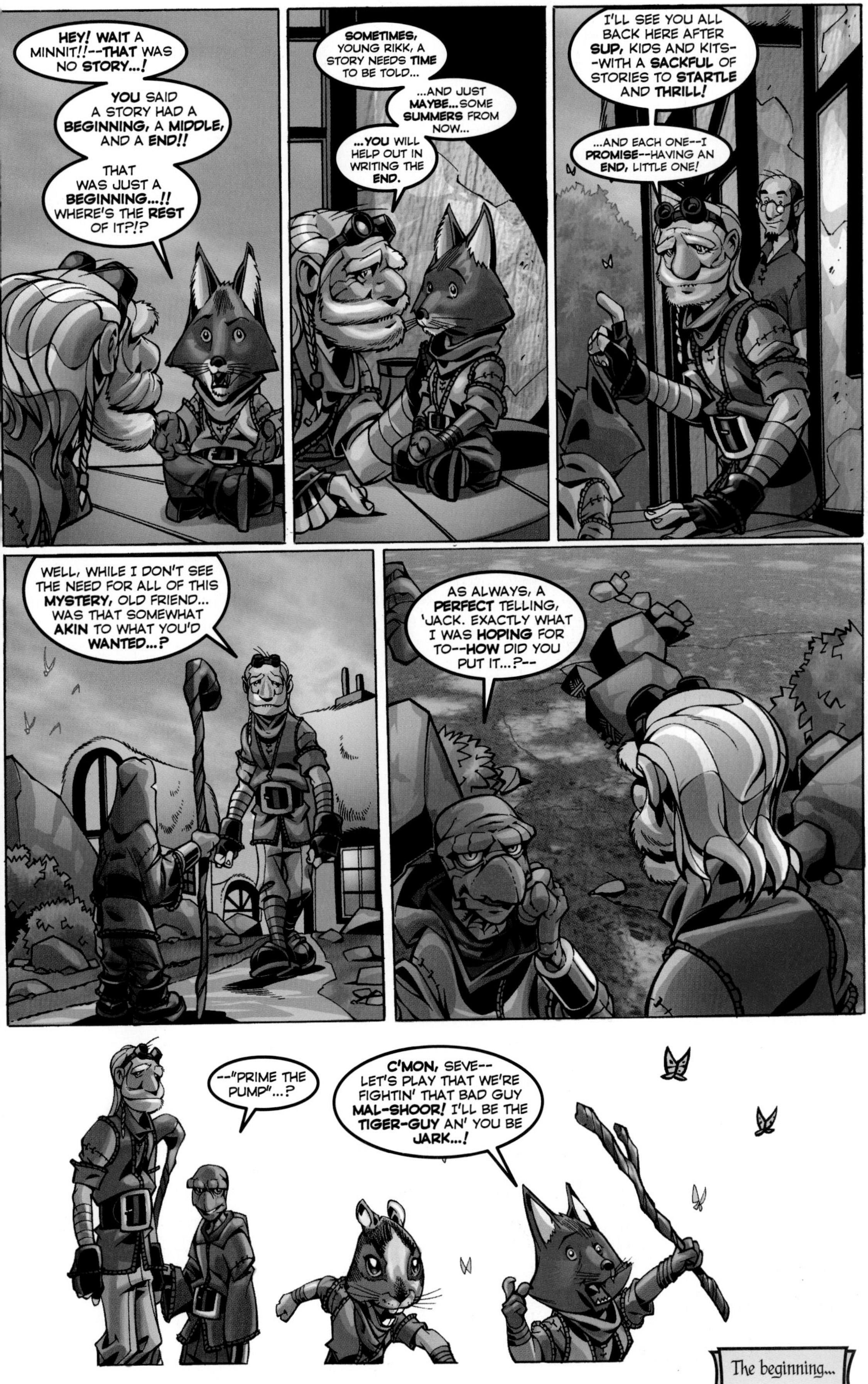
HEY! WAIT A MINNIT!!--THAT WAS NO STORY...!
YOU SAID A STORY HAD A BEGINNING, A MIDDLE, AND A END!!
THAT WAS JUST A BEGINNING...!! WHERE'S THE REST OF IT?!?
SOMETIMES, YOUNG RIKK, A STORY NEEDS TIME TO BE TOLD...
...AND JUST MAYBE...SOME SUMMERS FROM NOW...
...YOU WILL HELP OUT IN WRITING THE END.
I'LL SEE YOU ALL BACK HERE AFTER SUP, KIDS AND KITS--WITH A SACKFUL OF STORIES TO STARTLE AND THRILL!
...AND EACH ONE--I PROMISE--HAVING AN END, LITTLE ONE!
WELL, WHILE I DON'T SEE THE NEED FOR ALL OF THIS MYSTERY, OLD FRIEND... WAS THAT SOMEWHAT AKIN TO WHAT YOU'D WANTED...?
AS ALWAYS, A PERFECT TELLING, 'JACK. EXACTLY WHAT I WAS HOPING FOR TO--HOW DID YOU PUT IT...?--
--"PRIME THE PUMP"...?
C'MON, SEVE--LET'S PLAY THAT WE'RE FIGHTIN' THAT BAD GUY MAL-SHOOR! I'LL BE THE TIGER-GUY AN' YOU BE JARK...!
The beginning...

THANKS and Stuff...

Of course, while Mike and I get to have our names on the front cover of this lovely tome, we would be remiss not to take time out to offer thanks and recognition to those without whom Tellos would never have even gotten outta the gate.

First off, I'd like to thank my good pal (and sometime advisor) TOM DeFALCO for his glowing introduction and his RANDY O'DONNELL is The M@N partner, RON LIM, for the stunning pin-up of our guys with their guys. You should all run out and buy as many RANDY O'DONNELL is The M@N's as you can, 'cause, Kids, it's just FUN!!

Incidentally, Randy, Tesca, and Gemel, as well as the name Randy O'Donnell is The M@N, are all copyright and trademark Tom DeFalco and Ron Lim, just in case we miss it like...

...Last time, when we left out any of the requisite copyright information regarding PAUL SMITH'S beautiful pin-up of Serra and Rikk, with Chance and St.George from Paul and James Robinson's marvelous book, LEAVE IT TO CHANCE!! We'd like to take this opportunity to thank Paul as well, not only for the thrilling pin-up, but for his fantastic introduction to our first Trade Paperback, Tellos:Reluctant Heroes. Thanks, Paul—you are truly a 'Brother-in-Arms'.

Thanks too to ROB STULL, our fabulous Inker. Due to the erratic production schedule and such, Rob did so much to get the pages done as quickly as possible and we can't tell you how much we appreciate that, Rob. Of course, as always, there were times when we needed it yesterday and so it was great to know that we had friends that would also come through in the pinch. Thanks too to RICK KETCHUM, NATHAN MASSENGILL, and DEREK FRIDOLFS, for jumping in with the pen and brush when things got just too tight!

And, oh, how I wish we could dedicate a whole page just to sing the praises of PAUL MOUNTS...! Not only is PAUL probably the BEST Colorist in the business, bringing Mike's characters and landscapes to vibrant life, but he also handles the Lettering, Production, and much of the design work on Tellos. He is a friend, an advisor, and an indispensible member of the Tellos team. Thank you, Paul—a thousand times over.

And not to forget Paul's partner at BONGOTONE, KEN WOLAK, for the long hours of work he too has put into our colorful world!!

Also instrumental in getting out each and every issue of Tellos is the Gang at IMAGE. JIM, BRENT, BOZZI, KENNY, SEAN...They help out with Production, Presentation, Design, Solicitation, etc. and always tend to go above and beyond the call of duty when it comes to our little Tellos. Thank you, Guys! You make it fun!

And, of course, this book would be nothing without you, the ever-loyal Tellos READER! Dreams only come true when others come along and give it power. Thank you All, for making our little fantasy a reality!

And, personally, I'd like to take a moment to thank Dani Fermanich--Dani the Faerie, my Dani--who has stood ever-diligently by my side throughout the making of Tellos. Thank you, Dani, for your patience, your understanding, and your never-ending love. For saving me.

Todd
Autumn 2001

BUTCH WIERINGO

walked into Mike's house a little over six years ago and decided immediately that she'd live there. She was somewhat of a vagabond who had lived with several different families in Mike's neighborhood over the years-- but she would always be left behind when each family moved. She had primarily been an outdoor cat up until then-- but she was getting old and she and Mike mutually agreed that she would become an indoor cat from that point on.

It's not clear where Butch got her name (it's an odd name for a girl, as her vets keep telling Mike)-- and her exact age is in doubt. It's believed she's around 16 or so. She's diabetic and requires two insulin shots a day and is racked with painful arthritis-- but she still gets around fine and she's still got a wonderful, playful spirit.

She's been assured by Mike that if he ever moves from the neighborhood that she's going with him.

That suits her fine.

GRETCHEN ANN DEZAGO

first gamboled into Todd's life 16 whole years ago and swiftly became his best friend and confidant. She is a terrier mix with lots of personality, one ear up, one ear down, and is somewhat empathic, sensing when people she loves are down or depressed and giving them company and comfort. She is the best dog in the world, the princess. She goes to work each day with Todd, laying at his feet, offering story advice, and correcting his typos.

JAKE "THE TRICKSTER" DEZAGO

(aka. Puppet, Monkey, Barky Barkerson, Cliff) is obsessed with playing catch and squirrels. He is a Jack Russell Terrier and is chock full of energy, sometimes vibrating in place for entire seconds at a time. He is 8 years old and can jump to amazing heights. He has recently developed a compassionate side to mirror his older sister's, but has managed to retain his devilish nature.

More Tales To Tell...

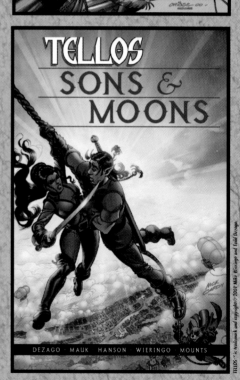